D1617382

The Balance of Consciousness
Eric Voegelin's Political Theory

The Balance
of
Consciousness

Eric Voegelin's
Political Theory

Kenneth Keulman

The Pennsylvania State University Press
University Park and London

Dedicated to my mother,
Lillian Frances Keulman

and to the memory of my father,
Paul Frederick Keulman

Library of Congress Cataloging-in-Publication Data

Keulman, Kenneth.
  The balance of consciousness : Voegelin and the mind's fate /
Kenneth Keulman.

  p.   cm.
  Includes bibliographical references.
  ISBN 0-271-00698-6 (alk. paper)
  1. Voegelin, Eric, 1901–85. I. Title.
  B3354.V884K48   1990
  193—dc20   89–28559

It is the policy of The Pennsylvania State University Press to use acid-free paper for
the first printing of all clothbound books. Publications on uncoated stock satisfy
the minimum requirements of American National Standard for Information Sciences—Permanence of Paper for Printed Library Materials, ANSI Z39.48-1984.

Contents

Acknowledgments

Enigmatic as it is to all but those concerned, a prefatory acknowledgment is an earned privilege for an author. According to one current fashion, a preface is meant to be a kind of playbill which lists the names of those who made any contribution to the production at hand. According to a second fashion, the preface is a provisional surrogate for the author's unwritten novel of ideas. In my view, a prefatory acknowledgment is neither. It is, rather, a page from that ledger in which one notes those persons who have so marked either one's life or work that it is impossible to think of either without thinking of them as well.

I remember with gratitude Eric Voegelin's graciousness in sharing diverse reflections on an extensive range of subjects over the course of frequent conversations—conversations that death broke off in January 1985. His remarks on these occasions were always marked by a combination of civility and incisiveness—whatever the subject. I am also grateful for the opportunity to read a number of unpublished manuscripts over the years. Many of these will eventually be published by Louisiana State University Press—the most notable being "The History of Political Ideas," which was begun in the early 1940s and completed over thirty-five years ago. Louisiana State University Press is undertaking the publication of Voegelin's Collected Works, which is projected at thirty-four volumes. I am grateful to the Press for permission to quote from passages of *Order and History.*

During visits to the Voegelin's Stanford home, it has also been my good fortune to experience the grace, intelligence, and wit which mark Lissy Voegelin's personality. Her hospitality repeatedly set intellectual inquiry in its proper place. I am endebted to her for permission to quote from unpublished manuscripts previously given to me by Eric Voegelin. The Hoover Institution Archives at Stanford University is a repository of the Voegelin papers.

Over a number of years I have benefited from the probing questions of Paul Caringella. It was he who clarified a number of issues underlying the initial conception of this work, and generously provided relevant materials.

I am also grateful to Frederick Crowe, of Regis College, University of Toronto, for demonstrating the way in which analytic scholarship may be fused with empathy for many human conditions. Warren Holleran has been of perennial assistance in fostering the process of critical thinking and remains one of the few scholars I know who can offer such assistance in the clarification of one's thought by being consistently affirming rather than threatening.

In addition, Stanley Hoffmann has made the Center for European Studies at Harvard University into a collegial environment in which I have found both intellectual challenge and personal friendship. The life of the Center is orchestrated remarkably by Abby Collins. I am grateful to both—and to many others—for continuously extending the hospitality of the Center to me.

Finally, my thanks go to Trudi Koziol of the Center for European Studies at Harvard University for the rare blend of competence and care which marked the preparation of the typescript. The same qualities marked the work done by Carol Cortazzo on the final version.

All translations are my own, with the exception of those passages noted from *Anamnesis*, which have already been translated in the English edition of the volume, translated and edited by Gerhart Niemeyer (Notre Dame: University of Notre Dame Press, 1978). In these instances, I have relied on the English edition.

Maintenant, sur une immense terrase d'Elsinore, qui va de Bâle à Cologne, qui touche aux sables de Nieuport, aux marais de la Somme, aux craies de Champagne, aux granits d'Alsace—l'Hamlet européen regarde des millions de spectres.

Mais il est un Hamlet intellectuel. Il médite sur la vie et la mort des vérités. Il a pour fantômes tous les objets de nos controverses; il a pour remords tous les titres de notre gloire; il est accablé sous le poids des découvertes, des connaissances, incapable de se reprendre à cette activité illimitée. Il songe à l'ennui de recommencer le passé, à la folie de vouloir innover toujours. Il chancelle entre les deux abîmes, car deux dangers ne cessent de menacer le monde; l'order et le désordre.

—Paul Valéry, "La Crise de l'esprit"

Preface

The current vitality of formal inquiry into the nature of mind is indebted to the claim that any discipline devoted to the study of the mind must analyze mental representations. The representational theory of mind is today a significant one. This vitality also reflects a renewal of interest in ethics and the perception that normative ethics do not inform unless they are based on insight into the nature of mental concepts. Wittgenstein's criticism in the *Philosophical Investigations* of the theory of knowledge and theory of meaning, accepted among empiricists following Russell, has been a decisive influence. This empiricist theory of meaning, along with its correlative theory of knowledge, appears to involve an erroneous description of the real conditions for using mental representations.

Among the specific matters within the theory of knowledge and ethics that need more precise conceptual analysis are the question of intersubjective comparisons between mental states and emotions; the limits within which an individual is immune to error in describing personal sensations; and the attribution of responsibility for actions. These questions have a place in intellectual history, and some of them extend as far back as Plato in the *Philebus* and Aristotle in the *Nicomachean Ethics*. The terms in which the questions are confronted and the theories of knowledge and meaning implied may vary. Many of the same distinctions, necessary to any adequate ethics, must be reevaluated in light of new epistemologies.

These types of inquiries are subject to increasingly precise clarification. They are significant if only because some cursory responses to them are taken for granted in most political and ethical arguments, or in law, economics, or psychology. They are also significant because our ordinary thinking is riddled with unreflective presuppositions comparing the states of mind of very different individuals and the possibility of attributing individual ethical responsibility to different types of people. Doubts that arise about claims to certainty on these questions are not limited to philosophers. They may also arise in any serious use of mental concepts. Philosophical doubts, raised by epistemology, are correlative with a more common unsureness that exists in discerning, for example, the operations of the will or the character of belief and imagination. Uncertainty about the plausibility of claiming knowledge of the external world of physical objects through sight and touch is a strictly philosophical doubt, in that it has little hold on us when we acquire and exchange information in the ordinary course of affairs or during the process of scientific investigation. One has to be perplexed already by the apprehensions of knowledge and certainty before comprehending the impact of skepticism about the external world. But the nature of the mind, and its relation to the body and the natural order of physical objects, is an independent enigma, and always stands in need of explication.

There is an additional reason why mental representations and the conditions of their application demand clarification, especially in our age: At different periods in history, less constancy exists between languages and the use of mental concepts than the use of physical concepts. The prevailing notion of the mind has significantly altered within historical memory. Even when we read Hume or any eighteenth-century discussion of the nature of mind, we are aware that the language of introspection, and consequently the language of ethical appraisal, is not completely correlative with our own. Anyone who knows more than one language, and who is familiar with the literature of more than one culture and one historical period, understands that the language offers some choice in ways of thinking about mental states. The distinctions that we choose to emphasize are in part a matter of our own interests, and we are not obligated to make in our own thought all and only those discriminations that are familiar in the conversation and writing of our contemporaries. We may conclude that some ordinary distinctions are insubstantial and illusory survivals of beliefs about the mind that can no longer be maintained; and we may have reasons for making distinctions that are no longer commonly acknowledged or acknowledged only in some other language, distinctions to which we attach value in reflecting on our own experience.

Finally, there is now a relatively new way of measuring the adequacy of representational theories of mind. Increasingly powerful computers and accompanying theories of their potential capacities together make the old conjecture of *l'homme machine* less tenuous and more tractable. Appropriate distinctions may suggest themselves that could not have been reliably imagined in advance of the facts. Some aspects of the multiple dilemmas of determinism and materialism can be focused and made sharper. The implications of this development for a computational theory of representation are apparent.

At the same time, it is salutary to recall the illusions of the early postwar years, when it was widely believed that the fundamental dilemmas of psychology and linguistics had been resolved and that an understanding of the remaining questions could now be achieved with the help of computers, sound spectroscopes, and similar products of recent technological advances. Today we can see that we are still far from comprehending fundamental questions; we still need new insights and concepts.

Knowledge and Politics

Until now, a common notion was that the significant issue for political thought was, What can we know? In *Knowledge and Politics,* Roberto Unger remarks that this notion was correlative with the belief that the way in which we resolve the dilemmas of the theory of knowledge in turn depends on the manner in which we address issues in political thought. The theory of knowledge, according to this understanding, is part of an investigation into the psychological question, Why do we, as individuals, act as we do? Political theory is concerned with the organization of societies. The branches of political theory are the disciplines that consider particular aspects of society: economics, law, government. If epistemology is fundamental to political theory, it must also be vital to these particularized areas of investigation. Likewise, if political theory has implications for the issues encountered in the theory of knowledge, disciplines such as economics, law, and government may cast some light on certain issues pertaining to the theory of knowledge.[1]

Unger admits that this type of perspective on the connection between knowledge and politics may appear strange. Epistemology seems interested in a number of technical puzzles that appear remote from a

1. Roberto Mangabeira Unger, *Knowledge and Politics* (New York: The Free Press, 1975), 3–4.

concern with the understanding of society. To devise a continuum of insight that spans the distance from epistemology to understanding individual behavior, from understanding individual behavior to the study of society, and from the study of society to the exercise of political choice, seems a fantasy. It appears anomalous to suggest that a correlation might exist between solutions to problems in the theory of knowledge and the theory of society.

Yet the assumption of such a correlation may be warranted in two ways. First, this claim permits a reconstruction of the dominant ideas of a social system. Through this reconstruction and the practice of critical reflection, we may be able to solve the problems generated by partial critiques of that system, which constitute the majority of available theories of a given society. Second, understanding the relationship between psychological and political ideas consequently serves as the key that allows a serious examination of the present system.[2]

Unger notes that the assumption from which the analysis begins is that the present state of psychological and political ideas has an affinity in one basic respect with the situation of European social thought in the mid-seventeenth century. Then as now, partial critiques of a still-dominant tradition could not be advanced further without being transformed into a total critique of that tradition.

Many movements, from the nominalism of Ockham to the political thought of Machiavelli and the theory of knowledge of Descartes, had attempted to dismantle the foundations of classical metaphysics in its scholastic form. Yet it was in the writings of Hobbes, his contemporaries, and his successors that the venerable psychological and political ideas of the schools were first impugned as a body of thought. Only at this time did it become apparent that theorists had not yet differentiated themselves from the medieval Aristotle; that the context within which they labored was flawed; that the notions about mind and society that exemplified this type of thought made up a unified system; and that this system of thought was based on certain metaphysical assumptions. The effort to understand the implications of these notions created a new body of doctrines—liberalism—which was even more coherent and comprehensive than the tradition it supplanted. The new system of thought, at first the creation of a small group of intellectuals, gradually became the shared possession of more diverse communities and the foundation of the modern social sciences.

2. Ibid., 4.

Today as then, a single set of concepts has been refined and criticized in a haphazard way. Current approaches to political theory are partial critiques of a style of thought they have neither rejected nor comprehended in its totality. Once again, however, reflection on the basic problems encountered by these traditions demonstrates the sway that the classical theory, in this instance liberalism, continues to exercise.

If this interpretation of our situation is accurate, we first need to articulate the concepts that shape and circumscribe the alternative modes of our thought. We must view the dominant theory of society all of a piece—not simply as a set of propositions about the distribution of resources and power, but as an overarching conception of mind and society.[3]

Political Reality

Over the past half-century, Eric Voegelin, a historian and political scientist, produced a demanding body of writing on the history of political theory from antiquity to the present. The foundation of this work is an inquiry into the nature of mind. The visible thread that runs through his writings is the evolution of consciousness and the notion central to that evolution—the polarity of contraries. Voegelin employs the notion of "political reality" to refer to the reality generated by the consciousness of specific individuals whose experiences and symbolic expressions produce a social field that also has the character of a historical field. The assumption here is that the problems of order in society and history arise from the order of consciousness. The theory of consciousness can for this reason be placed at the center of political theory.

Voegelin's unique contribution to political theory is an approach to history rooted in a study of the symbolisms of the history of order. This orientation, now common among historians of culture, along with a correlative move toward conceiving social life as organized in terms of symbols whose meaning must be discerned if we are to understand that organization and formulate its principles, has developed by now to formidable proportions.

3. Ibid., 5–6.

The hallmark of modern consciousness is its multiplicity, a multiplicity characterized by the dissimilarity of metier-formed minds. Voegelin's life project was to fashion a body of work that addressed the complexity and diversity of the modern world. A central part of his project was to remap the conceptual geography of mind, not so much solving traditional philosophical problems as dissolving them into consequences of misguided analysis. Voegelin's writings survey the multifaceted reality of power politics, historiography, and human development as important structures inextricably bound together and needing balanced treatment in a philosophy of consciousness and history.

The focus of this book is a consideration of theory of consciousness within the context of political theory. I first attempt to make explicit the theoretical framework of Voegelin's thought and then to demonstrate how he applies it interpretively to the historical materials on which it is based. Because the process of consciousness informs and foreshadows the field of history, an appropriate way to gain a critical understanding of political theory is through insight into the meaning of historical symbolisms. It is then possible to make a case for the centrality of theory of consciousness in political theory. These pages explore the relation between philosophy and politics and attempt to answer the question; Why is the problem of knowledge so central an issue for modern political thought and political knowledge?

The predominant tradition of thinking about mind is marked by an individualistic caste. According to this thesis, properly psychological states are all in a certain sense immanent to their subject. These states are not noncausally sensitive to any differences, social or political, in realities outside the boundaries of the person; in fact they do not involve the existence of anything outside the subject. In the process of indentifying mental states, this tradition neglects the significance of social institutions; it considers mind as though its states and contents were free of social influence. Yet a good argument can be made for the social nature of certain mental states.

In order to illustrate one approach to the critique of individualism, let us take as our target beliefs phenomena that are as properly mental as any individualist could wish. Let us imagine a certain divergence in someone's community, a divergence that does not causally affect the individual. The argument is that this difference would force us to attribute variant beliefs to the person, contrary to the individualistic thesis. If a variation in someone's culture, just on its own, can demand the attribution of different beliefs, then beliefs are culture-bound.

Certain beliefs involve relationships to contents that may change simply by virtue of an alteration of social fact; that is, without any change in the scope of an individual's psychology. Then certain beliefs are community-bound: They exist, and they are the beliefs that they are—in particular that they possess the contents that they have—only if an appropriate social context is in the offing.[4]

These types of considerations, which sketch the relationship between mind and society, knowledge and politics, are relevant for any examination of the work of Eric Voegelin. In an autobiographical memoir, Voegelin stated that the "motivations for my work are simple; they arise from the political situation. Anybody who lives in the twentieth century, as I did, with an awake consciousness ever since the end of the First World War, finds himself hemmed in, if not oppressed from all sides by a flood of ideological language, meaning language symbols which pretend to be concepts but in fact are unanalyzed *topoi*."[5] Voegelin maintained that his work emerged from experience, the actual experience of political disorder. This political situation was the aftermath of the First World War with the collapse of the Austro-Hungarian Empire, the ascendency of Bolshevism in Russia, the development of ideological politics in Western and Central Europe with its Socialist and Communist factions, and the emergence of fascism, national socialism, and the consolidation of totalitarian regimes by Hitler and Stalin. The origin of Voegelin's work, then, lay in the political situation of the twentieth century and the ideological language employed to describe it.

Thus a pronounced political orientation marks Voegelin's writings. The four books that he wrote during the 1930s all dealt with the political debacle that had already started and would shortly spread across the globe: *Rasse und Staat; Die Rassenidee in der Geistesgeschichte von Ray bis Carus, Der Autoritäre Staat; Die politischen Religionen.* "It is difficult," he once wrote, "to categorize political

4. These arguments are developed in detail in P. Pettit, "Wittgenstein, Individualism and the Mental," in *Erkenntnis und Wissenschaftstheorie*, ed. P. Weingartner and J. Czermak (Vienna: Holden-Pichler-Tempsky, 1983).

5. The quotation is taken from an unpublished transcript of tape-recorded interviews conducted by Ellis Sandoz in 1973. Quoted as [AM 96] in E. Sandoz, *The Voegelinian Revolution* (Baton Rouge: Louisiana State University Press, 1981) [at 28].

phenomena properly without a well-developed philosophical anthropology . . . "[6] Voegelin opened *The New Science of Politics* (1952) with the affirmation that "the existence of man in political society is historical existence; and a theory of politics, if it penetrates to principles, must at the same time be a theory of history." He later developed that theory of history in *Order and History*, and the inaugural sentence of the first volume (1956) articulated a *Programmschrift* for the entire project: "The order of history emerges from the history of order."

Thus the theory of politics that had been amplified into the theory of history (1952) was further developed in *Order and History* into the philosophy of order to be achieved by analyzing the trail of experiences and the symbols these experiences evinced in the field of history. The next principal reformulation came ten years afterwards. *Anamnesis* (1966) begins by articulating the theme of Voegelin's political philosophy in this way: "The problem of human order in society and history originate in the order of consciousness. The philosophy of consciousness is for that reason the centerpiece of a philosophy of politics." With this statement, the philosophy of politics was amplified by the experiences and symbols through which the process of consciousness expresses itself.

This series of epigrams provides a key to the direction of Voegelin's work. The concepts expressed in the first section of *Anamnesis* (written in 1943) articulate a theory of consciousness presupposed by both *The New Science of Politics* and *Order and History* and already of interest to Voegelin in his first book, *Über die Form des amerikanischen Geistes* (1928). That theory is spelled out in *Anamnesis*, specifically in the section entitled "What Is Political Reality?" The philosophy of order, Voegelin maintains, is the process in which the order of existence is discerned in the order of consciousness.[7] The philosophy of consciousness is the center of Voegelin's political theory, and following the publication of *Plato and Aristotle* (1957) his work focused on the process of consciousness as manifested in varied historical forms.

The language of platonic philosophy depends on political imagery. At the same time, the significance of this language and imagery, that is, Plato's discourse, indicates a transpolitical reality accessible to an as-

6. "The Origins of Totalitarianism," *The Review of Politics* 15, 65–68 [at 68].
7. *Anamnesis*, 11.

tute psyche. *This* reality experienced with *this* type of psyche was the actual norm on the basis of which the political standards and mores, along with the beliefs of citizens concerning them, were to be measured. The philosopher was the measure of the polis, Plato maintained, because the god was the measure of his psyche.[8] The actual experience for which the imagery of measurement was the symbolic articulation, the experience of being under a judgment more powerful than the rise and fall of cities, was the source of the philosopher's authority and the foundation upon which one raised one's own truth in opposition to the truth of the city.

The word *noesis* derives from the language of classical philosophy, specifically from the word *nous,* which signifies reason, intelligence, and mind. In the *Nicomachean Ethics,* Aristotle contrasts intelligence (*nous*) with calculative or discursive reasoning (*dianoia* or *logos*). Insofar as Voegelin understands political science as the noetic interpretation of political reality, the actual significance of the locution can be implied by stating that *noesis* is a rendering of political reality similar to that provided by Plato and Aristotle.[9] Thus, understanding the political orientation of Voegelin's work demands some insight into the political aspect of classical philosophy.

This schema obviates any interpretation of political science that patterns itself in terms of the method of the natural sciences. The noetic explication of political reality, conversely, develops out of the conflict that arises between the self-understanding of a society (as exemplified in its traditions, laws, and institutions) and the reflective individual's experience of both personal and social order.

Voegelin understood classical and stoic philosophy as an analytically elaborate articulation of the common-sense attitude or experience. In his later works, this insight into the relationship of sentiment and attitude vis-à-vis the world became a major tenet of his interpretive project. The first conclusion Voegelin reached, however, was political. Maintaining a continuous tradition of attitudes, sentiments, insights, and experiences of classical philosophy without the complex discursive trappings of academic language contributed to the intellectual climate of opinion and to the cohesion of a culture. He considered the example of Anglo-American constitutional democracy to be an exemplary instance of this.

8. *Laws,* 716c.
9. Aristotle, *Nicomachean Ethics* VI, 6, 1140b31–1141a8; *Posterior Analytics* II, 19, 100b5–14; Voegelin, *Anamnesis,* 284, 286–87.

Philosophy can thus serve as a means of critically evaluating the validity of symbolisms that function as sanctioned representations of the way in which a particular culture understands the world. In its critical dimension it is able to discern detrimental worldviews and offer alternatives through rational evaluation.

> A philosophy of politics is empirical—in the pregnant sense of an investigation of experiences which penetrate the whole realm of ordered human existence. It requires . . . rigorous reciprocating examination of concrete phenomena of order and analysis of the consciousness, by which means alone the human order in society and history becomes understandable . . . [Since] the consciousness is the center from which the concrete order of human existence in society and history radiates . . . the empirical study of social and historical phenomena of order interpenetrates with the empirical study of the consciousness and its experiences of participation.[10]

This statement may serve as a leitmotif for Voegelin's work. It is also the theme of this book.

10. *Anamnesis*, 8–9, 275–76.

Introduction

The manner in which modes of thought have changed over time has been the source of perennial speculation. The purpose of such interest may be to formulate a notion of what prompted developments in the ancient Middle East, Greece, or Renaissance Europe, where new ways of thinking seem to have preempted the old. The same types of issues have generated research on subjects like the displacement of magic by science and the evolution of rationality. In *The Domestication of the Savage Mind*, anthropologist Jack Goody suggests that this research has been further complicated by both the categories and the structure employed.[1]

Goody notes that the difficulty with the categories is that they are based on a disjunction both binary and enthnocentric. Occasionally the artless classifications of folk taxonomy are still used. We speak in terms of primitive and advanced as though human minds themselves varied in their morphology like machines of an earlier and later model. The rise of science is said to follow a prescientific age in which magical attitudes exercised controlling influence. This process is often described as the emergence of empirical from mythological thinking. More recently, there has been an attempt to overcome the problems summoned up by a description of the situation based on polarities through more constructively formulated dichotomies—the wild and domesticated (or cold and hot) thinking of Lévi-Strauss, and the closed and open circumstances deriving from Popper.[2]

The problem with the structure has been that it is either mainly nondevelopmental or else reductionistically so. While there is reason to be cautious of a developmental structure, much of the finest cultural analysis in fact begins exactly at this point. Even those who ex-

---

1. Jack Goody, *The Taming of the Savage Mind* (Cambridge: Cambridge University Press, 1977), 1.
2. Ibid., 1–2.

press these concerns, however, frequently deduce them from an enthnocentric interest connected with the evolution of modern industrial society. Once more, this approach implies a binary opposition. Its answer demands that we search among a wide variety of cultures for positive and negative instances in order to confirm our notions about the opposite elements. The search has an ethnocentric starting point. The dichotomizing of "we" and "they" in this way narrows the field of both the subject and its interpretation, leading once more to the use of binary categories.

Of no subject is this more indisputable than inquiries into the development of the human mind. Here the investigation confronts the problem of the participant observer. We perceive the issue not as an investigator studies geological layers, but from the inside outward. We begin with the understanding that significant differences exist between ourselves and others. We attempt to formulate the texture of these differences in general terms—the development from myth to history, from status to contract, collective to individual, ritual to rationality. Such movement tends to be articulated not only in terms of process but of progress as well. That is, it takes on a value dimension, a procedure inclined to misrepresent the way we see the type of development that has taken place, particularly when this is viewed in a comprehensive idiom such as, for instance, Lévy-Bruhl's division into prelogical and logical mentalities. The fact that problems relating to human thought are framed in such terms implies that sufficient documentation is hard to come by; or, to view the investigation from another perspective, that most documentation can be made to fit the categories. As for the framework, investigators straddle developmental and nondevelopmental perspectives. Yet once more the differences are ordinarily considered to be dualistic in nature, leading to the assumption of a single ethnographic approach rather than a multifaceted one.[3]

The Ethnography of Thought

Over the last half-century, an integral view of the nature of thought, considered in the sense of mental representation, has nonetheless

3. Ibid., 2–4.

developed out of these varied investigations. This view has been paralleled by the continuing advance of a markedly pluralistic understanding of thought in another, cultural sense as social reality. Such perspectives were initially framed as the "primitive mind" question, then as the issue of "cognitive relativism," and most recently as the dilemma of "conceptual incommensurability."

In *Local Knowledge*, Clifford Geertz describes the development of these approaches and makes a strong case for a diverse ethnographic orientation. I will here summarize an argument developed in a pivotal chapter of the book: "The Way We Think Now: Ethnography of Modern Thought."

The early form of the "primitive mind" characterization—that we the beneficiaries of the Enlightenment are characterized by thought processes marked by analysis, logic, and systematic testing, and that they, the savages, live among a *melange* of images, mysticism, and passions—has been attenuated as we have come to understand more about the way other cultures think. The misconception consisted of deciphering cultural elements as if they were individual manifestations rather than social institutions. The link between thought as process and thought as product is still in need of explication.

The second, the "cognitive relativism" framing of the question, was made up of a number of efforts to obviate this culture-is-the-mind-writ-large error. Specific cultural expressions were correlated with specific mental processes. Such research, though inconclusive, at least clarified the differences in the patterns of individual thought, given personal and geographic identities, and the observing, imagining, and reminiscing that people actually do.[4]

These studies, as Geertz points out, were not free of particularism. If various cultural activities produce distinctive patterns of mental functioning, it is not certain how people circumscribed by one culture are able to enter into the thought of people circumscribed by another. Since the research of cognitive relativists itself was based on an assertion of such discernment, this results in an ambiguous state of affairs.

The predicament became even more complex because correlative with the pluralization of the "product" aspect of thought, several unitive orientations to the "process" aspect were developing. These orientations are marked by the certitude that the mechanics of thinking

---

4. Clifford Geertz, *Local Knowledge* (New York: Basic Books, 1983), 148–49.

remain constant across time, culture, and environment. Yet the general drift toward universal notions of ideation has had an impact on the pluralizers as well. The basic identity of mental activity in the human race had persisted as a subliminal theme in their work. The core of that identity, though, was limited to the most basic capabilities, barely more than the capacity to learn, emote, abstract, and analogize. With the emergence of more provisional images of such subjects, this type of ambiguity appeared more and more unsatisfactory.

Yet thinking as it exists "in nature" is highly diverse, and it is sensible to take the question out of the domain of mentality and reformulate it in terms of cultural meaning. Structuralists—Lévi-Strauss and his followers—induce the principles governing the workings of the mind from culinary practices and the etiquette of eating. The product aspect of thought becomes so many random cultural codes, highly diverse, but which, when decoded, generate as their text the psychological invariants of the process aspect. What was previously viewed as an issue of the comparability of psychological processes from one culture to another is thus now perceived as an issue of the commensurability of conceptual structures from one community of discourse to another.

That thought is diverse as product and singular as process is an anomaly. But the character of that anomaly has to do with the enigmas of translation, with the way in which meaning in one system of expression is articulated in another—cultural interpretation, not mechanics of mind. In such a form the enigma may not be any more manageable than previously, but it does reformulate the issue as a question of the way in which culturally different individuals organize their symbolic world.[5]

All this leads Geertz to call for an ethnography of thought. The purpose is to emphasize a certain inclination of its nature as a historical, comparative, interpretive endeavor, the intention of which is to make enigmatic issues understandable by furnishing them with an informing frame of reference. It is founded on the premise that ideation is a cultural phenomenon. Like power or class, thought is a reality to be delineated by interpreting its expressions in the context of the activities that maintain them.

5. Ibid., 149–51.

Several practical implications follow from maintaining that thinking should be approached ethnographically. But Geertz suggests that this approach also arouses trepidation. What to some, standing in the social-fact tradition and its pluralizing tendencies, appears like the introduction of more valuable ways of thinking about cognition, looks to others, representatives of the internal representation tradition and its unifying characteristics, like a destruction of the bedrock of reason. The sociology of knowledge involved here is a question of conceiving cognition, motivation, perception, memory, imagination, and emotion as themselves explicitly social matters. How to achieve this, how to analyze symbol use as social action, is a complicated undertaking. The attempt to do so involves a consideration of the community as the forum in which thoughts are constructed and deconstructed.

At this point the imagery becomes political and the discontent of those for whom the mind is a reality apart becomes saturnine. This discontent is articulated in a number of ways: as an aversion to particularism, subjectivism, idealism, and, embodying them all in a kind of *bête noir*, an apprehension toward relativism. If thought is so contingent on culture, what is to guarantee its universality, its objectivity?[6]

Yet the perspective that one finds thought in a variety of cultural forms leaves a good deal more to say about the way in which separate individuals come to conceive reasonably similar things; about how thought frames change, how thought provinces are demarcated, how thought norms are maintained and acquired. Geertz points out that the ethnography of thought is a project that considers diversity seriously as itself an object of analytic description and interpretive reflection. The ethnographic approach can be rendered somewhat more sharply by tracing what it leads to when one trains it on the dynamics of the life of the mind.

The problem of integrating cultural life becomes one of making it possible for individuals living in different worlds to have an authentic, and reciprocal, impact on one another. If it is valid that a general consciousness exists that is made up of the interaction of a disorderly crowd of disparate visions, then the vitality of that consciousness depends upon creating the conditions under which such interplay takes place. For that, Geertz concludes that the first step is to accept the

6. Ibid., 152–53.

extent of the differences, the second to comprehend what these differences are, and the third to fashion a lexicon in which they can be articulated in the public forum.[7]

The Comparative Study of Civilizations

Because of the pressing nature of these issues, attested to by the current state of international relations in the world—a state in which international regimes have to learn to become devices for facilitating decentralized cooperation among egoistic actors—the comparative study of cultures and civilizations becomes significant. Such a study draws its research program from novel ways of relating to central questions that have been developing on the boundaries of comparative cultural history and comparative sociology. It concerns itself with civilizational traditions, structures, complexes, and most particularly with the analysis of intercivilizational and intercultural encounters. It examines them with specificity, using precise outcomes from across the world's history.

This new study proceeds in a manner very different from that of Spengler, Toynbee, Sorokin, or the older models of the study of civilization. From about 1950 to the present, a new discipline has emerged, one that analyzes semantic cultural structures in comparative terms. Max Weber inspired the more recent analytic perspective of civilization. This new model also draws on the work of research-oriented investigations of civilizational issues such as those done by Alfred Kroeber and George Sarton, medievalist Lynn White, Islamicist Gustav Grunebaum, and others like Mircea Eliade and Rudolph Otto. An important representative of this orientation was the work of the historian Joseph Levenson. His *Confucian China and Its Modern Fate* and *Revolution and Cosmopolitanism* are not histories in any ordinary sense. They are writings in a new genre based on an incisive knowledge of history, sociology, philosophy, and religion.

As far as we can tell, what Weber wanted to find out was how the world had taken on the character it had. He learned that if we actually attempted to do that, we would naturally need to know

7. Ibid., 161.

something about whether all places of the world are like our own. Obviously they are not; therefore it became critical to understand why things have one form in one place and quite another form in another. Thus he became involved in comparative historical analysis.

Weber turned to comparative historical studies of China, India, and ancient Judaism. He also planned a study of Islam, and a volume on medieval church structures. He did not live long enough to see these projects through. Before his death, however, he wrote a retrospection of his life, which appeared as the author's introduction to the collected essays in the *Sociology of Religion*. Unfortunately, because of the less-than-adequate scholarship in Germany, as well as the United States, that essay is usually assumed to have been written in 1904–5. It was actually the last paper to come from his hand before his death in 1920 and indicates the direction his thought had taken.

Weber made extraordinary contributions to understanding the civilizational study of history conceived in international and intercivilizational terms. Since Weber, historical studies have become increasingly pluralistic. This pluralism is indispensable to narrate the histories and comprehend the structures, not only of pasts as they can come to be understood, but also of futures in the making.

For a number of reasons, civilizational analytic models differ from other types of models currently in the ascendancy in Western scholarship. They place their emphasis on the specifics of cultures. They do not accept uniform schemas that rest on the assumption of universal invariant psychologies. They reject all unilinear evolutionary logic of irreversible development. They do not accept system theoretic models, which postulate general system structures as the foundation of all process. Civilization analytic models insist that if we are to understand our present, and our possible futures, we need access to the specificities of these diverse cultural traditions and must find a way of reaching into the roots of these structures as they have in fact related to one another. There are worlds in the making, but none of us can tell what shape they will have. The danger of accepting any uniform model is that the futures will be aborted because the pasts will have been stereotyped and frozen by alien molds that do not do justice to actual histories in process.

The historian and political philosopher Eric Voegelin began by asking a question rather like Weber's. He wanted to know how the world had become the way it was. He also wanted to develop an intellectual countervailing power against the political chaos of the times.

Voegelin combines an encyclopedic command of material with exceptional theoretical penetration. Readers are carried through an intricate analysis in history, politics, anthropology, philosophy, and religion, while they simultaneously receive an original and complex theoretical interpretation. Voegelin's perspective is achieved through critical experiential analysis and consequently stands up well under scholarly and technical criticism. His work is solidly built on a command of primary and secondary source materials and a philologist's competence in languages.

Voegelin's writings are marked by disciplined use of convergent data. By convergent data we mean here descriptions, measures, and observations—unstandardized facts that are at once varied, even somewhat miscellaneous, both in kind and degree of precision and generality. Collated and variously represented, these facts yet turn out to illuminate one another because the people they describe, measure, or observe are involved in one another's lives. Consequently, they differ from the type of data obtained from a census, poll, or survey, which gathers information about classes of individuals not otherwise related. The concentration on natural communities, groups of persons interacting with one another in many ways, makes it feasible to turn what appears to be a simple collection of diverse material into a mutually reinforcing network of social understanding.[8] Voegelin's writings are particularly notable for their emphasis on the raw material of experience. The veil of technical terminology, the range of familiar and strange sources and documents through which he pursues his line of inquiry, should not obscure the lucidity of language and expository technique. What is difficult about Voegelin's writing is the subject matter he explores, not his stylistic eccentricities. This subject matter ranges over a wide expanse of human experience and a variety of temporal and cultural horizons.

One of the themes we will first need to explore is the foundational one of the meaning of "human nature," giving attention to the political ramifications of this issue which, in the wake of developments such as Sociobiology, has again proven controversial.

8. Ibid., 156.

1

The Politics
of
Human Nature

As long as serious reflection on the nature of politics has existed, attempts have been made to connect such reflection with the nature of humanity. A great many thinkers who adhered to this tradition were confident that humanity possessed a "nature" and consequently articulated propositions about the conduct of life in society. Some speculators concentrated on the range of differences in conduct, but even radically divergent thinkers presupposed a collective fundament. Most believed that human beings need lives of stable interaction within an organized social system. This social system should be invested with coercive authority, including authority over life and liberty, a prerogative not ordinarily conceded as properly utilized by any other institution.

Human Nature and Political Thought

Notions of human nature are prominent in a number of ways in political theory. Principally, they often play a role in the legitimation of the state.[1] Theorists also consistently depend on conceptions of human nature to legitimate specific policies and more general policy positions. It is normative theory, justifications, to which these various presuppositions about human nature have contributed. The connection between empirical premise (about human nature) and normative conclusion

---

1. Aristotle, for instance, believed that the state was "natural," as was the requirement to obey its laws. *The Nicomachean Ethics*, trans. H. Rockham. Cambridge, MA: Harvard University Press, 1956, 311 (bk. X, ch. 9).

(justification) is in each instance a further, in this case normative, assumption. These normative assumptions—for instance, the opportunity for rational choice—are incontrovertible.

Some theorists, while maintaining that human nature is uniform in all nations and ages, emphasize the variety of human motivations.[2] Somewhat less significant than these, because of their implications for political theory, are varying presuppositions about two issues evaluated by the standards implicit in the first question: the degree to which individuals can be depended on to follow their objectives rationally, and whether differences among identifiable classes overshadow their similarities. All of this is founded on the presupposition that human nature, at least in these fundamentals, is relatively fixed. For those who believe in its indefinite malleability, the issue is irrelevant.

Throughout a great part of the history of Western civilization, differences of opinion with regard to these central questions have not been significant. More recent times have witnessed a change. By the middle of the twentieth century, speaking of human nature demanded audacity. Empiricists either maintained that not enough was known to speak of it, or were convinced that no such reality existed. Normative theorists, on the other hand, tended to deny it because of what were thought to be conservative implications.

Why did this change come about? Certainly the empiricists' need for precision and the normativists' need for change supply part of the reason. More generally, the prevailing relativism of the age fostered a similar orientation. The belief of the Age of Reason in its capacity to fashion propositions of universal validity yielded first to evolutionary theorists of human development, of history, and in some instances, of morality. Later, overarching theoretical systems, particularly in the area of political philosophy, lost credibility, and a more general skepticism gained ascendancy. Political theorists, both normative and descriptive, avoided propositions about definitive human qualities and theories derived from such speculation.

Along with the ambience of skepticism and positivism, more particularized causal factors contributed to the decline of theories of human

2. Hume thus states: "The same motives always produce the same actions; the same events follow the same causes. Ambition, avarice, self-love, vanity, friendship, generosity, public spirit—these passions mixed in various degrees and distributed through society have been, from the beginning of the world, and still are, the source of all the actions and enterprises which have ever been observed among mankind." David Hume, *Enquiries Concerning the Human Understanding*, ed. L. A. Selby-Bigge, 2d ed. (Oxford: Clarendon Press, 1902), Sec. VIII, Pt. I, 83.

nature. In the early years of the post-Reformation period, reasoning from ideas about human nature was common. Theories of human nature, along with frequently correlative secular theories of natural law, often displaced natural-law theories contingent on or at least more nearly related to theological notions of law. Yet it quickly became obvious that the preconceptions about human nature upon which these ideas were based varied greatly one from another. It was not novel for some theorists to hold a more optimistic outlook on the human province than others. Yet during the Christian era these differences were muted, while the ancient Greeks had placed more emphasis on the distribution of virtue among individuals than on a degree of virtue thought to be characteristic of all. Christian thinkers developed the notion that, while humans were naturally sociable and in their primitive state basically good, they had become depraved and could approach virtue only when held accountable to institutions of authority. Though Aquinas, in the spirit of Aristotle, maintained a more optimistic perspective on the individual than had been common, no dramatically altered implications for political theory were drawn from it. It remained for the seventeenth and eighteenth centuries to articulate formulas about preferable forms of government, such as Hobbes's defense of absolute monarchy and Rousseau's advocacy of democracy. Other writers arrayed themselves between these two poles. In this situation lay the seeds for skepticism about human nature as the cornerstone of political theory. Even a minor change in the original presuppositions—as in Locke and Hobbes—could produce a radical difference in the political conclusion. Of course, writers were suspected of meshing their presuppositions with their political leanings. It appears that during the course of European intellectual history, theories of human nature were frequently developed not objectively but according to whatever was required to furnish articulation and support to concrete social movements. Even more fundamental than the dilemma of objectivity, though, was the fact that such minor changes in presuppositions could lead to significant changes in conclusions. Could *the* correct presuppositions ever be determined with adequate precision?

To the variations expressed by theorists, diversity among cultures added reasons for skepticism about theories of human nature. Montesquieu supplies an early example of a writer who gave serious consideration to the immense variety of cultures, customs, laws, and forms of government and their mutual interdependence. Yet he did not abandon a concept of human nature. In Montesquieu's reflections on assorted travelers' tales, he acknowledges that diversity in human affairs is at least as significant as uniformity. Since his time, anthropologists have supplied much documentation of human variety, encouraging both political and moral relativism.

Psychology has joined anthropology in the process of attenuating faith in the existence of "human nature." This statement does not apply to all psychologists, yet it has provided the cornerstone for psychology in the United States during much of this century. In behaviorism, "human nature" is relegated to the "black box," and nurture has gained ascendancy. Consequently, the direction of "hard" behaviorism has opposed almost any concept of human nature for use by political theorists. Yet many who have been influenced by this thinking have been more concerned with denying that human nature is fundamentally self-seeking, competitive, and aggressive than that any such reality exists.

Finally, and closely related to the last point, the life sciences in general have recently been concerned with emphasizing human adaptability. Animals possess instincts; to a great extent they exist by them. These programmed patterns of dealing with the exigencies of life provide, for the lower forms specifically, the elements for their survival and occasionally the basis for their extinction when conditions change; at the least they fail to provide the means for coping with dramatic change. Here is where the higher forms of life, especially humans, with their relatively large brains, have an extraordinary advantage. The nature of the human race is to adapt to circumstances. Possibly that is the entirety of human nature, at least according to the extreme view.

Ideology

The twentieth century has thus been marked by the splintering of classical political ideas into many parts, one of which is the intensified development of ideologies. An analysis of these ideologies would begin with the pre-1914 concoction of racism, anti-Semitism, Darwinism, and antidemocratic elitism, but also take into consideration the changes in liberal and socialist thought. It would sketch the most formidable ideologies during the interwar years, deal with post-1945 era, and conclude with a consideration of ideology in the Third World.

One way of approaching ideology is to consider it as the philosophical justification of political authority. This century has generated the most virulent criticism and the greatest exaltation of ideologies.[3] Ideologies simplify complex matters; they stake out a claim to congenial notions and distill them into a program for political action. The most powerful ideologies—Marxism-Leninism, and National Socialism— "explain" the world and allow regimes to mobilize their people. They function as surrogate religions. Most ideologies are versions of the original idea of progress, which in the last part of the nineteenth century began to lose its liberal, humanistic orientation. They seduce by promising a better, redeemed world—whether by promoting racial purity, achieving a just and classless society, or prophesying a strong, national community that a messiah-like figure will lead to greatness.

In the so-called halcyon days of pre-1914 Europe, there were all too many harbingers of later disaster. The illiberal and irrational ideologies of those days lacked political resonance, but they permeated—especially in imperial Germany—many groups among the educated elite. In Germany, much of what was to take place following the Great War had already been anticipated before the war, including the pervasive sense of cultural despair. Many Germans reveled in "the decline of the West" before Spengler's tome ever appeared. They took a kind of bizarre solace in contemplating the end of this soulless, mechanistic world—in which so many of them prospered.

This mood, exploited by Hitler, made totalitarian action succeed the ideological thunder of ideas. Yet this process would have been inconceivable without the loss of confidence in reason and the vacuum of moral principles, or without Europe's alternate immersion in intellectual utopias and pessimism. The atmosphere of despair and rejection lasted through the Second World War.

The First World War intensified ideological conflicts. After the catastrophe of the Great War—when Europeans got their first taste of totalitarianism and the Germans more than a taste—the discontents and yearnings of the prewar period gained greater legitimacy. Some Germans now glorified the community of the trenches and thirsted for some form of continued militant fraternity. In Germany the post-

3. See, for example, Karl Dietrich Bracher, *Zeit der Ideologien: eine Geschichte politischen Denkens im 20. Jahrhundert* (Stuttgart: Deutsche Verlags-Anstalt, 1982).

war drama was played out in a seething, defeated, and divided country. During the Great War, Germans had been systematically deceived—thus the shock of the November collapse. The legacy was distrust and suspicion; there was no consensus about anything in Weimar, except possibly the injustice of Versailles. The rest was anxiety and resentment.

If utopia and revolution are commonplace in this century, it was not always the case. Where history has taken a tragic turn is in the triple movement: utopia conceived as a sterile monolithic harmony; revolution understood as a dogmatic commitment to violent change; sentiments of hope and belief transformed into an orthodoxy incompatible with dissent or critical opposition. Where history provides consolation is in its threefold hope: when utopian longing is a supple changing ideal of diverse virtues and dreams; when revolution signifies recourse to a difficult path of fundamental social reorganization without conspiratorial self-delusion and magic language, and where, whatever the commitment to principles of political action and moral aspiration, there exists dissent, tolerance, and a respect for humane reason.

Profound sources for the conflict between reason and passion have always existed. Emotion leads to utopian dreams and revolutionary aspirations; reflectiveness teaches caution and a course that must be wary of beguiling simplicities. We are tempted to intimations of Apollonian nobility, but something between the mundane and the penultimate is what we ordinarily settle for. Or is the authentic human condition to be found in what lies between?

The Critique of Modernity

During the nineteenth century, the belief in social progress and human perfectability was mainly associated with the tenets of political liberalism. Some thinkers, however, rejected such a faith, and tried to counterbalance liberalism's emphasis on the autonomous individual by stressing the fundamental contributions of society to human well-being. During this century, however, a significant shift took place. The most radical form of perfectionist philosophy came to be embodied in the doctrines of modern socialism. While the advent of the First World War had shattered the progressivist assumptions of nineteenth-century European liberalism, the success of the Russian Revolution, on the contrary, inspired similar if not more radical aspirations among those with socialist sympathies. The Soviet evocation of the "New Socialist Man" provided these critics with an even more explicit example of perfectionist ideology. Consequently, in time the move began from a critique of liberalism to a confrontation with socialism.

One of the responses to this situation has been an attempt to formulate an alternative to the modern order by those who were influenced by the Spenglerian scenario of the fatal decline of the West (volume 1 of Spengler's treatise appeared in 1918)—those who appealed to what they considered a more authentic constellation of values. This was not a new development in intellectual history. For more than two centuries—Rousseau's *Discours sur les sciences et les artes* (1755) is a suitable landmark for the epoch—questions have existed about the ascendancy and even the legitimacy of such fundamental modern notions as reason, science, progress, individual freedom, and technology. Ordinarily, these judgments are articulated with regard to what are considered antithetical notions such as nature, community, order, or imagination. Occasionally these antitheses are viewed as stable qualities of life, and the only issue is the dominant position attributed to reason and its allied characteristics by the Enlightenment. More frequently, however, the contrast is perceived as symbolizing a historical process in which an original, positively valued state (nature, cosmos, community) was displaced by the "modern" condition. And the conflict-ridden state of the twentieth century is then interpreted as evidence of the deleterious effects of disclaiming the original state of affairs.

Concentration on the Cartesian premises of empiricism also comes near to suggesting an original fallacy behind certain fundamental modern ideas, though the critics usually do not call for a return to premodern thinkers. Since the period of the 1850s, a number of significant works of German scholarship have concentrated on issues related to the nature and status of modernity and its fundamental attitudes. Marx's concern with understanding capitalism and tracing its beginnings from precapitalist economic and social formations, along with Nietzsche's celebration of the Renaissance, are early moments in this attempt. Yet these, as well as later attempts to define fundamental qualities of the modern age, resulted in no single clear understanding of modernity.

For later thinkers such as Heidegger, Husserl, Adorno, and Horkheimer, something seemed fundamentally askew in their tradition and their world. They frequently located the original fault as already evident in certain strains of Greek thought. According to their way of looking at things, it appeared that the modern age manifested the results of this fault embodied in the tradition. Karl Löwith, in *Meaning in History* (1949), maintained that some fundamental modern conceptions were secularized versions of what were originally notions stemming from medieval Christianity. He believed that this called into question the legitimacy of the self-understanding of the modern age as such.[4]

A New Politics of History

Another example of such historiographical analysis can be found in *The New Science of Politics,* by Eric Voegelin, published in 1952. Written as an analysis of modernity, it was influenced by the spectre of twentieth-century totalitarianism. The reality of an insanely destructive internecine European war between 1914 and 1918, along with its revolutionary aftermath, justified, if justification was needed, the notion of humanity and culture *in extremis* of final inauthenticity, of a descent into nihilism. It bore out the impotence of Cartesian-Kantian rational confidence, and the apocalyptic obsessions to be found in the great solitary artists and thinkers of the nineteenth century.

Thus the pressing task was to examine the significance of the breakdown of political order in a society and the characteristics of various movements that claimed special knowledge about the meaning of the world. The question taken up in *The New Science of Politics* was, How is it possible to account for the rise in modern Europe of two totalitarian regimes within twenty years of one another? Its author thought the answer would not be discovered through a simple analysis of election techniques or constitutional mechanics. In fact, totalitarianism in both its German and Russian forms appeared to be symptomatic of a more profound malaise that pervaded much of modern Western civilization. Voegelin called this crisis "gnosticism."

To raise the issue of gnosticism is to be forced to come to terms with the relation between politics and religion in the origins of Christianity.

---

4. These and other points dealing with the basic "critique of the Enlightenment" mentality are reviewed in Robert Wallace's translator's introduction to Hans Blumenberg's, *The Legitimacy of the Modern Age* (Cambridge, MA: MIT Press, 1983).

"Gnosis" is the traditional Greek name of a group or school of early Christian writers who were active in Northern Egypt (Alexandria) and Syria sometime between the years 30 and 300 of the Common Era. The name reflects one of the principal objectives of this group— namely, to determine the scope of "knowledge" (*gnosis*) as opposed to "belief" (*pistis*). More recently, contemporaneous non-Christian and even pre-Christian doctrines have also been classified under the term.

Most Gnostic writings employ Christian terminology related to a Jewish heritage. Many claim to offer traditions about Jesus that are secret, obscured from "the many" who constitute what, in the second century, came to be known as the "Catholic Church." These Christians are today known as Gnostics. Yet gnosis is not primarily rational knowledge. The Greek language distinguishes between scientific or reflective knowledge and knowing through observation or experience, which is gnosis. As the Gnostics use the term, it can be translated as "insight" since gnosis involves an intuitive process of knowing oneself. To know oneself, they maintained, is to know human nature and purpose, yet to know oneself at the most profound level is at the same time to know God. This is the secret of gnosis.

Voegelin was not interested in specific Gnostic teachings or principles in themselves. Rather, he believed that the modern problem centers on that specific form of consciousness which, in an attempt to articulate its own self-understanding, typically constructs a Gnostic system.

It was over sixty years ago that Eric Voegelin initiated his scholarly work amid the upheavals following the breakdown of the European order in World War I. Theories and worldviews that had satisfied previous generations were now found wanting in the passionate course of events that seemed to defy understanding. Although a wealth of conflicting conjectures, hypotheses, and theories sprang up, disorder remained all but inexplicable during the troubled time between the wars. Voegelin's consistently maturing thought, presented in a steady flow of publications over the last several decades, made a contribution whose significance is only now coming to be recognized. His controversial work, drawing on an ever-widening range of historical materials, focuses on three central themes: the philosophy of consciousness, of order, and of history, the three avenues along which he has conducted his search for understanding the human condition.

In his five-volume study *Order and History,* published between 1956 and 1987, Voegelin analyzed the development of Western self-understanding. *Order and History* is a work that rethinks both the substance and the process of Western intellectual history in an original way, throwing light on some of the most complex issues of our age. Beginning with an examination of Homeric mythology and proceeding to an analysis of Jewish theology and Greek philosophy, the *History* traces the West's increasing awareness of its fundamental relationship to forms of cosmological and historical order. It was as if Western thinkers discovered that their human nature existed only in its relationship to the order of society and nature at large. Within this order, however, tensions exist. Yet it is this realization of tension that constitutes the unique and consequently definitive quality of the human province. For those who are unable to bear the uncertainty that such a tension implies, this situation must be overcome. The inability to live within the limits of the human situation thus characterizes a certain type of modern mentality, one that attempts to escape the very tensions that define the human condition. The essential strategy for such a rebellion is to invest the world with an absolute quality. By acting as if the world had become sacred, this type of mentality can acquire once and for all the meaning that it previously lacked. In effect, security and certitude are gained at the cost of one's humanity.

The immediate consequence of treating the world as an absolute is to make the political order sacred. Thus politics, as that activity by which the world is organized, assumes a paramount significance and consequently takes on a totalistic cast. From within this perspective, individuals are charged with refashioning the world so that it eventually manifests the true and final design that is its appropriate form. The Promethean mentality attempts to achieve salvation within history, to definitively resolve life's tensions, uncertainty, and anxiety through political and historical activity. The fact that such a "resolution" is contrary to the limits of the human condition and thus impossible to achieve establishes both the irony and ultimate tragedy of this experiment. Implicit in this analysis is an insistence that this type of mind-set is operative within many of the major political movements of our time. In such instances, there is a tendency to absolutize the imminent and thereby detract from the bipolar quality of human nature.

The highly refined degree of discrimination and subtlety of perception that characterizes a work such as *Order and History* constitutes an evocative contribution to an understanding of the history of social and political order and disorder. Eric Voegelin is explicit about the dynamic motivating the writing of the *History*. In the preface to the first volume, he refers to the ideological presuppositions that have hampered the work of scholarly inquiry in the past, and then states that *Order and History* should not be read as a treatise that tries to exhume curiosities of a dead past, but as an investigation into the nature of the world in which we live presently. The current world social order is neither recent nor simple, but contains historical forces that present the analyst with a maze of complexity.

Likewise in this preface, he specifically refers the reader to his analysis of human nature and the problems involved in seeking a radical restructuring of the social order. He maintains that the prophet Jeremiah, for example, envisioned the transformation of Israel through a radical restructuring of reality. In this effort Jeremiah attempted the impossible. Voegelin maintains that the prophetic conception of radical transformation lies at the root of contemporary beliefs in the perfection of society, either through human progress or through revolution.

Thus, right from the outset of *Order and History,* the author affirms that the enterprise originates out of a sensitivity to the demands of the present—a time in which a great deal of what passes for the exercise of critical intelligence is in fact ideological discourse, the most common political form of contemporary gnosticism. The term "gnosticism" has in fact entered political argument as a synonym for ideology. The oeuvre must consequently be read as an "archeology of the present," an attempt to discern the lineaments of the human condition through the miasma of contemporary discourse. It can also be read as an example of the exercise of intellectual countervailing power.

In his *Programmschrift, The New Science of Politics,* which outlined an agenda of research that was subsequently to develop into *Order and History,* "gnosis" or "gnosticism" is the principal theme of the second section of the book. The work interprets gnosticism as a phenomenon that gives expression to the desire for a radical modification of human nature and the establishment of a transfigured society. It is gnosticism which, in this estimation, provides the key to understanding the nature of modernity.[5]

This judgment was refined in later writings to do justice to the complexity of contemporary society. This came about because of the necessity of expanding the inquiry into modern consciousness in order to

5. Eric Voegelin, *The New Science of Politics* (Chicago: University of Chicago Press, 1952), 107.

include an analysis of its Gnostic, hermetic, and alchemistic elements.[6] Initially, the phenomenon of gnosticism was an important element in this analysis of culture. Gnosticism was viewed as a reaction to the psychic tension induced by a world that had been de-divinized by Christianity.[7] In his more recent writings, Voegelin focused on Gnostic consciousness and its underlying rationale.[8] The Gnostic orientation can be seen not only as a search for certainty, a singular reaction to the tensions originally evoked by Christianity, but also as an example of a generic human proclivity. Thus the initial examination of gnosticism as a Western cultural phenomenon may be extended to assist in developing an anthropological perspective that has wider implications for the study of diverse cultures.

Voegelin consequently perceived a significant part of his task to be contributing toward the restoration of the "balance of consciousness." Plato and Aristotle established the balance, both in historical fact and as a premise of rational inquiry, and this is one of the central occurrences in the history of thought because it has been decisive for the life of reason in Western civilization until the present time. It is also a principal determinant of order in history.

In *The Ecumenic Age,* Voegelin notes that life in the world may become a pretense to be overcome by utopian hopes, as in apocalyptic movements; or that utopian hopes may become a projection, an imaginatively created illusion. One need beware of such distortions in order to maintain the type of stability that comes about when the balance of consciousness becomes comprehensible as constituting the very morphology of life itself.[9] In his writings throughout the years, Voegelin elaborated upon the varieties of "Second Order Realities" (as authors Robert Musil and Heimito von Doderer term this phenomenon) that can disorient the process of consciousness as it moves toward an exodus from reality or transforms its contents into utopian programs. To exceed the boundaries of this tension of consciousness

6. Eric Voegelin, "Response to Professor Altizer's 'A New but Ancient God,' " *Journal of the American Academy of Religion* 43 (1975), 765–89.

7. *The New Science of Politics,* 122.

8. An updating of Voegelin's notion of gnosticism can be found in James L. Wiser, "Voegelin's Concept of Gnosticism," *The Review of Politics* 42 (1980), 92–104. For a critical evaluation, see Richard Faber: "Eric Voegelin—Gnosis-Verdacht als polit(olog)isches Strategem," in *Gnosis und Politik,* ed. Jacob Taubes (Munich: Wilhelm Fink, 1984).

9. Eric Voegelin, *The Ecumenic Age* (Baton Rouge: Louisiana State University Press, 1974), 228.

that characterizes the human situation, various individuals seek some form of gnosis, the pretension to an irrefragable understanding of life's enigmas through knowledge. As an alternative, we may propose the "postulate of the balance": The achievement of differentiation of consciousness is ultimately human existence lived according to the balance of consciousness.

During the course of historical investigations, we may trace the fundamental advance from compact to differentiated consciousness, during which process existence became existence in historical form. The primary task of the historian is to move through the plane of theory into the foundational strata of generative experiences. The effort to trace the development of symbolic forms provides a framework for *Order and History.*

A reading of Voegelin's oeuvre raises the question of how extensively the phenomenological analysis of experience, which focuses on "the structure of the life-world," is brought to bear on biblical, Greek, and other material. This inquiry is a legitimate one since Voegelin's writings share an affinity with the central project of phenomenology. In one sense, his theory of experience and symbolization attempts to link phenomenology and history as points of a parabola. The theory of consciousness is the foundation of a phenomenological study of the search for order in society and history. The roots of this theory of history and interpretation of human experience lie in an understanding of consciousness.

The work of Eric Voegelin fits into the cycle of the rise, decline, and fall of theorizing about human nature. We are at present witnessing in many quarters a return to favor of human-nature theorizing. Yet it was never actually dead. Freud's *Civilization and Its Discontents,* for instance, articulated the pessimistic conclusions for politics that he himself drew from his psychological theory. Moreover, the general relativistic atmosphere that characterized so much of the first half of the century and was so unfavorable to notions of constant and universal human qualities has mainly given way to a greater willingness to postulate some constants in human affairs.

Yet agreement as to what form of polity human nature calls for is difficult to secure. Many argue that it points to liberal democracy, contending that both protection against tyranny and the fullest development of human potentiality can best be served by a democratic regime. These facts, assuming they are facts, provide not only reasons why democracy is desirable but reasons why individuals, as they become aware of their interests, will desire it and strive for it.

Certainly, both individual development and the political evolution toward which it points depend upon favorable circumstances, which may or may not prevail. Currently, many of those who think that some form of democracy is the wave of the future pin their hopes on the possibility of transforming human nature. Or, like Marx, they believe that the human being is essentially a friendly, cooperative, noncompetitive, community-loving creature whose "species-being," up to this time, has been obscured and twisted or prevented from developing by unfortunate circumstances.

It has become increasingly apparent that the problem of changing human nature runs much deeper than the old nature-nurture controversy. This way of stating the dilemma was a grand oversimplification since nature and nurture cannot be so sharply divided. The key concept today is "interaction," which in itself suggests the complexity of the problem. Also, it is recognized that even if environmental rather than genetic factors were dominant, the problem of directed change would remain intractable. The difficulty is that very early experience is apparently fundamental to the development of character, that is, "nature." How then escape the influence of the older generation, the family, or other members of the same generation who influence and serve as models for the young?

Theories of human nature are thus again becoming a prominent feature of political theory. Yet since what political thinkers have in mind frequently corresponds only minimally to the complex historical experience of life in the twentieth century, the claim of political philosophy to universal understanding is a tenuous one. Human nature is too complex to fit the manageable theories they devise. One by one, these theories are tested and found lacking—defeated either by the diversity of human behavior or by our inability to step outside our own class and culture. Consequently we promote socially constrained systems as universal truth.

2

Paradigms
of
Consciousness

The inquiry into the nature of human consciousness has negotiated an extensive and intricate history. Despite centuries of research, of attempting to coalesce two conjectural entities designated mind and matter; in spite of comprehensive investigations of the states of consciousness, of differentiating technical expressions such as intuition, representation, sensations, images—notwithstanding all this, the question of the nature of conscious intelligence remains a compelling one.

The term "consciousness" is widely used to characterize many mental states, and it possesses both intentional and nonintentional meanings. We can differentiate the question of what it is to be conscious of something from the question of what it is to be conscious. Thus consciousness involves not only awareness of one's own states, but the nature of these states themselves, whether one has cognizance of them or not. While attempts were made to explain aspects of the mind's self-knowledge according to pre-Cartesian psychological theories, the seventeenth century witnessed successes in mechanics, physiology, and the other physical sciences that posed a threat to this psychology. The intellectual climate of the present age resembles that of seventeenth-century Western Europe in any number of ways. One, particularly significant in the current context, is the widespread interest in the potential and capacities of automata, an area that fascinated the seventeenth-century mind as compellingly as it does our own.

The Mind-Body Problem

The history of the philosophy of mind appears to be a pendulum swing from the dualism of Descartes to the materialism of Hobbes, to the idealism of Berkeley, back to dualism, idealism, and materialism. Descartes's innovation was his explicit assertion that dimensions of mind exist that are not susceptible to mechanical or physiological explanation. Actually, this led Descartes to suppose that no explanation whatever could be provided for these dimensions of mind, which demonstrates the power of the prevailing paradigm. Descartes did not envision an independent science of mind that would be irreducible to physical science; and when he did attempt to explain "the passions of the soul," he offered an epiphenomenal physiological account.

But thinkers influenced by Descartes, particularly Locke and Leibnitz, did attempt to develop an independent psychology. They accepted the Cartesian argument that certain dimensions of mind could not be explained physiologically; but they rejected his view, and the prevailing view, that the only legitimate explanation was physical. It was this aspect of the Cartesian revolution that permitted philosophical grammar to flourish as part of an independent science of mind that was not reducible to the physical science of the time. Locke himself is clearly Cartesian in all relevant respects. He accepted the Cartesian hypothesis that dimensions of mind involving the normal use of language cannot be given a physical explanation, though unlike Descartes he went on to develop a theory of mind that was independent of physical theory. One could postulate that a revolution in the physical sciences made the Cartesian revolution necessary if there was to be any real theory of mind.

Mind in Evolutionary Theory

The inquiry into the structure of consciousness was initially called the mind-body problem, and it involved a complex reasoning process. But ever since Darwin, it has been transformed into a more scientific issue, it has become the question of the origin of consciousness in evolution. Where and by what means in the evolutionary process could the intricate tapestry of subjective experience have developed? And at what point did it evolve? Such thinking was initiated with the inception of modern evolutionary theory by Darwin and Alfred Russel Wallace, the coformulator of the theory of natural selection. After their dual announcements of the theory in 1858, both Darwin and Wallace struggled with the question of human evolution and its correlative dilemma of consciousness. But where Darwin discerned only continuity in evolution, Wallace did not.[1] This problem has been pivotal to the speculative themes of our age.

Over the years, a number of explanations have been advanced. The most comprehensive explanation asserts that the succession of subjective states experienced in introspection maintains a continuity extending indeterminately into the past through phylogenetic evolution and beyond into a basic property of interacting matter. Animals evolve; nervous systems and their mechanical reflexes increase in complexity; when some indefinite degree of nervous complexity is attained, consciousness emerges. This hypothesis was prominent in the first quarter of the twentieth century.

The contemporary formulation of the problem of consciousness has for its basis the nervous system itself. How often do we conceive of a thought as a particular neuron or a mood as a particular neurotransmitter? If a person is conscious, the center of that consciousness has to be in the brain. Currently we possess the techniques to investigate the nervous system directly. All that is necessary is to discover those parts of the brain that are responsible for consciousness, then trace out their anatomical evolution, and the problem of the origin of consciousness will be solved. Moreover, if we study the behavior of present-day species that correspond to various stages in the development of these neurological structures, we will finally be able to know with experimental exactness just what consciouness fundamentally is.

This appears to be an excellent research program. Ever since Descartes selected the pineal gland of the brain as the source of consciousness and was refuted by the physiologists of his day, there has been an intensive if often superficial search to localize where in the brain consciousness exists.[2] While thousands of careful neurophysiological and neuromorphological experiments of the last decades have not yet pinpointed empirically the engram of even the most fundamental association of the learning mind, they have provided direction to its theory.

1. To demonstrate such continuity was the intent of Darwin's second most significant work, *The Descent of Man*, 2d. ed. (London: J. Murray, 1874).

2. See Julian Jaynes, "The Problem of Animate Motion in the Seventeenth Century," *Journal of the History of Ideas* 31 (1970), 219–34.

Yet a double bind is involved in the foregoing type of reasoning, one that is tacit in the proclivity to translate psychological phenomena into chemistry and neuroanatomy. The presumption is that it is possible to know in the nervous system what is known first in behavior. Yet even if a complete wiring diagram of the nervous system existed, it would still not be possible to answer the fundamental question. It would still never be possible—from a knowledge of the brain alone—to determine if the brain contained a consciousness similar to our own. We first have to start from some conception of what consciousness is, from what is involved in the process of introspection.

At this point it seems premature to construct an entire paleontology of consciousness on the basis of brain research that is still in its nascent and most speculative stages. And it seems to be an exercise in *hubris* to assume that the genius of the past and its artifacts were due simply to an undifferentiated consciousness and not to a complexity equal to but different from our own. One could offer, for instance, many examples to demonstrate that the ancients were conscious masters of consciousness, able to perform along the spectrum of awareness to accomplish many different tasks. Recent cultural anthropology abounds with evidence of "primitive" peoples with minds as complex and capricious as our own.[3]

The term "mind" ordinarily refers to mental processes and dispositions for mental actions and reactions.[4] The problem of the evolution of mind is therefore not a false issue generated by a misconceived metaphysic. Rather, it is a matter of tracing the development of certain types of abilities, tendencies, capacities, and propensities in organisms and delineating the qualities or types of qualities upon which the existence of such characteristics depends.

Recent research in anthropology suggests that the prevailing view that the mental dispositions of the human race are genetically prior to culture[5] and that actual capabilities represent the amplification or extension of these preexistent dispositions by cultural means is not

3. For example, see Francisco Guerra, *The Pre-Columbian Mind* (London: Seminar Press, 1971); Claude Lévi-Strauss, *La Pensée Sauvage* (Paris: Librairie Plon, 1962).

4. See Karl Popper and John Eccles, *The Self and Its Brain* (New York: Springer International, 1977), 72.

5. Culture may be narrowly defined to include only post-tool-making symbolic patterns. For an argument that culture should be defined as "a learned pattern of the meaning of signals and signs" and extended through the entire world of living organisms, see T. Parsons, "An Approach to Psychological Theory in Terms of the Theory of Action," in *Psychology: A Study of a Science*, ed. S. Koch, 3:612–711.

correct.[6] The apparent fact that the final stages of human biological evolution occurred after the initial stages of cultural expansion implies that "basic," "pure," or unconditioned human nature, in the sense of the innate constitution of humanity, is so functionally incomplete as to be unviable. Tools, hunting, family organization, and later art, religion, and science molded people somatically; consequently, they are vital not merely to survival but to personal realization. Culture exerts a biological effect on the way skills are organized in the brain. The application of this revised understanding of human evolution leads to the hypothesis that cultural resources are ingredient, not accessory, to human thought.[7]

These are the central questions that David Hume maintained to be of preeminent significance: How does the mind function, and beyond that why does it function in such a way and not another, and from these two considerations together, what is human nature?

Cognitional Theory

To help us answer these questions in our time, we have cognitive science and its related disciplines: linguistics, psychology, Artificial Intelligence. Psychology has taught us about the penetration and reliability of our introspective knowledge. This is significant, because some theories of mind depend heavily on what self-conscious introspection is supposed to reveal. Cognitive psychology and artificial intelligence have produced models of cognition which, when activated within a suitably programmed computer, mimic closely some of the complex activities of goal-driven intelligence. The neurosciences have started to unravel the vast microsystem of interconnected brain cells that, in living creatures, appears to execute those activities. And evolutionary biology has revealed the long and intricate selective processes from which conscious intelligence has emerged over time.

In order even to attempt any kind of answer to these questions, there is currently a need to extend inquiry beyond the limit of reflective consciousness and rediscover the archetypal images and symbols in the neutral depths. In other words, the only way to go forward is to

6. Clifford Geertz, *The Interpretation of Cultures* (New York: Basic Books, 1973), 82.
7. Ibid., 82–83.

return to the origins and set out again from there. This calls for an attempt at a conceptual reformulation of the structure of consciousness—no simple matter since the history of the subject is an enormous confusion of metaphor with designation. For this very reason, a reconsideration of this history and the theory of cognition that may be formulated on the basis of historical reflection is appropriate.

Since its emergence about three centuries ago, historical consciousness has been one of the most significant developments of Western civilization. History has become a form of thought applied, knowingly or not, to nearly every area of human experience. There is no field of human action that cannot be studied, described, or made intelligible through its history.

Epistemology—the study of the conditions of knowledge, of how we know—can no longer be viewed as a secondary branch of knowledge. The awareness—the historical awareness—of *how* we know is the fundamental condition of philosophy today. Thinking about thinking is itself a form of thought, involving a kind of self-knowledge. It appears at a stage during the evolution of consciousness. The recognition of the historical dimension not merely of our existence but our consciousness opens the way to a new conceptual unity through historical philosophy, the very opposite of philosophy of history. The latter attempts to achieve the knowledgeability of history, but historical philosophy tries something else, more circumscribed but also more profound: It recognizes the historicity of human knowledge, with its inevitable limitations.

Systems are inadequate because they are human inventions, and in error precisely to the extent to which human beings, by failing to consider their limitations, try to force their recognitions into symmetrical "laws." This is the difference between historicism and historicity, the first being the (mostly German and idealist) recognition of the presence of history, so categorical as frequently to become abstract, and the second the recognition of the historicity of reason and reasoning. The evolution is from rationalism to historicism to historicity, not the other way around; or from the recognition of objective knowledge to that of subjective knowledge to that of personal and participant knowledge.

In order to develop some of these themes, we now turn to the writings of a distinguished historian of culture for whom the understanding of the mind's fate is paramount. The intent is to determine the parameters within which any theory of the mind must develop.

3

Consciousness and History:
The Search for Order

A great many scholars inaugurate their life work with intimations of a conceptual taxonomy and dedicate subsequent endeavors to elaborating its details. The instance of Eric Voegelin is more complex. The oeuvre is augmented by an extraordinary amount of historical knowledge, which, though systematically collated, frequently appears in the published theoretical writings only in such allusive form as considered imperative to document a position.

Eric Voegelin was born in Cologne, Germany, in 1901. After receiving his doctorate in law from the University of Vienna in 1922, he served on the Faculty of Law of that institution. In order to escape the Nazi regime, he came to the United States in 1938. He subsequently held positions at Harvard University, Bennington College, the University of Alabama, and Louisiana State University, where he was Boyd Professor from 1952 to 1958. Voegelin returned to Germany in 1958, where he became Professor of Political Science and Director of the Institute for Political Science at the University of Munich until his retirement in 1966. After his retirement from Munich, he was affiliated with the Hoover Institution at Stanford University as Henry Salvatori Distinguished Scholar, a title he held until 1974. He maintained an affiliation with the Hoover Institution until his death in 1985. Voegelin was a prolific writer. His major works include *The New Science of Politics; Science, Politics, and Gnosticism; From Enlightenment to Revolution; Anamnesis* and a five-volume work, *Order and History.*

After Voegelin received his doctorate, he served as assistant to Hans Kelsen, the originator, under the influence of neo-Kantian positivism, of the "Pure Theory of Law" and the principal author of the Austrian

Constitution of 1920.[1] This strenuous apprenticeship of diligent attention to texts manifested itself in all his subsequent research. In 1927 Voegelin published an article on Kelsen's legal theory in which he noted that the substance of law is not an eternal sacred order, but a compromise of contending social forces. This substance may consistently be changed by the elected representatives of people according to the desires of their constituents without endangering a transcendent law.[2]

Voegelin was not to remain bound by the effort to differentiate behavioral description from the constellations of experience that give significance to it. He discerned that he was engaged in a reductionist evaluation of law that failed to reflect upon the substantive experience that engendered it. It would not be an exaggeration to say that the fundamental orientation of the young legal scholar's intellectual life was determined by his rejection of positivism. From then on he would only accept concrete experience as binding evidence on his judgments, experience based not on perception, but the entire spectrum of consciousness. He would have to criticize ideas by penetrating to the experiences from which they originated, if in fact there were any, and then attempt to understand how these experiences related to one another in consciousness. He was, of course, aware that his standard and method had an extensive history in Western thought.

At the same time that Voegelin started to question the foundations of legal theory, he also came to fathom a similar reductionist problematic in Max Weber's writings. Weber's fact-value distinction derived principally from his dearth of knowledge of classical philosophy and Christianity; in exiling these foundational influences on the value structure of Western civilization, Weber was able to evade the perennial questions of the meaning of life and confine his analysis to homogeneous occurrences in social behavior and history.

Voegelin experienced the need to confront the questions that had been read out of consideration by Kelsen and Weber. In reading Othmar Spann, he became aware of the necessity to study classical philosophy. In the early 1930s he learned Greek as part of an effort to cope with a widening historical perspective and in increasing appreciation of the subtleties of language in the evolution of consciousness. In the early 1930s, the substitution by the Dollfuss administration of a Cath-

1. For a paradigmatic example of Kelsen's approach, see his *Algemeine Staatslehre* (Berlin: J. Springer, 1925).
2. "Kelsen's Pure Theory of Law," *Political Science Quarterly* 42 (1927), 276.

olic corporative arrangement for the 1920 constitution played a significant role in the development of Voegelin's understanding of consciousness and history. The leaders of the movement relied heavily on the papal encyclical *Quadragesimo anno* as the authoritative support for the social doctrines of the new order. Voegelin consequently began to inquire into the contents of many significant papal encyclicals, and then initiated a more extensive study of Christian origins. This fundamental concern with the religious foundations of his own and other civilizations thus took its point of departure from the exigencies of experience.

The occupation of Austria in 1938 forced Voegelin to abandon his professorship in Vienna and to go eventually to the United States. During this period, he began drafting a history of political ideas. Like Spengler and Toynbee, he was attempting to identify historical patterns, although by 1940 he was beginning to reflect on both the Hellenic prehistory of philosophy in myth and the Hebrew origins of Christianity.

It was becoming increasingly clear that ideas are not entities in history; the substantive realities are societies, which express their existence in history through a complex constellation of symbols. Voegelin initiated an inquiry into the modalities of symbolic forms through which societies give expression to their life and the problem of discerning the extent to which the symbolized experiences provide a basis of order.

This orientation is evident in *The New Science of Politics,* which explores the way a society represents itself symbolically in order to constitute its existence in history. The book's principal concern is the self-interpretation of the Western world that took place through the Christian experience and the subsequent distortion of those symbols in the modern era in ways that had been identified at the very origin of Christianity (through the original definition of gnosticism) as a threat to the Christian faith and the order that developed out of it. *The New Science of Politics* is a compressed case study of the way that a symbolic self-interpretation on which an order (both of the individual psyche and the society) has been founded can disintegrate when the experiences in which its truth is grounded are no longer present in the consciousness of those culturally representative individuals who articulate the variations on the original symbols. The instance is, of course, contemporary Western civilization, with the Christian symbols of a salvation beyond temporal history being transmuted into immanentist ideologies (and revolutionary mass movements founded on them). These ideologies promise an apotheosis of humanity and society within the future domain of world history.[3]

The Order of History

By this time, Voegelin's inquiry into the possibility of a theoretically intelligible order of history was well advanced. The initial volume of *Order and History: Israel and Revelation,* appeared in 1956, and *The World of the Polis* and *Plato and Aristotle* in 1957. Six volumes were originally projected; the final three were to be concerned principally with developments in Western civilization: *Empire and Christianity, The Protestant Centuries,* and *The Crisis of Western Civilization.*

Israel and Revelation opened with a statement of the orienting principle of the entire projected work: "The order of history emerges from the history of order." This epigram was both the *arche* and *logos* of *Order and History.* The types of order to be accommodated by the study were:

1. The imperial organizations of the Ancient Near East and their existence in the form of the cosmological myth.
2. The Israelite existence in historical form.
3. The *polis* and its myth, and the development of philosophy as the symbolic form of order.
4. The multi-civilizational empires since Alexander, and the emergence of Christianity.
5. The modern nation-states, and the development of modern gnosticism as the symbolic form of order.

In implementing the program, volumes 1, 2, and 3 (*Israel and Revelation, The World of the Polis,* and *Plato and Aristotle*) treated the first three types of order; the remaining two types were to be studied in volumes 4, 5, and 6 (*Empire and Christianity, The Protestant Centuries,* and *The Crisis of Western Civilization.*)

3. I have relied on William C. Havard, "The Changing Pattern of Voegelin's Conception of History and Consciousness," *Southern Review* 12 (Winter 1971), 49–67, for a significant amount of the foregoing biographical material.

Yet as the research progressed beyond the first three volumes, Voegelin gradually altered his intention of carrying the work to completion by means of a chronological, periodized history of the order and disorder of Western civilization alone. When the fourth volume, *The Ecumenic Age,* was actually published in 1974, its title and contents indicated that the conceptual framework had undergone considerable modification during the intervening years. In the introduction, the author describes not only a break with the program of *Order and History* but also the partial abandonment of his former views on the course of history, although the revised concept still issues from application of the original principle orienting the entire work.[4]

The turn that Voegelin's thought had taken between 1957 and 1974 was not expected. In writing the first three volumes, he conceived history as a process of increasingly complex understanding of the types of social order fashioned by various civilizations. Such order as can be discovered in the process, including digressions and regressions from the increasing differentiation, would emerge if the fundamental types of life in society, as well as the corresponding symbolisms of order, were presented in their historical succession.

A delay of more than seventeen years in the publication of a sequential work such as *Order and History* indicates that the author had encountered difficulties in his philosophy that required resolution. Thus the fourth volume breaks with the course originally charted, in which Voegelin presented life in society and the corresponding symbolisms of order in historical succession. The analyses in the three previous volumes were valid as far as they went, but the conception was untenable because it had not taken adequate account of the significant lines of meaning in history that did not run along lines of time.[5]

The Ecumenic Age—the age when the great religions, especially Christianity, originated—denotes a period in history that extends approximately from the rise of the Persian to the fall of the Roman Empire. A historical epoch that had philosophical and religious foundations succumbed to new societies of the imperial type. Thus volume 3, which concluded with a consideration of Aristotle, appears to have attained its denouement in *The Ecumenic Age* since the final volume, published posthumously, concludes the project with studies of prob-

4. See the introduction to vol. IV for Voegelin's reflection on the orientation of vols. I–III and on the reorientation of his thought, as exemplified in *The Ecumenic Age.*

5. *The Ecumenic Age,* 2.

lems that had originally initiated the entire undertaking. This concluding volume is more of a thematic inquiry than a chronological
reflection on the further historical unfolding of culture and the evolution of mind.[6]

The shift in the orientation of research was related to an alteration
in theoretical perspective: The historical studies revealed an increasingly complex constellation of problems associated with an interpretation of life in the world. The patterns of history produced through
phenomenal description (possibly a remnant of early exposure to philosophies of history from the eighteenth century to Toynbee) were perceived as theoretically subordinated to more extensive questions of
consciousness that made their appearance in several different forms in
virtually all phases of history. The analysis of recurrent civilizational
themes is not simply indulgence in a sophisticated form of literary-
historical onomatopoeia, but an attempt to delineate patterns of lived
historical experience. As in all efforts to move from the virtual infinity
of potential materials to explanatory theory, an ordering of extensive
knowledge of history into more comprehensive conceptual generaliza-
tion took place.

Substantial points of reference exist between this project and Dilthey's theory of history and attempt to define the authentic relations
between consciousness and historical fact. It may be from Dilthey that
Voegelin derives his fundamental and evaluative distinction between
the technical knowledge of the exact and applied sciences and the type
of insight aimed at in the *Geisteswissenschaften*. Voegelin's work
manifests a commitment to the concrete quality of human acts of perception and intellection.

The opening sentence of *Israel and Revelation* formulates an epigram for a philosophy of history in apparently precise terms: "The
order of history emerges from the history of order." According to
the fourth volume, *The Ecumenic Age*, the meaning was procedural:
the *knowledge* of the order of history was to emerge from a study of
the history of order, a history of five types of order, and symbolization
following one another from the cosmological order of the ancient
Near Eastern civilizations to modern "gnosticism." But within the
course of history another reality emerged: the epochal event of a quite
different type of history, evolving in consciousness. The event marked

6. *In Search of Order* (Baton Rouge: Louisiana State University Press, 1987).

the decisive advance from elemental to differentiated consciousness—existence became existence in historical form.

This project of historical research proved itself in the compendious, detailed historical analyses which filled all but forty-three of the twelve hundred pages of the first three volumes. Yet as we have already seen, the original project was abandoned. During the course of historical investigation, additional types of order and new lines of meaning were discovered, but efforts to fit the empirically observed structures into a chronological course of history were asymptotic. The previous research was still valid within the ambience of its purpose, but the fourth volume contains a nuanced emphasis on time, consciousness, and language as well as order and history. The movement and countermovement of history are portrayed more sharply, and greater attention is given to the origin of consciousness itself.

Order and History embodies the more patterned descriptions of the development of culture and the evolution of mind. Delineated here are the forms that have been employed to symbolize the experiences that have evolved out of the search for meaning. The nascent form was the myth, which manifested itself variously as cosmological, theogonic, or anthropogonic, and moved from elemental to more complex expressions. The other symbolic forms are philosophy and revelation, although imperviousness to this reality is also a historical phenomenon. The meaning of forms becomes attenuated through detachment from the experiences out of which they are generated. As in the instance of gnosticism, a "second reality" overlays the reality of daily life and disorients the individual and society.

Gnosticism

Voegelin is controversial for his appropriation of the concept of "gnosticism" in the analysis of contemporary intellectual and political patterns. His notion is founded on the way in which the term was employed in the ancient world, but is wider both in conception and extent. This presents historical and philosophical difficulties that are compounded by the recent increase of documentary material from the gnosticism of approximately the second to fourth centuries C.E., owing to the discovery of the Coptic Gnostic library at Nag Hammadi in Egypt.[7]

Ancient gnosticism tended to be apolitical. Voegelin's particular concern was with the forms that a claim to gnosis could take when there existed a desire to draw on the potency of such knowledge for the transfiguration of the present world. He discovered evidence of the development of these types of interpretation of gnosis in, for instance, the hermetic and magical traditions and speculative constructions of history such as that of Joachim of Fiore. This type of speculation served as historical background for such varied later developments as Hegel's notion of the absolute epoch, Comte's idea of a new age of Positive Science, and Marx's notion of a transformed human race in a communist society.

Because the ancient, classical form of gnosticism was oriented toward negation of the world rather than transfiguration, Voegelin's appropriation of the term is controversial. Also, besides what is known today as gnosticism, he later became concerned with a pattern of thought that was made up of many other strands, such as apocalypticism, magic, alchemy, and theurgy, as well as other modern derivations. The term is appropriate, though, as long as it is distinguished from the ancient doctrine that bears its name since both have in common the claim to absolute knowledge in the form of gnosis and the power deriving from that knowledge.

Voegelin's writings on Gnostic developments in history are marked by sudden leaps between, for instance, the ancient Gnostics and a medieval figure such as Joachim of Fiore or between Joachim and a modern thinker such as Marx. There are two reasons why transitions of this type appear so abrupt. One is that the historical literature on this subject is already vast, so that Voegelin presumes a certain familiarity with it and makes no attempt to spell out all the connections between the thinkers being analyzed. Another reason for the apparent suddenness with which the analysis proceeds from the gnosticism of one epoch to that of another is that Voegelin's published writings do not constitute all facets of his investigation. When he gave up the nearly completed history of political thought in the 1940s and went on to

---

7. The entire collection of Gnostic texts from Nag Hammadi, comprising fifty-two tractates, mainly Christian but also including Jewish, Hellenic, Zoroastrian, and Hermetic material, has been published in translation in *The Nag Hammadi Library in English*, ed. James M. Robinson (San Francisco: Harper and Row, 1977). The texts discovered were Coptic translations from Greek originals.

write *The New Science of Politics* and *Order and History,* many of the transitional steps spelled out in the earlier works were left tacit. Thus one wonders how the author proceeds, as he does in chapters 4 and 5 of *The New Science of Politics,* from ancient gnosticism to Joachim of Fiore in the twelfth century and from Joachim to the English Puritans of the seventeenth century. The intermediate stages were actually dealt with in the section entitled "The People of God" in the unpublished manuscript.

Gnostic orientations, in their specific historical incarnations, may show themselves in diverse forms, but certain basic qualities are proper to all of them. One common characteristic of gnosticism is its orientation toward dualism. Ancient gnosticism is well known for its negative attitude toward the world and the body, but dualism in a somewhat different form is a feature of immanentistic gnosticism as well. In the latter instance, the dualism is not one between this world and a Beyond but rather between the present world and a new one that is hoped for. Either way, the Gnostic experiences a sense of alienation from the present world and aspires to redemption from it. This redemption is to come through the transformation of the aspirant or the world.

The actual transfiguration may be imagined as taking place in a number of ways, but often it is expected to come about through some type of technical manipulation founded on a privileged form of knowledge. From this perspective, ethical preparation is not necessary in order for the transformation to take place. The historical *locus classicus* of this attitude is that of the Manichean Gnostics with whom Augustine associated in his youth.

Since the gnosis of the the Gnostic visionary is privileged information possessed only by the elect, not the universal tension of existence common to all, Gnostic movements tend to divide people into an elite (the knowers and masters of technique) and the masses, the ignorant who at best can be disciples of those who possess special knowledge. Depending on whether the particular Gnostic tendency is activist or contemplative, the elite may have as their role withdrawal into contemplation and asceticism or active inauguration of the New Age.

These tendencies were spelled out in *From Enlightenment to Revolution,* a portion of the unpublished history of political ideas written in the 1940s and the early 1950s (published in 1975). The book analyzes the sentiments and experiences that, beginning in the eighteenth century, led to the modern doctrine of progress which, it is main-

tained, contributed to the formation of the intellectual climate of opinion that made possible the totalitarian movements of the twentieth
century. Such thinkers as Voltaire, Helvetius, d'Alembert, Turgot,
Condorcet, Saint-Simon, Comte, Bakunin, and Marx are subjected to
intensive analysis. What is frequently regarded as the *political* crisis of
our time is demonstrated to be a deeply rooted crisis of the psyche.

A Theory of Politics and History

Eric Voegelin's later work was varied. A major collection of essays,
Anamnesis: Zur Theorie der Geschichte und Politik, was published in
1966. Most of the essays were written and published during the years
intervening between volumes 3 and 4, and provide some indication as
to whether a shift of orientation in thought had occurred and if so
what it entailed. The emphasis in *Anamnesis* falls on the development
of a theory of consciousness. The concept of "political reality" is employed to refer to the reality generated by the consciousness of actual
individuals, whose experiences and symbolic expressions produce a social field that also possesses the character of a historical field.

   In Search of Order, volume 5 of *Order and History,* was published
in 1987. Voegelin's death in 1985 cut short his work on the volume.
Although it is fragmentary, the theoretical presentation that he had set
for himself is essentially completed here. For instance, the volume's
opening essay on "The Beginning of the Beginning" involves a reflection on Genesis and develops an analysis of the paradox of consciousness and the complex of Consciousness-Reality-Language as the
texture of the experience symbolized imaginatively, with attention to
the truth and its deformation. Subsequently, "Reflective Distance vs.
Reflective Identity" investigates the deformative and formative forces
at work in modern philosophy, with particular attention to Hegel and
the German revolution of consciousness; it then considers Hesiod,
and finally reflects on Plato's attempt to formulate a language of
existential consciousness, especially as presented in the *Timaeus.*

   The vast enterprise of developing a theory of order and history is
not abandoned in this thin volume. But that theory is elaborated from
a different perspective. In the seventeen years between publication of
the first three and the fourth volumes of *Order and History* (1956–57
to 1974), the underlying philosophy of consciousness presupposed in

the earlier work (and of concern even in the author's first book in 1928) appeared in fully elaborated form in *Anamnesis* (1966). In the thirteen years following the publication of the fourth volume itself, and preceding and paralleling its publication, other writings have developed vital lines of inquiry that are completed in the fifth volume. Among the most crucial of these essays are "The Beginning and the Beyond" (a seventy-page manuscript written between 1975 and 1978 and left unfinished and unpublished), and published essays that include "Immortality: Experience and Symbol" (1967); "Equivalences of Experience and Symbolization in History" (1970); "The Gospel and Culture" (1971); "On Hegel: A Study in Sorcery" (1971); "Reason: The Classic Experience" (1974); "Remembrance of Things Past" (1978); "Wisdom and the Magic of the Extreme: A Meditation" (1981); and "Quod Deus dicitur" (1986).[8] These essays will appear in the first volume of the *Collected Works of Eric Voegelin*, to be published by Louisiana State University Press. Some of these writings, along with others, were at one time or another intended for possible inclusion in this volume; but that intention changed as the conception of the manuscript itself modified in the author's thinking, and there is no way of knowing with certainty how the book would have appeared had Voegelin himself lived to see it through publication. It is apparent, though, that "The Beginning and the Beyond" and "Wisdom and the Magic of the Extreme," together with "Quod Deus dicitur," belong to the same genre as that in which *In Search of Order* is cast.

Voegelin's research before his death included extensive work over the last decade into paleolithic symbolism. During the summer of 1977, for instance, he was engaged in the exploration of caves south of Paris with Marie König (author of *Am Anfang der Kultur*) in order

---

8. "Quod Deus dictitur" was published in the *Journal of the American Academy of Religion*, vol. 53, no. 3, 568–84, and incorporates about ten pages of the unpublished "The Beginning and the Beyond." Citations for the essays mentioned in the text are as follows: "Immortality: Experience and Symbol," *Harvard Theological Review* 50 (1967), 235–79; "Equivalences of Experience and Symbolization in History," in *Eternità e Storia*, 215–34 (reprinted in *Philosophical Studies* 28 [n.d.], 88–103); "The Gospel and Culture," in *Jesus and Man's Hope*, ed. D. Miller and D. G. Hadidian, 2 vols. (Pittsburgh, 1971), 2:59–101; "On Hegel: A Study in Sorcery," *Studium Generale* 24 (1971), 335–68, (reprinted in *The Study of Time* ed. J. T. Fraser, et al. [Heidelberg and Berlin, 1972], 418–51); "Reason: The Classic Experience," *Southern Review*, n.s. 10, 2 (Spring 1974), 237–64; "Remembrance of Things Past," in *Anamnesis*, ed. and trans. Gerhart Niemeyer (Notre Dame, 1978), 3–13; "Wisdom and the Magic of the Extreme: A Meditation," *Southern Review*, n.s. 17, 2 (April 1981), 235–87. Also, see "Response to Professor Altizer's 'A New History and a New but Ancient God?' " *Journal of the American Academy of Religion* 43 (1975), 765–72.

to perform onsite inspection of the petroglyphic symbols of the world's first known abstract artists.

A theme of much of the later writing is that underlying the more obvious and observable crises in the current public situation is the problem of the relativity of worldviews and ideologies. Individuals find they cannot be certain that any of the major perspectives orienting current history (such as Marxism, liberalism, or conservatism) are valid. Each of the modern paradigms claims to organize the human condition intelligibly. The relativity of historical perspectives generates a tension. The background of this personal and cultural predicament is the steady increment of mass organizations that fill with power the vacuum left by the loss of historical meaning.

Yet a sense of serene questioning draws Voegelin through a variety of languages and cultures, even back to our paleolithic ancestors, in exploring the richness of the world. His writings protest against the reduction of rationality to the instrumental reason predominant in advanced technological societies. The work stands as a critique of one-dimensional images of the human condition that attempt to reduce the complexities of life to single factors or principles.

The author of *Order and History* has not fashioned an abstract and logically closed system. From the inception of his research, he has attempted to understand the dilemmas of civilizations through their various historical manifestations, each of them in its own terms. Consequently, these pages teem with analyses of cultures, situations, texts, symbols, and experiences, each of which has illumined particular historical cases. Voegelin has consistently maintained that he proceeds empirically, that is, in deference to what actually has occurred in history. He has analyzed those occurrences so thoroughly, however, that one cannot possibly report on the quality and quantity of these analyses short of encyclopedic form. Comprehension of these materials can only occur through theoretical principles, some of which must have antedated the work on particular historical instances. On the other hand, the work of understanding historical manifestations of order yielded theoretical insights—one is almost tempted to say, *a posteriori*—and the perception of a context of history as a whole, in which these manifestations occur, or rather group themselves, was also a purely theoretical achievement. There is, then, an encyclopedic as well as a philosophical aspect to this work, so that the reader seeking to comprehend its philosophy is constantly drawn into excursions into previously unfamiliar terrain, except that these are actually not excursions but the main path of the inquiry. In the course of reading, then, it is necessary to discern the philosophical structure of the inquiry even while appreciating the wealth of insight into the anthropology of consciousness and culture.[9] Northrop Frye has put the issue concisely: "The synthesis of modern thought is the philosopher's stone of our age, and any such synthesis would have to contain, if it did not actually consist of, a philosophy of history."[10]

Western metaphysics, whether deliberately or not, has sought to transpose the essence of the person out of daily life. It has posited a pure perceiver, a fictive agent of cognition detached from common experience. This has been brought about through an artifice of introspective reductionism of the sort dramatized in Cartesian doubt and Husserlian phenomenology, and explains why metaphysics has loftily relinquished the study of perception to psychology, the understanding of behavior to ethics or sociology, the analysis of the human condition to the political and historical disciplines. Yet this process of abstraction has also issued in the resultant artifice of compartmentalization.

During the remaining course of this study it will be vital to give close attention to the words that are employed thematically. "The thought *is* the language," as Wittgenstein has stated. The use of the Word requires vastly more vigilance in the *sciences humaine* than it does anywhere else, for in the study of humanity, the Word engages the very being of its object. A technical vocabulary is merely a language within a language. A consideration of this technical vocabulary will at the same time be an attempt to discover the reality that the words disclose or conceal.

The most serious objection to the technical vocabulary currently employed to describe human beings is that it consists of words that split the person up verbally. But we cannot give an account of the splits unless we begin from the concept of a unitary whole, and no such concept exists, nor can any such concept be expressed within the current language system of the human sciences. The words of the current technical vocabulary either refer to the person in isolation from the other and the world, that is, as an entity not *essentially* "in relation to" the other and in a world, or refer to falsely substantialized aspects of this isolated entity. Such words are: mind and body, psyche and soma, psychological and physical, personality, the self, the organ-

9. Havard, "Voegelin's Conception of History," 65–66.
10. Northrop Frye, "The Shapes of History," in *Northrop Frye on Culture and Literature*, ed. Robert D. Denham (Chicago: University of Chicago Press, 1978), 76.

ism. All these terms are abstractions. We take a single individual in isolation and conceptualize various aspects of the self into "ego," "superego," and "id." In brief, we have an already shattered Humpty Dumpty, who cannot be put together again by any number of compound words: psychophysical, psychosomatic, psychobiological, psychosocial.

That which constitutes a person can be viewed from multiple perspectives, and one or another aspect can be made the focus of study. In particular, the human being has been seen as a person or thing—even as a machine. The same entity, observed from several points of view, gives rise to two entirely different theories, and the theories result in two entirely different sets of action. The initial way we perceive any given reality determines all our subsequent dealings with it. It is thus to Voegelin's merit that he reflects on the person as an integral whole, as the following passage illustrates:

> ... man is not a disembodied psyche ordered by reason. Through his body he participates in organic reality ... as well as in the realm of matter; and in his psyche he experiences not only the noetic movement toward order but also the pull of the passions. Besides his specific nature of reason in its dimensions of personal, social, and historical existence, man has what Aristotle called his "synthetic" nature. Of specific and synthetic nature together we can speak as man's "integral" nature. This integral nature ... Aristotle understands to be the subject matter of the philosopher's study *peri ta anthropina,* the study of things pertaining to man's humanity.[11]

Nearly every civilization preceding our own has been concerned with the *training* of people. They have been less interested in knowing what the person is than in discerning what the individual ought to be. A civilization capable of molding people does not ask too many questions about them or about a normative view of the human. Yet our own civilization, different in many respects from all the others, is the first not to hold any normative understanding of truth. Human beings, at their most powerful, are also the first to mistake exemplarity and success. Less and less do we imagine the humanity that we desire to be, and the concepts that governed the development of individuals are

11. "Reason: The Classic Experience," *Southern Review,* n.s. 10, 2 (Spring 1974), 240.

gradually disappearing. A Christian of the thirteenth century, or an atheist from the middle of the nineteenth, would say that we have fashioned problems of their certainties. Dante was not disconcerted by man, nor Balzac by the individual, nor Michelangelo by art.

The surge of questioning thought today, delving more and more into time and into the shadows of our lives, is increasingly wide-ranging. By extensive questioning we hope to reach out to the fringes of posterity and perceive the ferment that saves the work of the past from oblivion.

In order to derive an adequate comprehension of the orientation of Voegelin's work, it is necessary to understand the foundations of his analysis of the history of social and political order and disorder. The studies that led to the publication of *The New Science of Politics* and *Order and History* were concerned primarily with issues in political economy and philosophy of history. The results of these investigations, however, have extended far beyond these two fields. The basis of this retheoretization of politics and history has been a theory of experience and symbolization that ranks in significance with Cassirer's philosophy of symbolic forms and Jung's theory of archetypal experiences and symbols. The essays in *Anamnesis* introduced a theory and history of consciousness that may prove to be Voegelin's most significant achievement.

Understanding human nature and works has become a precondition for the survival of the species, as well as for the enhancement of the development of individuality. The search for that understanding is the central purpose of Voegelin's work and the source of its significance. He remained attentive to the expanding human sciences, which provide the empirical basis for a continuing effort to recover the theoretical foundations of a theory of history and consciousness.

In the past the anthropological study of consciousness has suffered from a surfeit of empiricism on the one hand and culture-bound theorizing on the other. Yet each attempt to penetrate more deeply into the makeup of human nature will pave the way for a more accurate understanding of fundamental similarities between forms of social life, such as language, art, and law, that on the surface appear to differ substantially. At the same time, we have the hope of overcoming the opposition between the collective nature of culture and its manifestations in the individual, since the so-called "collective consciousness" would, in the final analysis, be no more than the expression, on the level of individual thought and behavior, of certain space-time modalities of the universal laws that constitute the unconscious activity of the mind.[12] We would then be able to comprehend more accurately the mind's fate in the world.

We need once more to attempt an answer to the ancient platonic question: How do ideas work in the world? Put another way: How does consciousness, which seems so insubstantial, come to characterize and affect substantive reality? This is the question that haunts Western thought. The processes of the world are ensnared in its net. It is the principal question dividing schools of thought and ultimate attitudes toward life.

12. Claude Lévi-Strauss, *Structural Anthropology*, trans. Claire Jacobsen and Brooke Schoeph (New York: Doubleday, 1967), 64. Lévi-Strauss is speaking generically about anthropology in his comment about the "surfeit of empiricism." Yet it would not be difficult to apply the same criticism to the anthropology of religion: see, for example, Weston LaBarre's *The Ghost Dance* (New York: Doubleday, 1970).

4

The Order of Consciousness

The very first statement of *Anamnesis* expresses the main thrust of the author's political philosophy in these words: "The problems of human order in society and history arise from the order of the consciousness. The philosophy of consciousness is for that reason the centerpiece of a philosophy of politics." The essays published in the first part of *Anamnesis* (written in 1943) articulate the theory of consciousness presupposed by both *The New Science of Politics* and *Order and History*, already of interest to Voegelin in the late 1920s when he explored William James's understanding of consciousness in *Über die Form des amerikanischen Geistes* (1928).

The opening chapter of this volume consists of a critical study of the most prominent current theories, disclaiming both materialism and idealism. At the time there were several attempts to envisage consciousness as a stream of perceptions and scrutinize its temporal structure and relation to phenomena in this context. This was the orientation of James, Hodgson, Brentano, Husserl, and the Scottish School, but these attempts were of a highly speculative nature.

Voegelin came to believe that academic theories and methodologies relating to consciousness were of a highly restrictive nature, analogous to the narrow horizons of political mass movements. What he had discerned was consciousness in personal, social, and historical existence. He came to realize that it was necessary to demarcate the logical crossbearings of the concepts that we already know how to apply. Endeavoring to perform this operation on the concepts of the powers, operations, and states of mind has perennially been a major part of the work of intellectuals. Theories of knowledge, logic, political theory, and ethics result from their investigations into this field.

In 1943, in two extensive letters to Alfred Schütz,[1] Voegelin tried to

---

1. These letters were later published in *Anamnesis: Zur Theorie der Geschichte und Politik* (Munich: Piper, 1966), cited as *A*. English translation: *Anamnesis*, trans. Gerhart Niemeyer (Notre Dame, Ind.: University of Notre Dame Press, 1978), abbreviated as *AE*. The letters referred to are found in *A* 21–60. Only one is included in *AE* (14–35).

construct a different approach to consciousness. Voegelin considered Husserl's *Krisis* essay a significant epistemological breakthrough. Yet he remained dissatisfied by it, as "all epistemology is only a preface to philosophy." During the course of researching a "History of Political Ideas," he came to realize that these "ideas" are actually symbolizations rather than concepts. These symbolizations are rooted in actual life experiences; since the world is experienced in consciousness, the question of the way in which consciousness and the world interact must be confronted. Consideration of this dilemma led to the belief that the stream theories were inaccurate for other reasons as well. Most significantly, they construed cognition according to the paradigm of knowledge of phenomena and paid no serious attention to experiences of personal involvement—a significant agent of knowledge. Also, they studied cognition as a type of phenomenon understood abstractly. Yet consciousness is a specific process in which perception of the world is shaped by actual experiences. This belief moved Voegelin to embark on a period of recollection in order to bring the nature of his own consciousness into sharper relief. He strove to recall the nascent experiences that were significant in his own mental development. Through this *modus operandi*, he established a solid foundation for his theory.

On the Form
of the American Mind

In this chapter I want to consider the original critical evaluation of the stream of consciousness theories in *Über die Form des amerikanischen Geistes*, the theory articulated in the 1943 papers, and the most important subsequent developments of the theory.[2]

The first two chapters of *Über die Form des amerikanischen Geistes* take note of a difference between the philosophical issues that interested British and other European thinkers of the nineteenth and early

---

2. Though drawing on Voegelin's writings (including unpublished manuscripts) amplified by information provided by conversations with him over the course of a number of years, I have generally relied on the account of Voegelin's intellectual development during this period provided by Anibal Bueno in "Consciousness, Time and Transcendence in Eric Voegelin's Philosophy," in the *Festschrift* for Voegelin's eightieth birthday, *The Philosophy of Order*, ed. Peter Opitz and Gregor Sebba (Stuttgart: Klett-Cotta, 1981).

twentieth centuries along with those that concerned thinkers in the United States. In the area of philosophy of mind, the British were motivated by problems that arise from the relation of consciousness to the world outside the subject and from the time dimension of consciousness. This interest developed from a basically skeptical orientation. The American philosophers, on the contrary, did not consider the singularity of consciousness or its transcendence into the world outside of the subject as dilemmas. Peirce and James consider an undivided self and transcendence into the world outside the subject as basic presuppositions from which they interpret other phenomena. Voegelin's study of the work of the British philosophers in this area involves a critical evaluation of the most viable theories of consciousness of the time, and this evaluation was a significant element in the shaping of his own thought.

For Hume, all that can be known with certainty is the succession of perceptions that make up consciousness. All that exists beyond that "stream" is subject to doubt. Thomas Reid's work initiated a basic shift in the skeptical orientation. Reid maintains that the existence of the world outside the subject, as well as the flow of experiences of the self, can be known with certainty, but that this knowledge is founded upon common-sense principles, which are properties of the self. Consciousness and memory are two of these principles. Through consciousness one knows with certainty what the self is experiencing in the present. Memory is the basis of the knowledge one has of the experiences of the self once these experiences are in the past. Time originates from memory; it is not provided by intuition. In recalling a past perception, the mind has a representation of a "distance" between the past perception and the present moment, and we name that distance "duration." Consequently, according to Reid, the tension of belief and doubt is not between the stream of the self and the world outside the self, as it was for Hume, but rather between the present moment of consciousness and the temporally protracted existence of the self and its world. Reid understands the present self as the only actual existent, though he did not arrive at a skeptical conclusion. Thus, if the "common-sense principles" are called into question, the issue of the constitution of the stream of consciousness into a unity comes forth. This notion of consciousness, which was developed more fully by the later philosophers of the Scottish school (Stewart, Brown, Hamilton), led to a third stage of skeptical thinking, in which the present moment of duration is the only actual existent and the continued existence of the self and its experiences becomes dubitable. This standpoint makes up the "stream" theory of consciousness, and engenders the issue of the solipsism of the present moment.

Hodgson, Brentano, and Husserl attempted to develop a theory of perception founded on an investigation of the momentary duration of the vanishing point at the present moment in the stream of consciousness. Their ideas become dialectical when they are brought to bear upon the present moment of consciousness, and consequently become opaque.[3]

The logic of Brentano closely approximates Aristotelian logic. Brentano's world, in a sense, is a world without facts. The nominalist dilemma is that of navigating in a world devoid of universals. Since ideas are structural universals, it is possible to harbor the fantasy that they can do the work of authentic universals and that we will therefore escape the dilemma by introducing them. Brentano was so creative a nominalist that he believed he could make do in a world bereft of universals.

The representationalists maintain that a priori or conceptual knowledge exists and that to possess such knowledge is to have the ability to discern relationships among concepts. Brentano also assumes that a priori knowledge exists, but his world is empty of ideas. Since, for him, it is simply a figure of speech to maintain that a priori knowledge is the knowledge of relationships among concepts, he is consequently in the midst of a dilemma. Because of his nonrepresentationalism, he needs to search for a new method of predicating the difference between the two types of knowledge.

In a representationalist universe, knowledge is either indirect, that is, conveyed by means of an idea representing its intention; or direct in the wider sense, that is, having nothing "between" act and intention. This type of knowledge is either direct in the circumscribed sense or reflexive. Representationalism increases the need for a criterion, that is, for something "in" either the objective or the subjective constituent of the act that is present if and only if the latter's intention is actual and not just potential. The idea of a criterion is epistemological. A number of representationalists, including Brentano as a structural representationalist, believed that they had discovered one.

3. Voegelin's difficulties with Hodgson's theory are basically the same as those considered here. Hodgson makes dialectical the concept of time. Cf. *Über die Form des amerikanischen Geistes*, 57–59.

From the representationalist perspective, there is another reason that self-knowledge is an even better candidate for authentic knowledge. Indirect knowledge of others can at best be sustained by a criterion. Consequently, if one insists on an absolute guarantee, the only possibilities left are either direct knowledge of self or ideas (or both) or reflexive knowledge of self. Brentano demands an absolute assurance for knowledge. Nor, again, do any ideas exist in his universe. Since self-knowledge is therefore the only claimant, we are left with only one question: Is it direct or reflexive? The dialectical nature of perception cannot be reduced to rational categories by Brentano's analysis.[4]

The fundamental divergence between Husserl and Brentano on the question of the directedness of mental phenomena is that while Brentano attempted to resolve this problem by appealing solely to the two concepts of subject and object, Husserl employs a third, intermediary concept, which he refers to as the *noema* and introduces in order to explain the actual directedness of the mental phenomena. While Brentano attempts to describe directedness by referring to the object toward which the act is directed, Husserl, on the other hand, characterizes directedness by introducing the noema. This concept is correlative with Frege's idea of sense, and Frege was the only one who had employed the idea of sense to study contexts involving verbs for mental activities.

By employing a threefold division among the acting subject, the noema, and the object, Husserl is able both to retain Brentano's notion of the directedness of mental phenomena and resolve the problems where no corresponding objects exist. While Brentano maintained that the directedness of the act ought to be explained through the medium of an object toward which the act is directed, Husserl insisted that the directness of the act should be explained not by an object toward which the act is directed, but by a structure of consciousness when one performs an act. Husserl designates this structure the noema. The object, which is introduced to account for the directedness of consciousness, is *not* that toward which consciousness is directed, and this concept is a major distinction between Husserl and Brentano. What consciousness is directed toward will always

4. These points are made in Part III of G. Bergmann's *Realism* (Madison: University of Wisconsin Press, 1976).

be a physical object or anything else of which we are conscious. In many instances no such thing exists. We still possess directedness, however—that is, consciousness is always "as though" an object did exist.

By means of this theory, Husserl maintains Brentano's insight that acts should be as though directed toward physical objects. Husserl here appears to have resolved a difficulty in Brentano by separating what exists in the structure of consciousness and what exists in the external world. The notion of separating these two realities takes place as well in Husserl's study of perception. Here also, Husserl, particularly in his *Ideas*, uses Brentano as a starting point, and then demonstrates why one should modify him. Husserl initially analyzes the distinction that Brentano makes between mental and physical phenomena.

We have thus far concentrated principally on the mental phenomena, and we have noted that Husserl preserves Brentano's fundamental notion of the directedness of mental phenomena, but that he nuances it by employing a distinction relating to Frege's and Bolzano's distinction between sense and reference. Husserl has no further difficulty with the category of mental phenomena. He believes, though, that Brentano was in error when he analyzed physical phenomena. Husserl maintains that, in treating physical phenomena, Brentano has joined together two distinct realities. The two elements that should be distinct are what Husserl calls the objective and the material aspects of experience.

What are the material and the objective aspects of experience that should be maintained distinctly according to Husserl? He analyzes a number of Brentano's examples of physical phenomena. Brentano cites as instances colors and sounds. While Brentano maintained that physical phenomena exist *only* intentionally, Husserl thought that they exist in the same way that physical objects do. Husserl believed that in addition to physical objects and shapes, there are also colors and sounds in the external world. Like all objects, these can be experienced from different perspectives. The objective elements of experience for Husserl are thus shapes, sounds, colors, and the like.

Now we come to the material phases of our experience. These phases are, Husserl says, experiences that we undergo when our sensory organs are affected. When we see some object, or see the shape or color of it, we are affected in certain ways, and the experiences that we undergo are what he calls material phases of our experience. Another word he uses for this is *hyle*. He simply takes over the Aristotelian word for matter and says that the hyle are not objects that we perceive, or features of such objects—for example, colors. The hyle are experiences that we undergo when we see these objects, their colors, their shapes. So again he posits a distinction between what is the object of our act and what goes on in us. The material phases are things that go on in us; they have temporal coordinates—they start at a certain time and end at a certain time. But these temporal coordinates need not coincide with the temporal coordinates of the objective phase of which they are experiences. The color may remain there long after we have stopped observing it, so that temporal features of the color are different from those of the hyle we have. In Husserl's lectures on internal time consciousness, he has additional criticisms of Brentano because he finds the distinction between mental and physical phenomena in Brentano insufficient to account for the fact that we can experience something that lasts through a long period of time. Thus the object we experience has this long duration though our experience of it has only a short duration.

Husserl has found a unique way of describing perception. It is extraordinary that he compared sensory experiences to Aristotelian matter, which was not some object perceived, according to Aristotle, but nevertheless plays a part in perception, while Brentano, though an expert on Aristotle, never thought of comparing the physical phenomena to matter. There are good reasons for this, since Brentano lumped so many different things together and called them physical phenomena that he would not be likely to compare all of them to Aristotelian matter. Having divided Brentano's physical phenomena into two groups, Husserl found that one of these groups came close to the Aristotelian notion of matter and could appropriately be called hyle. Husserl consequently propounds a type of hylomorphism. What corresponds to Aristotle's "form" or *morphe* could, in a first approximation, be called the noesis, which informs the hyle. The noema, however, is an even better counterpart to the form, and the noesis is simply the temporal counterpart to the abstract noema. Thus, to sum up, the noema should be compared to the form, the noesis to the informing part of the consciousness, and the hyle to the boundary conditions that limit the range of neomata that we can have in a given case of perception. Neither the noema nor the noesis (nor the hyle) are objects of the acts whose noema, noesis, or hyle they are. However, they are the features through whose interplay our consciousness has directedness towards objects, the intentionality that Brentano claimed it to have.[5]

The differences between Schütz's and Voegelin's understanding of Husserl's *Krisis* essays concerned the question whether, in fact or intention, Husserl had moved into historicist interpretations but thought at the time that Husserl had not been guilty of them. Voegelin probably considered his repudiation of the *Krisis* a repudiation of Husserl's entire philosophy. He fixed upon formulations that presented one strand of Husserl's later thought, that is, the tendency to enter the field of philosophical idealism. Thus he entered a domain in which Voegelin's decisive orientations were to be found.

The Stream of Consciousness

Voegelin made only basic criticisms of the stream-of-consciousness theory in *Über die Form des amerikanischen Geistes*. His only affirmative judgment is that the dialectical puzzles of consciousness cannot be abridged to rational categories.[6] When he wrote his monograph, Voegelin did not possess the historical and philosophical background needed to articulate an incisive understanding of consciousness. For one thing, he was not familiar enough with the precedents of analysis of mind in antiquity. He did not know, for example, about the Heraclitian analysis of private and public consciousness, in the context of the *xynon* and the *idiotes,* or of Jeremiah's portrayal of prophetic existence. He attained the basic knowledge that led to his insights into the process of consciousness in 1943. As mentioned earlier, these insights are spelled out in two letters to Alfred Schütz, where Voegelin explains that his basic ideas developed in an encounter with the work of Husserl. The major features of this theory follow.

The stream notion of consciousness, the theory that consciousness is a flow of perceptions experienced at the vanishing point of the present moment, is untenable. No "stream" of consciousness exists, except when one's attention is guided toward certain types of simple perception. Time awareness seems to have a particular connection with the

---

5. This account relating to Husserl relies on themes expressed in Parts I and II of *Husserl, Intentionality, and Cognitive Science,* ed. Hubert L. Dreyfus, with Harrison Hall (Cambridge, MA: MIT Press, 1984).

6. *Über die Form des amerikanischen Geistes,* 20.

domain of sensory perception, and in particular with bodily sensations and auditory perception. Because of this, the choice of a simple
sense perception such as "hearing a tone" (Brentano, Hodgson, and
Husserl employ this example), as a model to analyze the nature of
consciousness is not an appropriate method for reaching an understanding of the problem.[7]

Concentrating on the vanishing point of the present moment does
not result in an insight into the nature of consciousness, but in the
realization that consciousness is lodged in the body since the experience of the flow takes place when concentration is directed to the
body's sphere. In this experience, however, that which transcends
consciousness does not become a datum of consciousness; what is
achieved is a momentary limit experience, an experience that makes it
possible to see a momentary approach to the *durée* of the body.

Thus, turning to the vanishing point does not lead to a foundation
for consciousness, and the efforts of Brentano, Hodgson, and Husserl
to discern a foundation for consciousness in the vanishing point are
not descriptions but conjectures. The only application for such conjectures is in fashioning models of the most rudimentary content of consciousness. But they cannot lead to a foundation for consciousness.
Also, concentration on the vanishing point is misplaced, for the concern of consciousness is to turn away from the flow in order to construct the world of meaning, which is, in a certain sense, outside time
and space.[8]

Consciousness is thus not constituted in the stream, but the experience of the stream is constituted in consciousness. Consciousness as an
ensemble does not flow. If consciousness is not a stream, then the task
of discerning the composition of that stream, which Husserl believed
to be a basic issue, does not ensue. Husserl posited an ego that organizes the stream into a unity. One may doubt that an ego in this sense
would be the agent of that organization. Instead, the ego appears to be
a phenomenon *in* consciousness. The ego would then be not a datum
of consciousness, but a complex symbol for various determinants of
the movement of consciousness.

An examination of consciousness in the context of the stream appears to be futile. The experience of consciousness is that two levels of
awareness exist—past and future. I recall an event not because it exists "in my past"; instead, I possess a past because I am able to have

7. *A* 38–39, *AE* 15–16.
8. *A* 39–41, *AE* 16, 18.

an already completed process of my consciousness present to me in the form of memory. Similarly, I do not "project" into the future, but have a future because I am able to project.

One way of speaking about the relationship between consciousness and the world would focus on the fact that we are able to date the succession of states of consciousness in temporal symbols.[9] We are also connected to the world through the relation of "object knowledge." This relation cannot be discerned from within, as Husserl believed, but only from without. The dialectical nature of sense perception cannot be overcome by logical categories.

Consciousness is elucidated in the dimensions of past and future, which are *present* to consciousness; that is, they are experienced in the present moment. Yet this moment is not a fixed point from which the phenomenon may be observed. To maintain that the past states of the process are understood to coalesce into a sequence would suggest prescience regarding the process as a succession of states. This understanding derives from causes other than the elucidation of the present moment of consciousness. Any cognitive orientation that places an extreme emphasis on the present moment limits itself to the solipsism of the moment and acknowledges that consciousness does not know whether the images it experiences in the present moment make up an order of succession. The "succession" experienced may be only an illusion.[10]

Consequently, (as Anibal Bueno points out in his essay for *The Philosophy of Order*), time consciousness is not an outgrowth of the fact that consciousness possesses a time form, but the result of a process of interpretation. This interpretation is founded on the symmetry between, on the one hand, the "past quality" and "future quality" of the images proffered in consciousness, and, on the other the recording of experiences with the aid of their connections to the history of the body, which in its turn can be recorded through its connections to occurrences in the world. Awareness of time as a linear sequence of experiences would thus be derivative, making it impossible to consider consciousness as in time. Consciousness is connected to world time by means of the body, but it is not *in* time.

These perceptions, which are hinted at in *Über die Form des amerikanischen Geistes,* bring up further issues. Does the fact that the linear

9. A 52f., AE 27f.
10. A 55, AE 31.

progression of experiences of consciousness is an inference—if accurate—mean that consciousness is not in time? In what way is it possible to characterize consciousness as atemporal? It is maintained that the world of meaning is outside space and time. Yet it may be said that meanings are atemporal solely in that they are engendered in abstraction from time. Also, the process of being cognizant of a nontemporal reality appears to be a temporal process. Likewise, how does the atemporal element of consciousness bear upon its temporal components? While these problems persist, a good argument is made for the case that the stream, though it is an element of consciousness, is not its core.[11]

When the representations of the mechanical world put forth by Galileo and Descartes appeared to demand that minds should be saved from mechanism by being represented as establishing a counterpart world, it was necessary to clarify the way in which the contents of this world could be discerned without the aid of sense perception. The metaphor of "light" was an appropriate one because Galilean science was so concerned with optics. "Consciousness" was selected to play in the mental world the role played by light in the mechanical world. In this metaphorical sense, the contents of the mental world were considered to be self-luminous or refulgent.

The paradigm was also used by Locke when he described the type of observational analysis that a mind is able occasionally to turn upon its own states and operations. He named this purported inner perception "reflexion" (or "introspection," as it is known today), appropriating the word from the common optical phenomenon of the reflections of faces in mirrors. The mind is able to "see" its own processes in the "light" given off by themselves.[12]

Yet even if a resemblance existed between an object's being illuminated and a mental operation's being conscious, it would not necessarily follow that the possessor of the process would perceive that operation for what it actually was. It may account for the way in which mental operations were ascertainable, but it could not give an account of the way in which we discern truths and elude or amend errors about them.[13]

11. Bueno, op. cit., 99.
12. Gilbert Ryle, The Concept of Mind (Chicago: University of Chicago Press, 1949).
13. Ibid., 162.

Reflective Consciousness

The preceding considerations imply certain conclusions. Consciousness is not a self-contained process that apprehends itself and is able, by analyzing its insights, to arrive at a comprehension of its own nature. Conversely, consciousness is a material process that understands itself to exist in a body and in a world. It consequently understands itself to be part of a wider reality which comprises it.

Voegelin came to a realization of the implications of this insight in 1943. It established the framework for his historical work. The manuscript on which he had already made much progress, his "History of Political Ideas," had directed him from "ideas" to the experiences giving rise to them. The exercises in personal recollection in 1943 provided a path back to the manner in which his own mind was formed by his early experiences of the world's wider reality, thus the significance of rooting his investigations in a theory that acknowledged that consciousness is materially constituted.

Consciousness is not able to become an object for itself. The only plausible starting point for a thinker is one's own consciousness, that is, all the prereflective experiences that have led one to pose questions about the nature of mind and the reality of which it is a part. These experiences may be described as moments of awareness that cause one to apprehend some part of reality as opaque, as something that calls for interpretation. A reflective individual's experiences of this type provide an openness to a diversity of questions about the nature of the world. These experiences are formative of a thinker's mind; they galvanize and provide direction to the process of thinking.

Eventually Voegelin chafed at what he considered the limited scope of issues with which most modern systems of thought were concerned. In order to unravel one's own intellectual position, it seemed necessary to probe one's consciousness in order to ascertain its constitution by the experiences of life if one desired to be mindful of his or her own cognitive presuppositions. This exploration had to begin with childhood to retrieve the formative experiences of life since they were vital elements in the current makeup of consciousness.[14]

The outcome of this attempt at recollection is an array of twenty sketches written in 1943, depicting particular childhood experiences. Here is one of them. The Petersberg (St. Peter's Mountain) could be

14. *AE* 12–13.

seen from the Voegelin family home. In the middle of the ridge, there appeared what the boy thought was a little toy house. One day he learned from a friend that the "toy" house was in fact a real house—a hotel. A new realization overcame the boy: that the house "up there" was small when he was below; that it was large when he went there and stood in front of it; that the family house, which was large, was also small when he stood above on the mountain and looked down on it. The experience was a disturbing one: He discovered that space is a strange matter and that the world he knew appeared differently if he stood at a different place in it.[15]

The recollection of childhood experiences is an effort to recall those archetypal episodes where the world made an impression on the psyche. The nature of these occurrences, though, cannot be ascertained only from these narratives, since such reminiscences can also be understood as creative acts that lead to experiences which inaugurate a search for understanding. Thus, philosophical reflection begins with the elucidation of one's own generative experiences, during which time questions about the nature of existence arise. In this state, one is able to bring rationality to bear on generative experience. It is through this type of reflective process that philosophical clarification of life is attained, and these types of experiences are constitutive of philosophical theories.

The foregoing sketch delineates Voegelin's understanding of the nature of consciousness following his theoretical reconstruction of the main issues involved in 1943. In *The New Science of Politics* (1952), and the first three volumes of *Order and History* (1956 and 1957), he developed the historical standpoint from which he would be able to explore the evolution of consciousness more extensively.

15. *AE* 42.

5

Theory of Consciousness

Anamnesis: On the Theory and History of Politics

Philosophy of consciousness is a term usually associated with Hegel or
with some attempt to resolve the Post-Cartesian problematic of the
relation between a knowing subject and an object of knowledge. *Anamnesis* (1966), articulates a philosophy of consciousness that is also a
theory of history and politics. *Anamnesis* spells out the theory behind
the process of retheoretization that Voegelin brought to the treatment
of historical events, patterns, creation of symbols, ideas, and institutions. The volume demonstrates the continuity of the hypothesis,
which was present from 1943, when Voegelin abandoned the project
of a history of political ideas and turned to that work on consciousness as history and history as consciousness. The essays in the book
thus form the basis for the process of retheoretization in which Voegelin had been engaged in his published work since *The New Science of
Politics* (1952).

Of the three parts of the book, the first is largely autobiographical.
A correspondence with Alfred Schütz clarifies, by way of a critique of
Edmund Husserl, objections to what are said to be the current misunderstanding of the problem of consciousness. Then a series of recollections from childhood set forth the central theme of the volume in its
simplest form. These recollections are followed by a previously unpublished essay on the theory of consciousness from 1943, a critical
breakthrough that identified the main problems and made possible
The New Science of Politics. That essay, then, was the beginning of the
reflection that led to the now fully formulated theory of consciousness
developed under the title, "Was ist Politische Realität?" in the third
part of the book. In between, Part 2 offers eight essays, most of them
previously published, as examples of retheoretization. Four of these,
namely, "Historiogenesis," the two chapters on Aristotle's concept of
nature and order by nature, and the last one, "Eternal Being in Time,"

are more than mere applications and must be regarded as pillars supporting the main structure.

Political theory, from this perspective, is not a set of propositions reducible to axioms, and that not because of inadequate intellectual efforts but because of the reality with which it deals and the problems of knowledge peculiar to it. For purposes of clarification, we may prefer to speak of the noetic interpretation of humanity, society, and history, a discipline that confronts society in the role of a critic. Yet one might ask: interpretation of what, and in what way? In matters of order we deal not with something like an alien object that we can view from without, but rather with a reality seen from the inside, ourselves participating in a larger reality that we know is not of our own making. The experiences of participating, of the reality in which we take part, and of ourselves as participants, are the source of order. Noetic interpretation, a later development, finds humanity already ordered and society already in existence. Consequently, noetic interpretation cannot start with a blank slate, something like Hobbes's state of nature. Noetic interpretation introduces a discursive philosophical interpretation of primary experiences and takes the place of more elemental symbolic forms. The knowledge it seeks is an exegesis of experience.[1] "All men desire to know," Aristotle's opening sentence in the *Metaphysics*, means that knowledge is prompted by desire and attraction, so that inquiry is both ignorant and knowing. Knowledge, therefore, does not deal simply with the subjective or relative or psychological. Its problems are not those of a clear-cut subject-object relation: Rather, the process is complex since we the knowers are participants, the terms of participation, and that in which we take part. While there is a terminological ambivalence here, it is appropriate to the situation. Consciousness is a two-way interchange between knower and known. That is why the process of knowledge has suggested to its interpreters the term *anamnesis*—recollection.

Noetic interpretation, its relation to the preceding mythical form of order, and the problems of deformation arising in its wake, form the materials from which a theory of consciousness may be fashioned. As the first attempt at noetic interpretation by the Greek classics may be considered mainly successful, it still serves as the starting point for contemporary philosophical inquiry. An analysis of the classical noesis can distinguish three dimensions. Deliberately setting itself off from

1. *Anamnesis*, 347.

the preceding myth, noesis: discerns the substantive structure of consciousness, the *ratio*; discovers itself, the light of differentiating consciousness illuminating the experience of existence in "tension"; and discovers the process-character of inquiry in the experience of moving from stages of less to stages of greater clarity and rationality.[2] At this point Voegelin goes beyond Plato and Aristotle and outlines what he calls the "new noesis." The Greek noesis essentially contended against the myth. After Aristotle, the symbols fashioned by the classical noesis (symbols among which it is possible to distinguish "indices" such as, for example, transcendence and immanence, and "type concepts" such as, for instance, the *spoudaios* of Aristotle or the *amathes* of Plato)[3] became separated from the experience for the exegesis of which they had been created. This led to a derailment of philosophy in the dogmatism of the schools where the manipulation of propositions was considered the main enterprise, as if the propositions themselves were a surrogate reality. Dogmatic philosophy entered into combination with Christian revelation, a combination that on the one hand brought forth an order of optimal rationality, the *doctrina Christiana,* but on the other entailed new deformations in the form of a dogmatic metaphysics, against which there arose the revolt movements of skepticism, enlightenment, and positivism. The new noesis, then, has to contend with dogmatism and ideology, and its problems differ from those of classical noesis, even though only in part. In unraveling the various facets of cognition that explain deformations and ideological revolts, we are able to construct history as the movements of consciousness in its ongoing inquiry.

To the three dimensions of the classical noesis, Voegelin adds three of his own findings: (a) that of the "perspective of reality," the angle of view of consciousness determined by the human situation that leads one to speak of the perspectivism of all human knowledge; (b) the dependence of consciousness on object, which means that consciousness, rather than spinning on itself, is always conscious of something, so that there arises the possibility of misunderstanding, and illusionary, or deliberately false imagery; and (c) the inescapability of "reality" as that which must concern consciousness, so that the structures of reality are the form in which consciousness and thinking moves.[4]

2. Ibid., 288–89.
3. *Anamnesis* "Sprachliche Indizes und Typenbegriffe," 315–23.
4. Ibid., 303–6; 311.

Here we obtain the yardsticks enabling us to make significant distinctions between different variants of reality or to discern the loss of reality. Consciousness will inevitably form images and representations of reality as of something other than itself, but can and occasionally will form images that miss reality and sometimes even substitute an ersatz-reality, or, as Musil has called it, a "Second Reality."[5]

Such analytical work makes it possible to trace the relation of successive historical phases of human intellectual development to each other, finding everywhere the same endeavor to obtain insight into the nature of reality. Thus the myth preceding philosophy was not false to reality but merely elemental, less differentiated than noetic interpretation. From the point of view of the present order, which is oriented by noetic representations, the myth and every kind of prephilosophical form of thought are indispensable recollections to remind us of the authentic concern of philosophy. On the other hand, it is possible to locate the origins of disorder first in academic dogmatism and then in the ideological revolts occasioned by that dogmatism. A pattern of decline appears here, which Voegelin sums up in an essay entitled "Immortality: Experience and Symbol" (1967).[6] He traces two movements, from noetic insight to academic dogmatism to ideological revolt, the first beginning with the Greek classics and the second with the formulation of Christian doctrine. In the wake of the second, with its two more centuries of dogmatic philosophizing, there follow two more centuries of ideological revolt from which, he believes, stem the ambiguities besetting us today.

The task Voegelin set out to accomplish was to recover the elements of order in a time of disorder. This task has demanded a supreme intellectual effort, yet the difficulties of the effort have left their mark on the work itself. One could imagine other revisions of the kind that Voegelin himself has steadily introduced in his work. For instance, one wonders whether the pattern of declining order from insight to dogmatism to ideology does not occupy too central a place and could not have been moved over to take its place with other processive patterns. One further question: History, in this analysis, is essentially the movement from one form of order to another, a decisive role being played in this movement by noesis. Yet could not "history" also have another meaning: The existential order of Israel that replaced the Middle East-

5. Ibid., 309, 311.
6. "Immortality: Experience and Symbol," *Harvard Theological Review* 60 (1967), 235–79.

ern order of the myth, and consisted in the cognitive response to a single event—the Exodus? This unexpected event, coming outside of and apart from the rhythm of sacred times characterizing the order of the myth, created for the first time an indestructible past as well as a hopeful future. In its way, it was as much an alternative to the myth as Greek noesis, so that the myth was replaced not only by noetic interpretation but also by history as a mode of existence, and "history" would stem not only from leaving behind past forms of order but also from Israel's experience of a singular-event-theophany. In past writings Voegelin also emphasized this aspect, but it seems somewhat neglected in *Anamnesis*. These minor critical remarks cannot diminish the significance of the achievement: A theory of consciousness that attempts to keep in focus and balance the processes of cognition, fundamental human experiences, the existential character of order, and the historicity of human affairs.

The Phenomenological Alternative

Voegelin's changing conception of history and consciousness developed in dialogue with phenomenology, especially with the writings of Husserl. The work of principal interest is *Anamnesis*. Some of the titles of the essays indicate movement in the direction just suggested: An intensified emphasis on the order of existence, ontology, and a process theory of reality. These examples include "What Is Right by Nature?" (1963); "What Is Nature?" (1965); and "Eternal Being in Time" (1964). "What Is Political Reality?" (1966) includes a section on "The Consciousness of the Ground." Consequently, we will briefly look at this theory of consciousness in relationship to phenomenology.

The phenomenological movement[7] focused disciplined attention on the analysis of constellations of human experience—on the "structure of the life world."[8] This inquiry has evoked significant attempts to discover a reflective orientation that can do justice to these experi-

7. The classic foundational works for phenomenology are those of Edmund Husserl: *Husserliana, Edmund Husserl, Gesammelte Werke* (The Hague: Martinus Nijhoff, 1950). Twenty-four volumes have been published thus far. Vols. I–IX primarily contain unpublished writings and relevant working notes.

8. This is in fact the title of a book dealing with phenomenology: Alfred Schütz and Thomas Luckmann, *The Structure of the Life-World*, trans. Richard M. Zaner and H. Tristram Englehardt (Evanston: Northwestern University Press, 1973).

ences without reduction or distortion. In France, the most well known of these sustained reflections have been carried out by Sartre in *L'être et le néant* and by Merleau-Ponty in *Phénoménologie de la perception* and certain later fragmentary writings. Sartre possessed a keen sense for life situations, and his oeuvre is marked by penetrating description. But his dualistic ontology of the *en-soi* versus the *pour-soi* was seriously qualified by the author himself in his Marxist work, *Critique de la raison dialectique*. Merleau-Ponty's most prominent work is a significant contribution to the phenomenology of the preobjective world of perception. But aside from a few brief hints and sketches, he was unable, before his death in 1961, to develop carefully his ultimate philosophical perspective.

Heidegger is the only contemporary thinker who has formulated an ontology that claims to do justice to the stable results of phenomenology and the living thought of the present. His early work, *Sein und Zeit*, is a highly original contribution to foundational thought. Yet Heidegger himself has apparently recognized the exaggerated anthropocentrism or subjectivism of its point of view, which he attempted to balance out by a contrapuntal emphasis in his later writings.

Thus Heidegger does not reflect on cosmological civilization, which grounds its symbolization in myth. The myth develops when a society acquires civilizational existence beyond the level of tribal organization. The human race's initial articulation of the order of its existence is that it is a participation in the order of the cosmos.[9]

Heidegger's uncompromising view is that the existential interpretation of history as a system of knowledge aims only at the verificaton of its origin from the historicty of *Dasein*.[10] He does not acknowledge historical learning as a starting point for the solution of the problematic of history because he thinks that such an approach prevents sufficient penetration into the essence of history since the very object of historical knowledge would prove a hindrance.[11] Heidegger rightly points to the origin of historical inquiry from history as a phenomenon: It is because humanity *is* history that history exists. Yet within the context of his phenomenological ontology, the unilateral relation Heidegger posits ought rather to be a mutual one: History as a discipline and history as a phenomenon presuppose each other. To take as

9. What Voegelin calls "der kosmischen Primärerfahrung (*Anamnesis*, 315); also in vol. IV of *Order and History*, 68–75.
10. *Sein und Zeit* (Freiburg: N. Niemeyer, 1927), 376.
11. Ibid., 375.

a starting point the fact of historical scholarship is no obstacle on the path toward the essence of history.

To recognize the culture-boundedness of human existence is to admit its historicity. The project is to arrive, by way of historical reflection, at the "historicity of *Dasein*" itself. In this *Dasein* one discovers how it derives its "being history" from the self-reflection which links past, present, and future, and thus is capable of conferring upon the past a unity which it by itself is lacking. What explicit historical scholarship did for its object is accomplished in this instance by self-reflection, the implicit historical knowledge embodied in *Dasein*. And in this case as well, it must be clear that history as a phenomenon and history as an intellectual discipline presuppose each other. The starting point of a phenomenological study of history must be the praxis of historical studies.

Voegelin is one contemporary thinker who does reflect on the significance of cosmological civilization.[12] We have seen that, besides the historical character of all his work, the writings are also marked by concern with more explicitly philosophical questions. The opening chapter of his first book—*Über die Form des amerikanischen Geistes* (1928)—for example, was entitled *"Zeit und Existenz."*[13] One could perceive this work in cultural thematics as a remedy for the ahistorical limitation in Heidegger's enterprise. The project has an affinity with that of phenomenology. In one sense, it is an attempt to link phenomenology and history as points of a parabola. *Order and History* is unique in its project of unveiling the coinherence of rational understanding and biblical faith as the primary ground of Western civilization.

The philosophy of consciousness is the theoretical foundation for this phenomenological study of the search for order in society and history. This philosophy of consciousness underlies and emerges from *Order and History*. The empirical survey of the expressions of reason in the search for authentic order is primarily a philosophical anthropology. In his earlier work, *The New Science of Politics*, Voegelin employs the term "philosophical anthropology,"[14] but replaces it in studies published later with the expression "philosophie

---

12. *Israel and Revelation*, Part 1, 13–110.
13. *Über die Form des Amerikanischen Geistes* (Tübingen: J. C. B. Mohr, 1928) 19–52.
14. Consult page 25 of his introduction for a statement of the significance of philosophical anthropology for an understanding of metaphysics.

des Bewusstseins"[15] (philosophy of consciousness). This is a refinement of the earlier term insofar as it indicates the area from which order is fashioned as the order of consciousness.

The collection of essays in *Anamnesis* is a synopsis of the epistemological foundations of the theory of politics that are developed in *Order and History*. Most of the essays were written and published during the years intervening between *Plato and Aristotle* and *The Ecumenic Age,* and provide some indications as to whether there has been the type of shift of orientation in thought alluded to earlier, and if so what it has entailed. These essays testify to a receptivity to contemporary conceptualizations of the experience of order.[16] The theme of *Anamnesis* centers on the belief that philosophy of consciousness is the core of political philosophy. Since problems of social order originate within the consciousness of the individual, Voegelin sought a way to overcome what he judged to be the inversion of political philosophy in neo-Kantian epistemology, value-related methodology, historicism, and ideological historical speculations.[17]

These essays are a contribution to the philosophy of consciousness that is the foundation for Voegelin's work. This is the order of human existence that all the varied experiences and symbolizations of order are an attempt to express, the source from which the experiential types and symbolizations of order arise, the center from which the concrete order of life in society and history radiates.[18] Voegelin's study of history and his theory of politics is thus an inquiry into the experiences that order and penetrate all the dimensions of life.

His investigation consists of two phases: an examination of the range of concrete experiences and symbolizations of order, and an

15. In *Anamnesis.* The beginning of Voegelin's actual work on the problem of consciousness dates back to 1943. *Anamnesis* was not published until 1966.

16. In this connection, see Voegelin's account on pages 19 and 20 in *Anamnesis* of his decision to abandon an extensive "History of Political Ideas" after he had completed the greater part of the work because he considered its orientation obsolete on the basis of his further researches into "experiences [as opposed to 'ideas'] of order." *The History of Political Ideas* will be published by Louisiana State University Press.

17. "Die Probleme menschlicher Ordnung in Gesellschaft und Geschichte entspringen der Ordnung des Bewusstseins. Die Philosophie des Bewusstseins ist daher das Kernstück einer Philosophie der Politik.

Das die Misère der Politischen Wissenschaft—durch ihre Versunkenheit in neukantische Erkenntnistheorie, wertbeziehende Methode, Historismus, beschreibenden Institutionalismus und ideologische Geschichtsspekulationen—nur mit Hilfe einer neuen Philosophie des Bewusstseins zu beheben sei, war mir schon in den zwanziger Jahren klar." Ibid., 7.

18. "Das Bewusstsein ist das Zentrum, von dem die konkrete Ordnung menschlicher Existenz in Gesellschaft und Geschichte ausstrahlt." Ibid., 8.

analysis of consciousness that can relate various phenomena as equivalences of experience and symbolization in the one reality of the person.[19] These two realities are interdependent because the analysis of consciousness arises out of an attempt to understand the historical phenomena of order, and concrete historical experiences and symbolizations can be comprehended only in relation to the analysis of consciousness. Voegelin selected the various essays in *Anamnesis* in order to demonstrate the way in which a philosophy of consciousness emerges as the theoretical penetration of the foundations of even more extensive complexes of materials. They are meant to illustrate the connection between the analysis of consciousness and the phenomena of order. Just as consciousness is the center from which the concrete order of life in society and history radiates, so the realities of social and historical phenomena of order reach into the empirical data of consciousness:[20]

> Das wichtigste Ergebnis dieser Arbeit war die Einsicht, dass eine 'Theorie' des Bewusstseins im Sinne von ein für allemal gültigen Propositionen betreffend eine vorgegebene Struktur unmöglich ist.[21]
>
> (The most important result of this work was the insight that a theory of consciousness in the sense of a set of propositions valid once and for all concerning a fixed structural configuration is impossible.)

The position held here is that a theory of consciousness develops only in interaction with the empirical investigation of concrete historical phenomena. While it is true that the theoretical analysis arises out of the dilemmas of empirical inquiry, it does not mean that this examination cannot also be treated as a separate question insofar as there are difficulties that are not to be resolved by uncovering more phe-

19. See Voegelin, "Equivalences of Experience and Symbolization in History," in *Eternità e Storia*, 215–34.
20. "Die Einzelstudien sollen auf die Strenge des empirischen Zusammenhanges zwischen Bewusstseinsanalyse und Ordnungsphänomenen aufmerksam machen: So wie das Bewusstsein das Zentrum ist, von dem die konkrete Ordnung menschlicher Existenz in Gesellschaft und Geschichte ausstrahlt, so reicht die Empirie der gesellschaftlichen und geschichtlichen Ordnungsphänomene in die Empirie des Bewusstseins und seiner Partizipationserfahrungen hinein." *Anamnesis*, 8–9.
21. *Anamnesis*, 7.

nomenological materials. These problems concern the context in which new empirical data are to be understood.[22]

Thus it is evident that a theory of consciousness is a question in its own right. The core experience of order from which implications for the order of society derive is part of the emergence of order in history. This is the theoretical foundation for the phenomenological reflection on the search for order. The roots of this conception of interpretive history lie in a theory of consciousness. It is consequently important to locate the foundations of Voegelin's empirical studies in his anthropology.

The problem that arises in the empirical investigation of the search for order is that of relating the different symbolic forms to one another. This is a foundational question of order in Western civilization. Once the different experiences and symbolic forms have emerged, there begins the long history of rivalry among the different sources of insight. The conflict between the ways of truth is the underlying issue of Western intellectual history from the interweaving of Hellenism and Christianity to the present.[23] The task is to attempt a clarification of the relations existing among the different symbolic forms that have contributed to the formation of the present society.

This project involves overcoming the dichotomy between reason and revelation on the basis of an anthropology founded on a dialectic of engendering experiences and expressive symbolizations.[24] Experiences and symbolizations may be differentiated in the sense of the subjectivity's being transparent to itself in its exegesis of consciousness and the reality of which it is conscious. Symbolizations detached from engendering experiences cause the phenomenon of dogmatization. The context then becomes a "second-order reality"—an eclipse of reality.[25]

We may view experience and language as correlative. The language symbol articulates the experience: It is *analytical, differentiating*. Articulating implies developing the structure of the whole and giving further expression to it. Myth, an intracosmic story that explains the nature of reality, is elemental: It comprehends the whole, unconcerned about its structure. Its language is also elemental. The narrative is not

22. The opening essays in *Anamnesis* are methodological reflections which preceded the publication of vols. I–III of *Order and History* by twelve years.

23. *Plato and Aristotle*, 219.

24. *Israel and Revelation*, 407–14.

25. For Voegelin's development of this notion, see his article "The Eclipse of Reality," in *Phenomenology and Social Reality*, ed. Maurice Natanson (The Hague: Martinus Nijhoff, 1970), 185–94.

contingent upon the words used in relating it, in contrast to ritual or poem. When we reflect on symbolic language, we mean language *after* the break with myth—the language of differentiating consciousness. Every advance solidifies knowledge into the proper analytical vocabulary that reveals questions for further exploration and produces subvocabularies, rectifications, deeper structural insights. What are the necessary conditions for such an analysis? Any material that does not facilitate the process of understanding is excluded: visual symbols, certain archaic symbolisms, visions not translated into structural insight. *Order and History* began with a fundamentally simple diagnosis, a clear strategy for the task ahead. In *The Ecumenic Age* the complexity of the analysis begins to approach the complexity of history itself.

The Husserlian Problematic

In "Remembrance of Things Past" (1977), the introduction written by Eric Voegelin for the English translation of *Anamnesis*,[26] he recalls that in 1943 he had arrived at an impasse in his theoretical formulation of issues in the traditional province of intellectual history. His previous investigations had brought him to the realization that the center of a theory of politics had to be a theory of consciousness.

He became increasingly aware that the traditional construction of an intersubjective ego as the subject of cognition did not apply to an analysis of consciousness. The truth of this observation about the limitations of the traditional construction was not contingent on the proper functioning of a subject of cognition in the Kantian or neo-Kantian sense, but on the objectivity of an individual's consciousness when confronted with certain subjective deformations. An analysis of consciousness has no instrument other than the consciousness of the analyst. The quality of this instrument, then, and consequently the quality of the results, is contingent upon the horizon of consciousness; and the quality of the horizon will depend on the analyst's willingness to inquire into the various dimensions of the reality in which one's conscious life is an event. A consciousness of this type is not an a priori structure, nor is its horizon a given. It is, rather, a continual

---

26. *Anamnesis*, trans. and ed. Gerhart Niemeyer (Notre Dame, Ind. University of Notre Dame Press, 1978).

process of expanding, articulating, and self-correction—a continuous effort to avoid the illusion of considering the reality of which it is a part as an object external to itself, an object that consciousness can master by shaping it into a system.[27]

The concern here is thus with mind embodied in personal, social, and historical life. Voegelin was aware that this horizon of consciousness—more comprehensive than the traditional construction of an intersubjective ego—was not simply a personal idiosyncrasy, but was in fact the very fabric of the social and historical reality in which he was living.[28] It is not surprising, then, that he considered the formulation of a theory of consciousness his principal task.

The formation of a theory of consciousness that Voegelin attempted in 1943 emerged after years of studying Husserl's phenomenology and a continual dialogue with Alfred Schütz about its significance. The discussions between Schütz and Voegelin reached a turning point when, in 1943, Voegelin was at last able to obtain a copy of Husserl's *Krisis der Europäischen Wissenschaften,* which had been published in 1936. They both agreed that the work of Husserl was the most incisive analysis of certain phenomena of consciousness then available; but they also had difficulties with the analysis as it appeared in the *Meditations Cartesiennes* of 1931, and they believed it was impossible to apply the phenomenological method, without more extensive development, to the social realities that were their primary concern.[29]

27. Ibid., 4.
28. Voegelin writes: "My own horizon was strongly formed, and informed, by the restoration of the German language through Stefan George and his circle, the renewed understanding of German classic literature through Gundolf and Kommerell, the understanding of Platonic philosophizing, and especially in the Platonic myth, through Friedlaender, Salin, and Hildebrandt, by the impact of Marcel Proust, Paul Valéry, and James Joyce, by Gilson and Sertillanges, whose work introduced me to medieval philosophy, by Jasper's existentialism and, through Jaspers, by Kierkegaard, and by Spengler's *Decline of the West* that was based on the conception of civilizational cycles developed by Eduard Meyer whose lectures I still heard as a student in Berlin." Ibid., 5.
29. It may be possible to suggest a new direction for Husserl studies on intersubjectivity, today. This direction focuses on the relation between the individual "I" and a collective group of others, or, in other words, on the connection between the individual subject and Husserl's communal spirit.
In carrying out the overall task of suggesting a new direction for Husserl research on intersubjectivity, the following may serve as a guide: The publication of Husserl's text, "Gemeingeist II: personale Einheiten höherer Ordnung und ihre Wirkungskorrelate," *Husserliana,* XIV (The Hague: Martinus Nijhoff, 1956–58), which was written in 1918 or 1921, and two appendices to that text: appendix XXV, which was written in 1921 or 1922, and appendix XXI, which was written in fall 1922. Also to be taken into consideration are Husserl's analyses of the structure of society as they are formulated in his articles, "Die Idee

In the *Logische Untersuchungen* (1900) and in *Ideen zu einer reinen Phänomenologie und phänomenologishcen Philosophie* (1913), Husserl, in opposition to psychologism and historicism, radically distinguishes the *irreal* object of thought from the real act of thinking. The ideal entity that is the object of thought is distinguished from the real act of thinking by its repeatability as contrasted with the inherence of the real act in an irrevocable temporal flow. The ideal object is not an actual part of the temporal acts that intend it—thus the impossibility of the reduction of logic to philosophy, or the conflation of philosophy as an expression of the *Zeitgeist*.

In a number of his later works, Husserl responds to what he understands as the hegemony of objectivism. Husserl perceives the existence of a critical state in the sciences and more generally in European civilization. The crisis is not internal to the sciences (for instance in the case of indeterminacy in physics); rather it concerns the exclusive incarnation of rationality in these disciplines and their inability to serve as the foundation of a "philosophical culture." The critical situation concerns "was Wissenschaft Überhaupt dem menschlichen Dassein bedeutet hatte und bedeuten kann."[30] ("what science in general had meant and could mean for human existence.")

Objectivism encloses the impulse of rationality within the sphere of the sciences. From Husserl's point of view, this presents two difficulties. On the one hand, it fosters a split between the province of science and the world of lived experience. It obscures the relation of the world of ideal constructs and mathematical models to the world of lived experience. On the other hand, the limiting of the sphere of rationality to the scientific enterprise facilitates the rise of pseudorational as well as irrational philosophy. Husserl wrote this work during the rise of fascism. In his interpretation of history, brought forth as a reaction to this critical situation, Husserl wants to establish that the destiny of the West is capitulated in terms of the primacy of rational-

---

einer philosophischen Kultur: Ihr erstes Aufkeimen in der griechischen Philosophie," in *Erste Philosophie* (1923–24): *Erster Teil, Kritische Ideengeschichte*, ed. Rudolf Boehm, Husserliana VII; and " 'Erneuerung' Ihr Problem und ihre Methode," *The Kaizo-La rekonstruyo*, III, 1923.

Nevertheless, despite the indisputable excellence of Husserl's studies on the structure of society from 1918 or 1921 to 1923, we should not assume too readily that they represent Husserl research with an acceptable new orientation to the study of intersubjectivity. Rather, the viability of this new orientation must be critically examined.

30. Edmund Husserl, *Die Krises der Europäischen Wissenschaften und die Transzendentale Phänomenologie*, Husserliana VI (The Hague: Martinus Nijhoff, 1954), 3.

ity, and to understand the sciences as an accomplishment of subjectivity elaborated on the basis of human experience of the life-world.

In his inquiry into the origin of Greek philosophy, Husserl seeks the advent of a subjectivity that makes up the "eternal ideas"—the ideal objects that consciousness intends but are transcendent to the consciousness that intends them. He searches for the origin of this subjective accomplishment in the transformation of cultural life:

> Natürlich hat der Einbruck der theoretischen Einstellung, wie alles historisch Gewordene, seine faktische Motivation im konkreten Zusammenhang geschichtlichen Geschehens . . . ein historisches Faktum, das doch sein Wesenmässiges haben muss.[31]

> (Naturally the outbreak of the theoretical attitude, like everything that develops historically, has its factual motivation in the concrete framework of historical occurrence . . . a historical fact that must nevertheless have something essential about it.)

The "eternal ideas" are the corollary of a subjectivity that in Greece for the first time is freed from practical, limited life interests in the world typical of all natural worldviews. These limited, practical life concerns are replaced by a will to truth—the attempt to know the world as it is.[32] The project that organizes the horizons of the theoretical attitude is a rational knowledge of the world as it is. The subjective attitude and the ongoing project that is its corollary are for Husserl the purpose of Western culture inasmuch as this theoretical orientation becomes the basis of a society which "sie soll sich nicht mehr von der naiven Alltagsempirie und Tradition sondern von der objektiven Wahrheit normieren lassen."[33] (" . . . henceforth must receive its norms not from the naive experience and tradition of everyday life but from objective truth.")

The constitution of truth as universality necessarily implies the idealization of experience since what is true is not this particular experi-

31. Ibid., 331–32.
32. Husserl writes: ". . . der Mensch wird zum unbeteiligten Zuschauer, Überschauer der Welt, er wird zum Philosophen; oder vielmehr von da aus gewinnt sein Leben Empfänglichkeit für nur in dieser Einstellung mögliche Motivationen für nuartige Denkziele und Methoden, in denen schliesslich Philosophie und er selbst zum Philosophen wird." Ibid., 331.
33. Ibid., 333.

ence or its object but the ideal object intended by this experience. The subjective achievement of idealization makes possible the transition from measurement to mathematics in Greece. Geometry, as well as being the achievement of a subjective act, is also the institution—of this achievement. Later, when Galileo proposes the mathematization of nature, he has no need to inquire into the origins of geometry, "in die Arte, wie die idealisierende Leistung ursprünglich erwuchs."[34] (". . . into the manner in which the accomplishment of idealization originally arose.") Nature itself being extended can be made intelligible by the acquired science of mathematics. Not only nature as extended, however, but its qualitative aspects can by an indirect mathematization be made intelligible through the same mathematical concepts. The sensible qualities—"secondary qualities"—are the subjective effects of the interaction of extended bodies in space, and this causal relation can be expressed by the functional dependence of numbers.

According to Husserl, Galileo's mathematization of nature is not achieved without a price. Galileo's failure to trace geometry back to the life-world upon whose basis the act of mathematical idealization is founded makes his works "entdeckender und verdeckender."[35] (". . . a discovering and a concealing.") This failure renders Galileo incapable of recognizing the "objectively true nature" as "ein wohlpassendes Ideenkleid"[36] ("a well-fitted *garb of ideas*"), fitted on, or over, the life-world. This objective nature comes to be regarded as authentic reality, whereas the experienced life-world is perceived as an effect of true nature, the merely subjective appearance of authentic reality. For Husserl this disjunction between the *Lebenswelt* and the world of scientific rationality, along with the disappearance of the life-world as a theme for systematic rational investigation, frames the problem for all subsequent philosophical inquiry. It is the underlying or hidden problematic for modern philosophy.

The themes that dominate Husserl's theory of history are a return to its origins and the reassertion of a teleology become obscure to itself. His goal is a reconciliation between the person as subject and the person as the object of science, since it is their disjunction that ultimately constitutes the crisis. The moment of restoration is a return to the life-world—"the things themselves"—as a lost foundation. Yet this

34. Ibid., 26.
35. Ibid., 53.
36. Ibid., 51.

strategy is problematic because an intelligible world is the product of an order generated by the practice of a discourse determined by laws. A return to the things in their silence—prior to and founding discourse—is not possible.[37]

Husserl's imperative return to the "things themselves" is of course not an invitation simply to gaze at the objects in one's personal environment, but rather to discover in their organization the achievement of transcendental subjectivity prior to mathematical or scientific idealization. For Husserl the "order of things" emerges from the activity of a transcendental subject.

Historical Anthropology

Rejecting a philosophy of historical totality does not lead to an empiricist historiography in which all intelligibility other than simple narration is discarded.[38] Yet if the unity of continuous history based on the totalization of a subject is rejected, what unity, or unities, can be discerned in history and how are they consolidated?

In the introduction to *The Ecumenic Age* we read:

> When I devised the program [*Order and History*] I was still laboring under the conventional belief that the conception of history as a meaningful course of events on a straight line of time was the great achievement of Israelites and Christians who were favored in its creation by the revelatory events, while the pagans, deprived as they were of revelation, could never rise above the conception of a cyclical time. This conventional belief had to be abandoned when I discovered the unilinear construction of history, from a divine-cosmic origin or order to the author's present, to be a symbolic form developed by the end of the third millennium B.C. in the empires of the Ancient Near East. To this form I gave the name *historiogenesis*.
>
> The discovery disturbed the program seriously. There was more at stake than a conventional assumption now disproved. For the very unilinear history which I had supposed to be en-

---

37. *Anamnesis* (Niemeyer), 10–11.
38. See "Historiogenesis," in the *Festschrift für Alois Dempf* (Munich: Albert, 1960); reprinted in *Anamnesis*, 79–116, and in *The Ecumenic Age*, 59–113.

gendered, together with the punctuations of meaning on it, by the differentiating events, turned out to be a cosmological symbolism. Moreover, the symbolism had remained a millennial constant in continuity from its origins in the Sumerian and Egyptian societies, through its cultivation by Israelites and Christians, right into the "philosophies of history" of the nineteenth century A.D.[39]

The introduction also relates how the plan for the originally projected six-volume linear "course" treatment of *Order and History* was broken by the refractory nature of the materials emerging from the study of historical orders and their symbolization. The search for order had produced symbolizations of experience that were not congruent with an easily discernible pattern of movement from compactness to differentiation through the emergence of philosophy, revelation, and Christianity. Instead, the historical evidence revealed parallel movements that do not fit into any time line and consequently have to be comparatively explored in their fullness without respect to their chronological relations to one another.

As a consequence of this reorientation in thinking, both *The Ecumenic Age* and the fifth and concluding volume of this work, *In Search of Order,* consist of a series of discrete studies about the symbolization of order as manifested at various times and places throughout history, as well as some special studies about the emergence (and in some instances the symbolic distortion) of the experience of consciousness among a variety of individuals who have shaped our understanding of meaning and order.

One can see from the foregoing remarks how it may be possible to call Voegelin an empiricist, but only in the sense that for particular forms of philosophy, empiricism is a residual category for any type of thought not committed to the resolution of history into expression. In its Marxist guise, this idealist problematic substitutes the class consciousness of the proletariat for a transcendental subject, and the notion of reification for that of expression.

Within the context of what has been said earlier on theory of symbolization, the form of knowledge is made up of a series of cross-references of things to other objects and of all things to their origin. The explanatory strategies founded on this discursive formation are

39. *The Ecumenic Age,* 7.

the several ways in which objects can resemble one another. The world is a text that must be read and interpreted. Knowledge is exegesis; beneath the manifest text is a hidden text that must be discovered. Beneath the variety of empirical languages is a natural language in which things have their authentic names.

Order and History does not elaborate a theory of transition from one discursive formation to another. Nevertheless, clues for a theory of transition lie within Voegelin's text. In the concluding pages of *The Ecumenic Age,* we read:

> The 'stop-history' Systems which dominate the contemporary scene can maintain the appearance of truth only by an act of violence, i.e., by prohibiting questions concerning the premises and by making the prohibition a formal part of the System.[40]

During the period in which he was evaluating the work of Husserl, Voegelin continued his correspondence with Schütz. The first essay he wrote and sent him was a critical analysis of Husserl's *Krisis* essay.[41] But that was not sufficient. He had to formulate the alternative to Husserl's conception of an egologically constituted consciousness, and a formulation suggested itself as possible, at least on principle.

The attempt to discern the comprehensive structure of consciousness, however, raises a foundational issue in epistemology. If the abstract statements about the structure of consciousness were to be accepted as valid, they had first to be recognized as valid in the concrete. Their truth rested on the lives of persons who were able to articulate their insights and consequently generate the language of awareness. The truth of consciousness was simultaneously abstract and concrete. The process of verification had consequently to penetrate through the engendered symbols to the inaugurating experience; and the truth of the situation had to be ascertained by a responsive sensibility that could verify or falsify the engendering insight. The process was further burdened with the impossibility of separating language and experience as independent entities. Causal experience did not exist as an autonomous entity—only the reality as articulated by symbols. At the other end of the process of verification, responsive sensibility did not exist as an autonomous entity either—only an expe-

---

40. Ibid., 330.
41. Later published as "Brief an Alfred Schütz über Edmund Husserl," in *Anamnesis.*

rience that could articulate itself in language symbols and, if necessary, modify the symbols of the engendering reality in order to allow the symbols to render the truth of reality encountered more adequately. Consciousness exists, and becomes more refined within the tension between experience and symbolization. Neither the experiences nor the symbols can become autonomous objects of investigation for an observer. The structure of consciousness reveals itself through participation in the life process. It is essentially historical.

These types of insights, again, led Voegelin to abandon a nearly completed, multi-volume history of political ideas that he had been writing during the 1940s and early 1950s as untenable, and to replace it with a study of the order that emerges in history from life experiences and their symbolization, and from the processes of differentiation and deformation of consciousness.[42]

---

42. Cf. Teil I-Erinnerung, of *Anamnesis* (37–60).

6

Symbolism and Historicity

Words confine infinity. Symbols guide the spirit, beyond the powers of the finite state of becoming, into the realm of the infinite world of existence.
                        —Johann Jakob Bachofen,
            Versuch über die Gräber Symbolik der Alten, Werke

In our attempt to achieve some perspective on the changing pattern of Voegelin's conception of history and consciousness, we initially saw that his orientation in the 1920s had a positivistic bent. We looked at some of the personal and intellectual experiences that prompted explorations of the mythic and symbolic foundations of modern political ideologies. This investigation exists on a continuum with the 1940s work on a comprehensive history of Western political ideas, which in turn resulted in *The New Science of Politics* and *Order and History*. Later, I want to examine in more detail the revisions that *The Ecumenic Age* brings to the original program of the *History*. With this fourth volume, *Order and History* has become an explicit description of the process of differentiating consciousness, a theory of consciousness in itself.

This project attempts nothing less than a recovery of the intellectual substance of Western civilization. Such a restoration is conceived of as occurring through a return to original sources of experience such as classical philosophy. One of the central concerns here is to narrate the chronicle of the history of consciousness, not a history of ideas, but rather of *experiences* that led to the discovery and exploration of consciousness itself. Voegelin has dedicated much of his effort to the exploration of classical philosophical consciousness as a source for understanding the present time. During the course of this inquiry, he concentrated on developing a theory of symbolization.

The *raison d'etre* of the symbol lies in the human urge to express that which is inherently inexpressible.[1] This desire may well be that impelling force that sponsors all creative endeavor, the attempt to effect a restitution of a positive and affirming experience of order in a new form and on a more refined level. The energy and interest currently dedicated by Western civilization to science and technology were once devoted to mythology by ancient peoples,[2] who added speculative and theorizing propensities to these efforts. The symbolic meaning of a phenomenon links the human with the cosmic, the casual with the causal, disorder with order, and it justifies a word like *universe* which, without these more extensive implications, would be meaningless, a dismembered and chaotic pluralism.

One of the errors in many theories of symbolization lies in opposing the symbolic to the historical. Starting from the premise that there are symbols—and, in fact, there are many—which exist only within their own symbolic structure, the inappropriate conclusion is then drawn that nearly all events that appear to be both historical and symbolic— in other words, to be decisively significant in history—may be perceived simply as symbolic matter transformed into legend and then into history. A number of scholars have taken exception to this misconception. Mircea Eliade asserts that:

> The symbolism *adds* a new value to an object or an activity without any prejudice whatever to its own immediate value. In application to objects or actions, symbolism renders them "open"; symbolic thinking "breaks open" the immediate reality without any minimizing or undervaluing of it: in such a perspective this is not a closed universe, no object exists for itself in isolation; everything is held together by a compact system of correspondences and likenesses. The man of the archaic societies becomes conscious of himself in an "open world" that is rich in meaning. It remains to be seen whether these "openings" are but so many means of evasion, or whether, on the contrary, they constitute the only possibility of attaining to the true reality of the world.[3]

1. Théodule Ribot, "La Pensée Symbolique," *Revue de Philosophie* 49 (1915), 386–87.
2. C. G. Jung, *Symbole der Wandlung*, 20ff.
3. "Le symbolisme *ajoute* une nouvelle valeur à un objet ou à une action, sans pour autant porter atteinte à leurs va leurs propres et immédiates. En s'appliquant à un objet ou à une action, le symbolisme les rend 'ouverts.' La pensée symbolique fait 'éclater' la réalité

Eliade in this passage clearly has in mind the distinction between the historical and the symbolic. It is also possible to discern the plausibility of a bridge linking both forms of reality in a synthesis. The hint of skepticism in the concluding words should be ascribed to Eliade's predominantly scientific training at a time when science, with its emphasis upon the analytical approach, has achieved admirable results in every sphere of life without the overall organic pattern, that is: "multiplicity in unity." This scientific disaffection has been well defined by Martin Buber: *Imago mundi nova, imago nulla.* The world today lacks its own image because this image can be formulated only by means of a universal synthesis of knowledge—a synthesis which, since the Renaissance and the *de omni re scibili* of Pico della Mirandola, has progressively become more difficult.

Thus the symbolic in no way excludes the historical since both forms may be seen as reciprocal expressions of one meaning on different levels. In the matter of religion, for example, Jung agrees with Eliade in his belief that the psychic fact "God" is a collective archetype, a psychic existent that must not in itself be confused with the concept of a metaphysical God. The existence of the archetype, (that is, of the symbol) neither postulates a God, nor denies that God exists.[4] Yet although this is, strictly speaking, unquestionable, it must surely be agreed—if only in theory—that the universality of an archetype affirms rather than denies the reality of the principle in question. Consequently the symbolic, being independent of the historical, not only does not exclude it but, on the contrary, tends to root it firmly in reality because of the parallelism between the collective or individual world and the cosmic. And because of the great depth of the hidden roots of all systems of meanings, a further consequence is the tendency to espouse the theory that all symbolist traditions, both Western and oriental, spring from one common source. Whether this source once appeared in time and space as a primeval focal point, or whether it stems from the "collective unconscious" is quite another matter. The

---

immédiate, mais sans l'amoindrir ni la dévaloriser: dans sa perspective l'Univers n'est pas fermé, aucun objet n'est isolé dans sa propre existentialité: tout se tient ensemble, par un système serré de correspondances et d'assimilations. L'homme des sociétés archaïques a pris conscience de soi-meme dans un 'monde overt' et riche en signification: il reste à savoir si ces 'ouvertures' sont autant de moyens d'évasion, ou si, au contraire, elles constituent l'unique possibiité d'accéder à la véritable réalité du monde." Mircea Eliade, *Images et Symboles* (Paris: Gallimard, 1952), 177–78.

4. Jung, *Symbole der Wandlung,* 85–86.

road toward understanding the human province goes from the study of conscious content to that of unconscious forms.[5]

Explanatory Power

Critical thought requires the complementarity of theory—a body of concepts, propositions and interpretations, to assist in organizing the welter of rapidly moving historical events. The test of any theory lies in the extent to which it aids in the comprehensive understanding of concrete social and historical events past and present, and in its capacity to be a reliable guide in the future.

One significant phase in the development of cognition is the appearance of the symbolic function. The ability to symbolize makes it possible to operate on new levels. At this stage we are not restricted to acting on objects in the immediate environment, because the symbolic function allows us to evoke the past. Recently, both the research and theoretical concerns of a significant number of anthropologists have once again been directed toward the role of symbols—religious, political, and even economic—in social and cultural processes. Whether this revival is a belated response to developments in other disciplines (psychology, linguistics, philosophy, to name only a few) or a return to a central concern after a period of neglect is difficult to say. Whatever may have been the cause, there is no denying a renewed curiosity about the nature of the conjunctions existing among culture, cognition, and perception as these connections are revealed in symbolic forms.

In the preface to volumes 2 and 3 of *Order and History,* the author writes: "*Order and History* is a philosophical inquiry concerning the principal types of order of human existence in society and history as well as the corresponding symbolic forms." A good case can be made for the notion that the field of symbolization in the present time has moved away from the representation of an objective reality toward the expression of subjective emotional states.[6] Voegelin's contribution toward a theory of symbolization is an attempt to return to the classical

5. This is the contention of Claude Lévi-Strauss, *Structural Anthropology,* trans. Claire Jacobson and Brooke Schoepf (New York: Doubleday, 1967), 24.

6. J. E. Cirlot, *A Dictionary of Symbols,* trans. Jack Sage (London: Routledge and Kegan Paul, 1967), ix.

function of symbolization. An *entrée* into this particular understanding of one of the ways in which the mind works may be gained through his theory of symbolization.

Symbolizations of Order

Eric Voegelin began as a student of the history of political ideas. Gradually he realized that no such entity existed, except in a trivial sense. The ideas were not speculations about political society or more or less arbitrary inventions of gifted thinkers or rationalizations of emotional attitudes and vested interests. They were part of a more comprehensive reality of a process of symbolization extending over the entire realm of expression and interpretation as it is encountered in the very form of political society and the world of thought and art. Reflecting on the symbolizations of order as they unfold in history, he has tried to uncover the foundations laid by the Greeks.

Thus Voegelin did not initiate his career as a philosopher; rather, as a teacher of jurisprudence at the University of Vienna, he was led to philosophical speculation on account of an experience with the fragility of constitutional democracy in many European states after World War I. He perceived that institutions are founded on ideas, or symbols of self-interpretation shared by a people, and that if such interpretations are shattered, the institutions will be as well.

Consequently, Voegelin embarked on a lifelong quest for the contours of political reality, a quest that led from the immediate context of the political struggle in concrete societies to the concepts that animated that struggle in an individual national society, to the ideas that bound together a particular civilization, and further, to the comparative structure of political ideas in the varied civilizations that have emerged in world history. As this search expanded in scope and time, it also increased in depth; for the orienting concepts of civilization had to emerge from somewhere, and that "somewhere" was the depth of human consciousness. So the domain of empirical political reality expanded from constitutions to the concepts that undergird them, from these ideas to the experiences of participation in political and social reality of which the ideas were expressions, and finally to the comparative study of experiences of order and disorder in the psyche of representative human types—philosophers, sages, and prophets.

Voegelin would have opposed the view that he was presenting his own merely personal or subjective framework for political evaluation, both because he repudiated idiosyncracy in philosophy and because he considered the language of values to represent a bygone era of methodology. Nonetheless, he would also have conceded that we must employ that language if we want to make ourselves understood, and he was aware that any attempt to recover a classical understanding of political theory in our time initially appears idiosyncratic.[7] Voegelin evaluates political ideas and regimes on the basis of an understanding that derives from a comparative study of symbols concerning order and disorder that have appeared over time. In fact, he characterizes history as a "trail of equivalent symbols in time and space."[8]

In order to comprehend the meaning of a symbol, care must be taken not to interpret it literally. To interpret the language of Plato or Aristotle or the *Iliad* or the Bible literally is to dogmatize and deform it, for symbols are indices pointing to the motivating experiences of the individuals who articulate them. A more discriminating approach would be to relate symbols intended to clarify political reality to the experiences that engender them. If the symbols are detached from their experiential context, then thought degenerates into the dogmatic formalism of the various "schools," whether Neoplatonic, stoic, or scholastic, with their desiccated disquisitions on essences, substances, and accidents. From there to the rejection of philosophy itself by those modern intellectuals disenchanted with the detached symbols, seen in their literal opaqueness from the outside and therefore regarded as irrational,[9] is but a short step. Voegelin discovered years ago that the fundamental philosophical problem is the nature of reality.[10] Unfortunately, this is exactly the problem that many modern philosophers tend to neglect or assume to have been resolved in some commonsense fashion or regard as meaningless and "unverifiable." If, however, one attempts, as Marx did, to abolish the "problem of reality," one also abolishes philosophy.

A philosophy worthy of the name—that is, one in which symbols are recognizably equivalent to other symbols that facilitate the under-

7. Voegelin, "Equivalences of Experience and Symbolization in History," *Eternità e Storia*, 215–34. Voegelin discusses the problem of so-called "value-relativism" in *The New Science of Politics* (Chicago: University of Chicago Press, 1952) (e.g., cf. 20).

8. Voegelin, "Equivalences," 233.

9. Voegelin, *From Enlightenment to Revolution*, ed. John H. Hallowell (Durham, NC: Duke University Press), 1975, 21.

10. Ibid., 257.

standing of complex issues,[11] will acknowledge that reality is not a disorderly flux of events but an intelligible process. Since philosophers are situated within the process rather than at some Archimedian point outside of it, they cannot, in any Gnostic sense, discern its meaning as a whole. The answers to the foundational questions of life remain opaque. Nonetheless, philosophers are also aware that they possess the faculty of reason to cast some light on these questions.

The most fundamental human experience is the anxiety-laden one of the actor in a drama who knows neither his part nor the play nor in fact what exactly he himself is. To be certain about this world, to be certain about their own role in maintaining the order of things, was an urgent necessity for early humans—their "vital problem." Humanity requires knowledge not only about *how* things are and *how* they work, but also about the meaning of things. Early humans expressed their understanding in symbols created to render intelligible the relations and tensions between God and humanity, world and society, within the limits of experience and oriented by it. These symbols interpret the unknown in analogy to that which *is* known or believed to be known. A characteristic feature in the process of symbolization is the attempt at making reality as intelligible as possible through fashioning symbols that interpret the recondite dimensions of life by analogy with the really, or supposedly, known. These formulations have a history insofar as reflective analysis, responding to the exigencies of life, renders symbols increasingly more commensurate with their function. Compact segments of knowledge are differentiated according to their constitutive parts, and the intelligible itself eventually comes to be distinguished from *terra incognita*. Consequently, the history of symbolization is an evolution from elemental to more complex experiences and symbols.

Another representative characteristic in the early phases of the development of symbolization revolves around cognizance of the analogical nature of symbols. The realization expresses itself in diverse ways, consonant with the problems of cognition through symbols. The order of the world can be represented analogically by employing more than one experience of partial order in existence.

In this process of reciprocal clarification, contemporaneous and incongruent symbols develop. Those who fashion them endure such a situation since this type of dialectic does not effect the adequacy of the symbols themselves. If any quality is characteristic of the early history

---

11. This theme is developed more fully in "Equivalences of Experience and Symbolization in History," referred to in previous notes.

of symbolization, it is the diversity of interpretations of reality, the acknowledgement and forebearance accorded divergent symbolizations of the same reality. The diversity of symbolizations is correlative with an awareness of the unity of truth sought by means of numerous symbols. This early forebearance extends far into the Greco-Roman period and finds its classic expression in the diatribe of Celsus on Christianity as introducing disorder among the gods.

The early permissiveness implies that the order of human life can be portrayed analogically in diverse ways. A symbol is authentic insofar as it represents the truth to the extent that it can be comprehended. This indulgence, however, reaches its boundary when one realizes that the analogical nature of symbolization is limited by the adequacy of symbols to make authentic order transparent. The actual variety of symbols may consequently be considered a deficiency, and efforts may be made to bring a number of symbols into a rational, hierarchical order.

This entire process transfers the task of understanding from a mysterious level to an intelligible plane. The symbol becomes not only a form of expression and interpretation but a form of continuous investigation. By means of symbolization, it is possible to explore the unknown vicariously. Such explorations either yield new discoveries or create new difficulties in understanding, difficulties that require adjustment or change in the symbolism. The history of symbolization is consequently the history of ongoing search for more profound understanding. It is also the history of refusals to understand, refusals also made in the mode of symbolization, where knowledge of the *how* is substituted for knowledge of the *why*. This comes about when symbols of human dominance are substituted for symbols of the order of the cosmos.[12]

Cosmological Civilizations

The historical-critical method, frequently employed in *Order and History*, consists of an analysis of collective thought over a period of time. These types of studies deal not with the growth of knowledge in the individual, but with the historical evolution of a set of notions on a

---

12. See the introduction to vol. I: "The Symbolization of Order." On the issue of "human dominance," see *The World of the Polis*, 16–19.

given subject matter. After having analyzed the historical development of a particular notion, the attempt is then made to discern a parallel between individual acquisition of knowledge and development of collective knowledge. In other words, a psychological model is employed to study the evolution of collective thought.

Order and History opens with a study of the imperial civilizations of the ancient Near East, representing what is called the "cosmological" stage of civilization. Here society is constituted in the image of hierarchical order and conceived as a *cosmion,* a small model of the world. "World" and "being" are not yet differentiated. Man knows himself to be a part of

> the great stream of being, in which he flows while it flows through him . . . the same stream to which belongs everything else that drifts into his perspective . . . We move in a charmed community where everything that meets us has force and will and feelings, where animals and plants can be men and gods, where men can be divine and gods are kings . . . where things are the same and not the same, and can change into each other.[13]

Vegetative rhythms and celestial revolutions furnish the model for the order and operations of society. We recognize the image of a society in the era of myth, an era only now drawing to its close as the last handful of stone-age people are being drawn into the vortex of twentieth-century civilization.

It is usually accepted that modern ways of thinking differ from primitive thought processes only with regard to consciousness, and that the unconscious has hardly evolved since the Upper Paleolithic Stage. Oneirocritical symbols, then, are not strictly different from mythical, religious, lyrical, or primitive symbols, except that a kind of *demi-monde* is intermixed with primary archetypes. This demi-monde consists of the remains of images drawn from reality, which may lack symbolic meaning and may be physiological expressions—merely memories—or possess a symbolism related to the material and primary forms from which they originate.

The creation of the imperial civilizations of the ancient Near East represents a step beyond tribal organizations.

13. *Israel and Revelation,* 3.

To establish a government is an essay in world creation. When man creates the cosmion of political order, he analogically repeats the divine creation of the cosmos. The analogical repetition is not an act of futile imitation, for in repeating the cosmos man participates, in the measure allowed to his existential limitations, in the creation of cosmic order itself.[14]

Cosmological symbolization requires, therefore, a point of physical connection between cosmos and empire, an actual place at which the stream of life flows from the cosmos into the empire. This point is the "center of the world," the *omphalos*. (There is still a navel-shaped stone in Delphi, marking the Greek center of the world; Jacob laid down a stone in the place where he dreamed of the ladder on which the angels moved from heaven to earth and back; the name of the city of Babylon itself means "gate of the gods.") Babylonian mythology is thus a symbolism that expresses the self-understanding of this civilization and relates every factor of political order—political constitution and organization, rights and duties of rulers and subjects, property rights, rules of justice—to human participation in a sacred world.[15] In this type of civilization, life in its most mundane aspect bore meaning because it was understood as life in an inseparable, ordered community, rising and falling like the ever-recurring cycles and rhythms on earth and in the skies.

Within the relatively brief span of five centuries, from approximately 800 B.C.E. to about 300 B.C.E. there occurs an extraordinary series of "speculative outbreaks," a movement to a more complex level of understanding. This occurs in Israel at the time of the prophets, in Greece with the genesis of philosophy and tragedy, in India with the rise of Buddhism, in China with Confucius, the tradition that has come to be personified in the name Lao-tzu, and other classical philosophers. An unforseen break with cosmological myth occurs, and what had been one unified experience of an existence in which the boundaries between world, gods, and human beings were fluid now unfolds into a more complex experience of order.[16] The "charmed community" of cosmological myth becomes a tenuous relation between clearly separated participants; "world" becomes "nature," an auton-

14. Ibid., 16.
15. Ibid., 24–26.
16. *The World of the Polis*, 3–4.

omous environment interacting with the human race; society, no longer a *cosmion*, must orient itself toward the new source of order. Later, the opposition of state and individual will come into perspective. Humanity itself, taken out of the mutable relationships within the cosmological community, now stands opposite both world and society. This new detached situation of the human race finds expression in the Aristotelian symbolism of "essence" or "nature" as that without which a thing would not be what it is: Humanity is humanity, and what makes it so is "human nature"; human nature therefore does not and cannot change, not just by definition but because the notion of a change in human nature is contradicted by humanity's irrevocable experience of being what it is, distinct from all other creatures. Such are the bare coordinate notations that mark the human province in the world. They give no idea of the drama or the depth of the three symbolizations that finally fused in Western civilization: the revelation on Mount Sinai bringing the Chosen People and its unseen God into their mutual presence; the Greek transition from myth to philosophy fully articulating the new structure of order and discovering the *agathon* as the unseen goal toward which the individual turns, the way a part of the whole turns toward the whole from which it does not want to be separated; and the Christian symbolism of the Incarnation.

The newly manifested order is authoritative in nature. Now that the human race knows its place in this order it can look back and discover its past; the unity of the race from its origins to the present has become apparent. But equally apparent is the break in existence in time. Humanity has discovered the past as that which was, and is no more, and it has become aware of the open horizon of its future. But this discovery, while it gains a new truth about order, neither gains all of the truth nor establishes an ultimate order of mankind. The itinerary of humanity through time is an unfolding mystery: "[W]e neither know why mankind has a past nor do we know anything about its goal in the future."[17] As human life assumes its new historical form, the question, Where does history lead? arises by necessity and proves perplexing. We only know what has already happened. It is possible to make exiguous steps toward envisioning the future, but not to see its end or even the direction it will take. Only because we stand where we do can we conceive of the course of history as a scheme of directional progress. But this conception is an illusion.

17. Ibid., 5.

The History of Order

We begin to understand the title *Order and History* as indicative of an inquiry into the nature of the order in which we live presently. The study of this order leads back to its threefold origins in Israel, Greece, and Christianity, decisive moments that transform the earlier order into a more complex one. There is thus a history of order, heuristic like all history. From this history of order emerges the order of history, its structure. This is not a structure of progress from primitive times to ever "higher" civilization, except in its material aspects (an essential part of the sequence of historical events but not helpful in revealing the structure of history). A study of order does not have the purpose of manifesting the primitivism, naïveté, logical deficiency, or general benightedness of ages past, but, on the contrary, shows people with the same nature as ours, struggling with the same problems as ours, under different conditions and with less complicated instruments of symbolization. There is a symmetry between everyday life and the liminality endemic in archaic society, but an asymmetry between the two in modern society. What has changed since the origins of the human race is not human nature but human consciousness of order. The distinction between prehistoric and historic times according to the absence or presence of written documentation is purely technical. The essential distinction is between pre-"historic" human existence not yet open to the dimension of history and human "existence in historic form."

The historical character of this enterprise is nowhere better exhibited than in the insistence on locating the first appearances of new symbolizations in historical time. For this reason one may reject any phenomenology of ideas that collects and classifies its specimens (for example, myths of renewal, hierophanies, and the like) without attention to their location in history. The "same" myth may mean very different things in different historical contexts, and a typology of myths and ideas is misleading unless based on chronology. The fact that a new type appears at a given time and in a given situation may be more significant and illuminating than the comparative description of that type. And the study of the conditions that give rise to a new type is not just a matter of placing it in its proper environment; such questions arise when the former answers are no longer adequate. The history of symbolizations is therefore the history of the search for understanding fundamental human dilemmas, whatever the result of the search may be. And since new problems are most acutely felt when new experience clashes with old ways, the formulations found by the creators of new symbolisms are likely to be more penetrating than those of their late successors who no longer experience the problem in its pristine urgency and poignancy. All this applies not only to ideas, beliefs, and theories, but also to symbolizations of fundamental knowledge in the form of the constitution and operations of a society, or in any of the other forms in which self-understanding is articulated.

History is thus the process by which humanity articulates its own nature. This process is heuristic. The experiences that shaped Western civilization illuminate the past, not the future: History thus has no knowable meaning, no essence or shape that can be grasped at any time. Furthermore, even what is understandable about human nature is not explicitly known at all times to all societies. How, then, is a historical philosophy possible?

One answer is that history is made wherever people live, but that its philosophy is a Western symbolism, the way that Western society articulates its own mode of existence.[18] To articulate means to differentiate, to specify explicitly. The philosophy of order and history is thus the symbolic form of Western self-exploration in the light of the experience that has formed this civilization. And this light illuminates not only the new form of existence, but, by contrast, earlier modes of existence as well:

> [Without] the creation of history as the inner form of existence in opposition to the cosmological form of order, there would be no problem of the history of mankind; and without the discovery of the logos in the psyche and the world, without the creation of philosophical existence, the problem of history would not be a problem of philosophy.[19]

A historical philosophy is therefore not a universal discipline. It arises at the confluence of the three symbolizations of the new truth or order—the Israelitic, the Greek, the Christian—of revelation, philosophy, incarnation. The Church Fathers who first gave expression to philosophy of history perceived that. Clement of Alexandria names the three sources of truth about order that flow together to make possible

18. Ibid., 23.
19. Ibid., 7.

the articulation of Western existence in historical form.[20] The symbolic instrument of this expression is philosophy.

It may well be that the Greek creators of this symbolization understood the new reality of order better than their late successors, who live in it without recalling the conditions of occupancy. The Hellenic philosophical breakthrough opened up exploration in every direction. "World" became visible as ordered and lawful; humanity could look upon it as an observer exploring its laws and its order. This opened the way to scientific understanding. But this way left humanity's vital problem untouched. Only to the extent that man was part of the world, a natural object, could he undertake to understand himself scientifically. For the understanding of man as man, for the exploration of his relationship to the source of newly manifested order, a different symbolization was needed. At its heart was the Greek discovery of the soul.

This was an authentic discovery. One need only recall that even Homer as yet has no conception, nor in fact a word, for soul. (As a consequence, he did not have a word for body either, for the discovery of the soul is the discovery of a differentiation.) What the Greeks discovered was of course neither a material nor a psychological entity. They discovered the fact that humanity can become aware of the order of existence because humanity itself is a part of this existence. The world could be explored when its relative autonomy was seen; the nature of humanity and the nature of its knowledge came into view when its autonomy was recognized as being only partial. As Plato says, when the Demiurge mixed the stuff from which to fashion the world soul, a little bit was left over, and out of it he made man's soul. This is a tale, a *mythos,* conveying an essential truth about the faculty of aspiring and knowing. We recognize the process of articulations: Bodily life, emotions, and knowledge will be further articulated into knowledge of what is actually there, trust with regard to visible reality, and knowledge regarding pure abstract forms.[21] The soul becomes the model order that furnishes symbols for ordering society analogically in its image, and the symbolism of the soul unfolds to provide the model

20. Clement of Alexandria, *Stromateis,* VI.
21. With this differentiation of knowledge, the symbolism of the soul spanned the entire range of human experience. In the course of the Enlightenment its meaning was lost: body became the object of physiology, knowledge the object of epistemology, and what was left became a psychology of faculties of the mind. This faculty psychology failed. Its modern successors are psychologies without psyche and *logos,* a situation that makes the recovery of these lost symbols both possible and necessary.

for social order. Society can therefore no longer be ordered in the image of the universe: Since the truth of life is experienced by the well-ordered individual, a well-ordered society must be what Plato in a well-known phrase calls "man writ large."

Because of its complexity, it is worthwhile to spell out some of the implications and consequences of the foregoing philosophical symbolism.

1. The form of this type of articulation differs fundamentally from the cosmological forms of symbolic expression. The articulation is systematic: no element must be overlooked, each element must be defined, the relationships between the elements must be fully explored. In identifying the soul as the locus of fundamental experience and, by its very nature, as the locus of highest knowledge, philosophy sees the world as a manifestation of the *logos*. This makes possible an exploration through reason of the entire life-world.

2. In the order of knowing, a lower part is reserved for *doxa,* commonly translated as opinion, as opposed to *sophia* or knowledge. According to Plato, those who have love (*philia*) of wisdom are called philosophers. Plato calls others who love opinion, or *doxa,* *philodoxers.* There is, then, a correct and incorrect type of knowledge concerning the order of society. This is what *philodoxers* deny, and philosophers assert.

3. Since philosophy is here understood as a Western symbolism within which any analytical questions about the nature of order and history must be framed, there are no philosophies—only philosophy and *doxa.* This is not to restrict the study of philosophy to the Greek tradition. Philosophical reflection is marked by a continual concern with the adequacy of the symbols of order. Much that was once adequate is adequate no longer. What Plato and Aristotle fundamentally said about the order of political society is still of significance. What they said out of their experience as citizens of the Greek city-state no longer applies. The new forms of political order in which we now live require a new and different symbolism.

4. Just as it is possible to distinguish adequate from inadequate symbolizations of order, so one can distinguish order from disorder in the individual and in society. Understanding order does not mysteriously produce "values" and "goals." But serious reflection can tell us what is in order and what is not.

5. The Greeks explored ways of achieving the most refined development of the person through ordering human life and activity. At the apogee of their civilization, *paideia* was considered to be the education of the individual toward full maturity, that is, toward living in consonance with the human condition. But just as an individual may strive for this consonance, so one may also close oneself to it. This closing of the person is a *nosos*, a disease and the source of disorder. A society that attempts to divorce itself from the source of order opens itself to disorder.

The Historical Dimension
of Theory of Consciousness

As we have seen, the historical dimension of Voegelin's theory of consciousness was developed in *The New Science of Politics* and the first three volumes of *Order and History*. I want here to suggest the implications of that work.

Our fundamental prereflective experience is not a form of object knowledge. There cannot be a separation between a knowing subject and a known object because the subject is a part of the process it knows. Object knowledge (intentionality in Husserl's sense) is only a substructure within our awareness of this larger reality. Ultimately this comprehensive reality is a process that becomes comprehensible itself in the consciousness of individual human beings.

The historical aspect of this process consists in the record of the many who have expressed their experiences in language symbols. Reflection on these symbolizations provides a path to understanding history since it is by means of these symbols that societies articulate their own understanding of human life. The historical pattern of these symbolizations is consequently the key to the history of order from which "the order of history emerges," as stated in the opening sentence of *Order and History.*

What the pattern of symbolizations indicates is the development from compact to differentiated forms. The primeval form of symbolization is the cosmological myth. But in the course of history other forms of symbolization have arisen that articulate a more adequate understanding of the world than the ancient myths. *Order and His-*

tory distinguishes three major moments in the differentiation of human consciousness: the Israelite revelation, Greek philosophy, and Christianity.

The development from compact to differentiated forms of consciousness is a fundamental one in the evolution of cultures. The terms "compact" and "differentiated" refer not only to the symbolizations, but also to the characteristic forms of consciousness that generate them. Voegelin also discerned what he terms "deformed" symbolizations, which he attributes to the deformed consciousness of those who fashion them. The principal types of deformation in this category are the modern Gnostic and apocalyptic symbolisms.

Interpreting past symbolizations is difficult. Because a consciousness is a concrete individual process, any description of the nature of consciousness in the abstract must initially be true in the consciousness of a specific individual. Any abstract statements about consciousness are founded on the experiences of a particular person, who has to articulate these experiences in language. Statements about the nature of consciousness are consequently marked by both a concrete and abstract aspect. Thus, when an interpreter attempts to understand a text, the process of interpretation must penetrate from the language symbols to the engendering experiences. The validity of these experiences can only be determined by an experiential response on the part of the interpreter. This response is an attempt to recover or reenact the original experience.

The engendering experiences and the symbols through which they are expressed, however, are not separate objects. All the interpreter has to work with is an experience articulated in certain symbols. Also, in the process of reenactment, experiential response does not exist as a separate reality, but again as an experience that must be given expression in language symbols. Language alters, if need be, the symbols of the engendering experience in order to fashion a new symbol that more adequately expresses the validity of the experience.

In the first three volumes of *Order and History,* these principles were applied to Israelite revelation and classical Greek philosophy. Voegelin's study of Greek philosophy is of significance in the development of his theory of consciousness since experiences that engender philosophical reflection make explicit the nature of the mind itself. In these experiences, consciousness attempts to interpret its own logos.

The engendering experiences of Greek philosophy—the human condition of ignorance and search for the ground of existence, wonder, the platonic eros, Aristotle's "immortalizing," the *nous*—are of major significance in Western thought. Through them the psyche discovers itself. The historical import of classical Greek philosophy results from a balance of human consciousness that Plato and Aristotle established both in fact and as a postulate of their thinking.

In the seventeen years between the publication of the third and fourth volumes of *Order and History,* Voegelin continued to reflect on the nature of consciousness. The most systematic statement of the new insights he attained in this period is found in two papers published in 1964 and 1966.[22]

The foregoing developments in Voegelin's theories have significant consequences for his understanding of the mind. Of particular importance is his analysis of compact, differentiated, and deformed modes of consciousness. We have seen that one of the basic notions in Voegelin's theory is that deformed consciousness fashions deformed symbolisms about the nature of reality. In his last major work, *The Ecumenic Age,* Voegelin adds another dimension to this theory. In the great noetic differentiating events of the Ecumenic Age, humanity discovers itself as possessing consciousness, discovers consciousness as the locus of experience. The succession of noetic insights through generations of thinkers constitutes a progressive series of experiences of differentiation, a "noetic field of consciousness." As this field of noetic consciousness develops in time, it comes to be recognized as possessing a structure and an ability to move progressively toward more and more differentiated knowledge. In those who experience them, the differentiating events produce consciousness of epoch, an awareness of before and after. The new insights reduce the old truth of the cosmological myths to the status of "pseudos." In other words, these differentiating events constitute history.

22. "Eternal Being in Time" (1964) and "What is Political Reality?" (1966), published in both the German and English versions of *Anamnesis.*

7

Historical Form

We saw earlier that during the course of historical investigations, Voegelin traced the fundamental advance from compact to differentiated consciousness—existence became "existence in historical form."[1] If understanding the history of order and the order of history is even to be approached, the main concern is to pierce through the level of theory into the fundamental level of engendering experiences. The dominant theoretical design characterizing *Order and History* is an effort to trace the emergence of consciousness by analyzing experiences of order and the resulting symbolic forms.

At this point, it is appropriate to look at the experiences that resulted in the creation of the historical form, a development that dominates the philosophy of order and history. The parameters of this study do not allow even casual analysis of the symbolic form of the myth. Likewise, any treatment of the form of philosophy has to be restricted to a brief consideration of its relation to the historical form itself.

From this perspective, the experience of the sacred gives rise to historical form. In the primary instance of Israel, the constitutive event is the revelation on Mount Sinai. In the comparable Hellenic experience, the form of philosophy develops from the time of Xenophanes' realization that " 'The One is the God' "[2] to Aeschylus's descent into the depth of the soul to reach a decision for *Dike* and the platonic vision

---

1. Ellis Sandoz's essay, "Voegelin's Idea of Historical Form," originally published in *Cross Currents* 12 (1962), 41–67, and later revised for inclusion in *The Voegelinian Revolution* (Baton Rouge: Louisiana State University Press, 1981), remains a solid guide to this theme of *Order and History*. In this section I have tried to encapsulate some of the salient points of his discussion along with a number of my own observations. I have in places employed a different linguistic idiom which renders a variant interpretation of certain of the issues associated with this theme.

2. Aristotle, *Metaphysics* I, 968b, 18. Xenophanes A 30. Kathleen Freeman, *The Pre-Socratic Philosophers: A Companion to Diels, Fragmente der Vorsokratiker* (Oxford: Basil Blackwell, 1953).

of the *Agathon*. These corresponding experiences were later appropriated by Christianity.[3] Other parallel events of a decisive nature took place contemporaneously in the India of the Buddha and the China of Confucius and Lao-tzu, but their qualities are disparate. A significant characteristic that they hold in common, though, is that in each instance they broke with the myth.

The mandate of understanding these events materializes as a principal task of *Order and History*. It needs also to be said that social order, however profoundly affected by the new understanding, remains the order of a plurality of concrete societies. Efforts at making this order intelligible find expression in symbols, and the first significant category of symbols is the *cosmological form*. The varied symbolisms in myth and ritual of the cosmological form build upon the fundamental experience of the cosmos. According to this schema, the cosmos itself provides the overarching order into which the human race must fit itself if it is to survive, and suggests its order as the model of all order, including that of society. The strength of the elemental symbols lies in their secure foundation in the readily experienced reality of visible and palpable vegetative rhythms and celestial revolutions that pervade the natural world and the cosmos and, seemingly, human society with them. This primordial experience of life is the source of an enduring dilemma: "The many need gods with 'shapes.' When the 'shapes' of the gods are destroyed with social effectiveness, the many will not become mystics but agnostics."[4]

The problem of "gods without shapes" arises at this point. The cosmological form collapses, existence in historical form is initiated, and a fundamental restructuring of individual and political life takes place. Plato symbolizes this new direction as the *periogogé*, the turning about of the soul.[5] In Judaism and Christianity, it is the *conversion*, the removal of a society from the secular realm to constitute it as the representative of the *civitas Dei* in historical existence.[6]

The line of reasoning from harmony to a grasp of the resonances of truth goes back at least as far as Pythagoras, and is also important for Plato. To delineate the main burden of foundational intellectual inquiry as a "correspondence to" the questions advanced is to make philosophical propositions accurate in a unique way. There can be no

3. *The World of Polis*, 8, 11ff.
4. Ibid., 239.
5. *The Republic*, 518d-e.
6. *Israel and Revelation*, 10–11.

real exactness, no responsibility where question and answer are not congruent, where they do not derive from a common axis—the very fact of existence.

In spite of the vagueness of its mode of expression, this may seem to be a persuasive statement, and one that separates this form of inquiry from its positivist critics. Within the context of this division, it challenges Descartes and the Cartesian foundations in all subsequent models of rational, scientific knowing. For Descartes, truth is determined and validated by certainty. Certainty, in turn, is situated in the *ego*. The self becomes the center of reality and relates to the world outside itself in a probing way. The *ego* is knower and user. For a "correspondence" notion of truth, on the contrary, the person and self-consciousness are not the axis, the appraisers of life. The essential connection to otherness is not, as is the case with Cartesian and positivist rationalism, one of utility. It is, rather, a relation of responsibility, both to and for. Consequently, if philosophy is co-respondence that makes articulate, that renders audible and is answerable to the summons of existence, we must turn to the "thinkers," not the pragmatic knowers. In the obscure efficacy of original meaning in Greek words, we may find authentic philosophical thought.[7]

With this type of orientation toward cognition, it would be good to look at what takes place with the appearance of historical form.

The authority of the myth dissolves, and existence in the elemental cosmological form differentiates. Society and its order, which have until now been symbolized as an analogue of the cosmos and its order (or as a "microcosmos"), tend to become symbolized as analogous to "the order of human existence . . . ") or as a "macroanthropos."[8] This newly differentiated order of society could be designated as the anthropological form. The historical form and the anthropological form are not the same, although they are differentiated out of the cosmological form together.

The order of *universal humanity* unfolds in time and space beyond the orders of the individual societies. This is the problem of the historical form. The universality of the human race is first evinced (it can be seen in retrospect) in the parallel development throughout the world of the cosmological myth of the common symbolic form of the same humanity. Consequently, the order of the ancient Near Eastern civili-

7. For the development of this theme, see the first chapter of George Steiner's *Martin Heidegger* (New York: Viking Press, 1978).
8. *Israel and Revelation*, 5ff.

zations was cosmological in form. By the time of Alexander, however, humanity had moved through Israel and Greece and so into historical existence.

> Israel alone constituted itself by recording its own genesis as a people as an event with a special meaning in history, while the other Near Eastern societies constituted themselves as analogues of cosmic order. Israel alone had history as an inner form, while the other societies existed in the form of cosmological myth. History, we therefore conclude, is a symbolic form of existence, of the same class as the cosmological form; and the paradigmatic narrative is, in the historical form, the equivalent of the myth in the cosmological form. Hence, it will be necessary to distinguish between political societies according to their form of existence: the Egyptian society existed in cosmological, the Israelite in historical form.[9]

The Horizon of Intelligibility

Without Israel, history would not exist—only the eternal recurrence of societies in cosmological form.[10] There is an important difference between existence in cosmological civilizations and historical existence. Does this mean, for instance, that Egypt had no history? The answer to this question depends upon the principle of compactness and differentiation.[11] Since human nature in this scheme is invariable and since the range of human experience is always present in its full dimension, cosmological civilizations are not devoid of history. In cosmological civilization, sacred experiences rise up into consciousness from out of the vast reaches of the unconscious. But this can be discerned only in retrospect, only after the experience has broken through and differentiated fully, only after it has created a historical

---

9. Ibid., 124.
10. Ibid., 126–27.
11. Voegelin articulates this interpretive principle in the following propositions: "(1) The nature of man is constant. (2) The range of human experience is always present in the fullness of its dimensions. (3) The structure of the range varies from compactness to differentiation." *Israel and Revelation*, 60.

present. The loosening of the authoritative hold of the myth facilitates inquiry into the nature of the physical world and presages the development of science.

As a form in which society exists, history has the tendency to include the entire human race—as it did on the first occasion in the Hebrew Bible. The proclivity of the historical form to extend its domain of meaning beyond its present into the past raises several dilemmas.

First, the struggle to find meaning assumes, at the most basic level (in primitive societies and cosmological civilizations), the form of ritual, myth, and play. At the opposite end of the range of experience, it takes on the form of history. The phrase "the meaning of history" must be used in a nuanced way. On the one hand, history is not a finite unit of observation susceptible to analysis by the methods of the natural sciences. On the other, it is not possible to fashion a system in the manner of Hegel, Marx, or Comte. For those disposed to approach history in either of those ways: "History has no knowable meaning (*eidos,* or essence) . . . ,"[12] and

> Canaan is as far away today as it has always been in the past. Anybody who has ever sensed this increase of dramatic tension in the historical present will be cured of complacency, for the light that falls over the past deepens the darkness that surrounds the future.[13]

Second, to the extent that history possesses objectivity, it does so as a consequence of personal experiences and the elaboration of these experiences in the accounts of individuals to whom they occur. These accounts render intelligible the field of history in which the event took place, and symbols fashioned for explanatory purposes are of a general type. The makeup of each such event provides a principle for understanding individuals and cultures by relating human existence to its degree of approach to the historical form.[14] In every instance of a new historical present, the great discovery divides the stream of life into the Either-Or of life and death, and divides time into the Before-and-After.[15]

---

12. Voegelin, *The World of the Polis,* 2.
13. *Israel and Revelation,* 129.
14. *Israel and Revelation,* 130; *The World of the Polis,* 2.
15. *The World of the Polis,* 5.

The approbation or denial of the representative authority of the witnesses to what is really at stake in the human condition is to be respected as a historical reality. Just as for Plato this reality and the responsibility of impartiality could be stated as "every myth has its truth,"[16] so a more complex historical present does not negate the authenticity of a historical present of a more fundamental level. This present is not destroyed when it becomes a retrospective past for a complex experience of order. Consequently, the opposition to a more profound understanding of the nature of order, and the simultaneous existence of more simply ordered cultures, along with more complex ones, is part of the historical process. To view these more simple societies as "primitive" is an instance of cultural chauvinism.[17]

Since symbolic expressions are restricted by the empirical horizon of those who formulate them, the Pauline historical present, after being normative for almost two millennia, has become inadequate. Modern philosophy needs to integate the even more comprehensive past with a Western historical horizon that has become global.

The third dilemma concerns the loss of historical capital. In this instance, perplexity about history becomes a real issue. From the present of a society in historical form there falls a ray of meaning over the past "from which it has emerged; and the history written in this spirit is part of the symbolism by which the society constitutes itself."[18]

From this perspective, then, history is a symbol; symbols can become deprived of their substance; the vacant symbol can still be employed for intentions at variance with its function as the medium of constituting existence in historical form. The Spengler-Toynbee historiographic projects are a significant example. These are manifestations of the tension between the Judeo-Christian historical form (in which Western civilization still exists) and the loss of marrow that it has undergone. The *raison d'etre* for the Spengler-Toynbee endeavors can be discovered in a lack of insight into the real dilemmas that the West faces. Their single-minded concentration on history is an indication of an apprehension that historical form, as it was achieved, might also be lost.[19] This is, in fact, the reason for a modern preoccupation with a

16. *Israel and Revelation*, 11.
17. See A. J. Toynbee, *A Study of History*, 2d ed., 12 vols. (Oxford: University Press, 1935–61); (1935) I, 90ff; II, 54ff; cf. VIII (1954), 272–313; XII (1961), 292ff, 665ff. This analysis appears in *The World of the Polis*, 12ff.
18. *Israel and Revelation*, 132.
19. Ibid., 133.

crucial period in culture that is more sensed than understood. The actual results of Toynbee and Spengler should not be taken at face value. They should, rather, be regarded as symptomatic manifestations. Their degree of confusion supplies an index of the seriousness of a situation that reveals history about to be overcome by the civilizations.

> The shift in accents [i.e., the preoccupation with the sheer mechanics of civilizational process as opposed to any concern with an originating historical present] is so radical that it practically makes nonsense of history, for history is the exodus from civilizations. And the great historical forms created by Israel, the Hellenic philosophers and Christianity did not constitute societies of the civilizational type—even though the communities thus established, which still are carriers of history, must wind their way through the rise and fall of civilizations.[20]

The Tension Between Historical Form and Civilizational Form

The tensions between the civilizations and history must claim our attention at this point. History "is the exodus from civilization." Any reduction of history to civilization is lacking in subtlety of analysis. Again referring to Toynbee and Spengler, Voegelin remarks that neither accept the principle that experiences of order, as well as their symbolic expressions, are products of a civilization but not its constitutive forms.[21]

Before elaborating on the consequences of this reduction of history to cycles of civilizations, it might help to clarify the relationship between historical form and civilizational form. A society's *form* is the interpretation of institutions and experiences of order.[22] It becomes manifest in constellations of related symbols that literally constitute a society and order it in a distinctive way. A symbolic form of existence creates a society. In the process of being preserved and reaffirmed through ritual observances and reiterated experiences in the tradition

20. Ibid.
21. Ibid, 126.
22. Ibid., 60.

of the founding experience,[23] the symbolic form sustains the society. In this manner, a society attains and retains its cultural identity. Consequently, a society's civilizational form is its mode of participation in the process of experience and symbolization of order that extends indefinitely into the future. Seen under this aspect, a civilization's form has historical singularity that can never be absorbed by phenomenal regularities because the form itself is an act in the drama of humanity striving for consonance with the truth of existence. This very striving, descriptive as the dynamics of human nature, *is* history.[24]

Why, then, does a tension exist between history and civilizations? Specifically, how can the historical form be both the constitutive form of Western civilization and, simultaneously, be said not to have constituted a society of the civilizational type?

The tension arises, in part, because of a failure to distinguish between a civilization as a mechanical concatenation of institutional phases (divisible into periods of genesis, growth, and decay) that succeed one another *ad infinitum,* and a civilization as a mode of participation in the process of striving for fidelity to its understanding of the nature of existence. The phenomenological civilizational theory tends to preempt the field of history with the result that human life is reduced to perennially recurring cycles of civilizations. Thus the essential meaning of history becomes lost. Societies constituted by the historical form are not civilizations because history, as a form of existence, is the course of order for the human race. A civilization is bound to the lasting and passing of existence. It has to maintain its consonance with the mundane order of existence as well as with the transcendent order, and it must be cautious not to mistake one for the other or to lose the balance between the rival orders that life inexorably demands.

A further aspect of the tension between history and the civilizations clarifies when the question is posed: What type of society does the

23. For an analysis of revelation and the people's response from Moses through the prophets, see I, 428ff. The Sinaitic revelation is analyzed at I, 406ff. and on page 417. The experiences founding the Greek form of philosophy present a similar problem. "What philosophy is, need not be ascertained by talking *about* philosophy discursively; it can and must be determined by entering *into* the speculative process in which the thinker explicates his experience of order" (II, 170). This important statement also articulates the main principle of Voegelin's method: the procedure it prescribes is followed with rigor and intensity throughout *Order and History.* The Hellenic experience is possibly best portrayed in connection with Socrates' *zetema* in the *Republic* (368c ff.) at III, 82ff.; see also, 112ff.

24. *Israel and Revelation,* 63.

historical form constitute? We have already observed that history tends to become universal history, as it did in the Hebrew Bible. Western civilization, as we have seen, has articulated its mode of participation in the form of history's process; that is, in a universalist, noncivilizational existential form. This is of far-reaching consequence. The Western historical form established by the Judeo-Christian tradition and Greek philosophy is the constitutive form of Ecumenical society. This is the conclusion that must be drawn from the theory of historical form.[25]

The truth articulated by the Western historical form is not the circumscribed truth of a civilizaton, nor is it the equally parochial truth of one "higher-religion"[26] among others. It communicates, rather, the most profound experiences that have occurred to human beings throughout history. Its validity is universal. It is the *representative* character of the bearers of the truth of life for humanity that is the essential point, not the ostensible parochialism of their location in this or that particular ethnic, geographic, or civilizational horizon.

The Mosaic experience brought about a freedom from existence in the form of cosmological myth. Yet once the adequate expression for an experience of order has been developed within the cosmological form, it does not disappear from history when revelation becomes the organizing center of symbolic form. The new symbols pertain primarily to the relationship between God and the human race and to that among persons; the old symbols validly order life for the world. A problem that "is insoluble on principle" emerges at this point: that of achieving a balance between "the life of the spirit and life in the world." Exclusive consonance either with immanent order or with transcendent order results in spiritual or physical suicide.[27]

It is the movement away from existence in cosmological form depicting the implicit line of expansion of the historical form that seems to be reflected in the contemporary expansion of Western civilization to global proportions. This raises the issue of the destiny of the West, in the sense of the meaning that the order of a society has in relation to its own development and decline.

---

25. See the section entitled: "The Meaning of History," *Israel and Revelation*, 126–33.
26. Cf. Toynbee, *A Study of History*, IV, 222ff.
27. For the problem of balance in the wake of the Hellenic experiences of transcendence, see *Plato and Aristotle*, 255; for the dilemma in Christianity, see the observations concerning the Sermon on the Mount in the same volume, 266ff.

History reduced to civilizations implies the destruction of Western historical form. It is with the intention of avoiding this possibility that Voegelin wrote *Order and History;* or, to recall the words of Richard Hooker, it is to guarantee that "Posterity may know we have not loosely through silence permitted things to pass away as in a dream."

8

Condicio Humana:
Neoclassical Elements
in Cultural Interpretation

Neoclassicism

Anyone who is temperamentally incapable of embracing the modern politics of cynicism is compelled to reexamine the classic assumptions about human nature. One of the most pressing concerns of our generation is refashioning our knowledge of the mind into a more extensive general theory of human nature, culture, and history.

It is on the amplification of a circumscribed set of patterns that Western civilization, its capacities for cultural memory and response, appear to depend.[1] The translation of images of order from one cultural epoch to another is a paramount means of such amplification. Neoclassicism is founded on a premise of timelessness. It assumes the equilibrium of generic human characteristics and thus of expressive forms. All translation from the canon, all mimesis, all citation is therefore synchronic.

Elements of Cultural Inquiry

A body of work such as that of Eric Voegelin manifests a profound appreciation for classical and neoclassical traditions. In an essay "On Classical Studies" (1973),[2] he initiates his reflections on the character of classical scholarship by citing Wolf's definition of classic philology

---

1. J. B. Leishman's preface to *Translating Horace* (Oxford: Cassirer, 1956) is an excellent introduction to the problem of the authority and transmission of classic forms in Western literature.
2. "On Classical Studies," *Modern Age* 17 (Winter 1973), 2–8.

as the study of human nature as manifested in the Greeks,[3] whose effort to arrive at an understanding of their humanity culminated in the creation of philosophy as an inquiry into human nature.

The essay proceeds to specify some of the constituent qualities of philosophical reflection. A human nature, a definite structure of existence, circumscribes the boundaries of the human. The human being is a questioner (*aporein*) and seeker (*zetein*) for the origin, the direction, and the meaning of existence. The desire to know, the questioning and seeking itself, the direction of the questioning, are the experiential complex, the *pathos*, in which the reality of participation in existence (*metalepsis*) becomes transparent. The central concern of the philosopher's endeavors is the exploration of this reality, of the platonic *metaxy*, as well as the articulation of the exploratory action through language symbols, in Plato's case of his myths.

The process by which human beings become conscious and articulate is one where human nature becomes transparent to itself as the life of reason. Man is the *zoon nous echon*. Through the life of reason (*bios theoretikos*) humanity realizes its freedom.

In the Greek manifestation of classical studies, human nature has achieved the state of noetic consciousness and developed the symbols for its self-interpretation. The level of development of reason in the Greeks has set critical standards for the exploration of consciousness. The achievement, however, is not a final possession, an heirloom to be handed on to later generations, but a paradigmatic action to be explored in order to continue under the conditions of the present time.[4]

Voegelin concludes his reflections on classical studies with the designation of two general areas in which no major advance of the discipline beyond its present state seems plausible without recourse to, and continuation of, the Greek noetic project. He maintains that if anything is characteristic of the present state of the historical disciplines, it is the discrepancy between the extensive amount of material and the poverty of their theoretical penetration.

> Whenever I have to touch on problems of the primitive myth or the imperial symbolism of Egypt, of Israelite prophetism, Jewish apocalypse, or Christian gospels, or Plato's historical conscious-

3. Friedrich August Wolf (1759–1824) originated the discipline of philology. The work on which his reputation still rests is the *Prolegomena ad Homerum* (Halis Saxonum: Orphanotrophel, 1795).

4. Voegelin, "On Classical Studies," 3–5, 7.

ness compared with that of Deutero-Isaiah, of the Polybian ecumenic consciousness compared with that of Mani, of magic or hermetism, and so forth, I am impressed by the philosophical and text-critical work done on the sources, but I feel frustrated because so little work is done to relate the phenomena of this class to the structure of consciousness in the sense of noetic analysis.[5]

Second, one of the premier achievements of the Greek struggle for insight into the nature of order, both against the older myth and the sophistic climate of opinion, is the exploration of deformation and its varieties. Again, Voegelin believes that very little is done to explore this achievement, to develop it more extensively, and to apply it to the modern phenomena of deformation.[6] As did Heidegger,[7] Voegelin also maintains the assumption that Greek beginnings, especially the origins of philosophy in the pre-Socratics, were a privileged moment in Western intellectual history, not merely a *point de départ* for later "developments" but, literally, a stopping point to which later thought must refer.

Theory

Voegelin employs the terms "theory" and "philosophy" somewhat correlatively. He generally uses the word philosophy in what he understands to be its platonic sense, that is, as the love of wisdom respecting the ground of existence, or the world-transcendent *arché*.

"Theory" is occasionally employed to mean the articulation in propositional form of the results of philosophical inquiries. Theory is the prose and philosophy the poetry of investigation into the nature of life. However, since theory is only a part and not the entirety of philosophy, philosophy is obliged to employ (though critically and self-

5. Ibid., 7–8.
6. Ibid., p. 8.
7. See, for instance, Heidegger's essays: "Der Spruch des Anaximander," in *Holzwege* (Frankfurt a.M.: V. Klostermann, 1950): "Logos," "Moira," and "Aletheia," in *Vortrage und Aufsatze* (Pfullingen: G. Neske, 1954). Also see *Einführung in die Metaphysik* (Tübingen: N. Niemeyer, 1953). A general discussion of Heidegger's classicism can be found in Werner Marx, *Heidegger and the Tradition* (Evanston: Northwestern University Press, 1971).

consciously) the language of intimation when the eye of theory has reached its outermost limits. Voegelin implies this when he states in *Anamnesis* that the most important result of his analysis of order and history was the insight that a theory of consciousness is impossible in the sense of a set of propositions valid once and for all concerning a fixed structural configuration. This is because consciousness is not something "given" that can be described from the outside, but rather an experience whose *logos* can be brought to light only through the meditative exegesis of itself.[8] The illusion of theory has to be abandoned before the reality of the meditative process. The character of consciousness must be explored from within by the process of meditation, through which the mind obtains continuously deepening insight into its own *logos*.[9]

Voegelin's work is a contribution to understanding the significance of order in society. *Anamnesis,* or recollection, is the symbol originally chosen by Plato to designate the process of discerning the order of existence. Remembrance or recollection becomes "the activity of consciousness, through which what has been forgotten—that is, the knowledge latent in consciousness—is brought into the specific presence of consciousness."[10] Political philosophy is then an empirical enterprise in the sense that it is an investigation of experiences. One of the tasks of contemporary philosophy is to bring to remembrance experiences which, while once known, have been permitted to sink into forgetfulness. This will mean, specifically, the recovery of the insights of Greek philosophy, yet does not imply that Plato and Aristotle have pronounced the final word on the subject of order and existence. Foundational thought is characterized by a certain inner tension that gives it a suppleness, making it more adequate to the comprehension of reality than more apodictic expressions of thought. Voegelin's own thinking reveals this tension quite dramatically. To overlook the interrogatory aspect of his work would be to receive a distorted impression of his thought.

Voegelin's affinity for philosophical skepticism—he displays consid-

---

8. Voegelin, however, does not intend to denigrate theory as such. Rather, he calls into question inadequate conceptions of theory. Consequently he describes his own *New Science of Politics* as articulating a "theory of politics."

9. Ibid., 7.

10. ". . . die Tätigkeit des Bewusstseins, durch die das Vergessene, d.h. das im Bewusstsein latente Wissen aus der Unbewusstheit in eine spezifische Praesenz des Bewusstseins gehoben wird." Ibid., 11.

erable respect for Hume, Santayana, Michael Oakeshoot and Camus—
is testimony to the heuristic quality of his mind. At the same time, this
quality leaves him vulnerable to criticisms of inconsistency and ambiguity by both sympathetic readers and proponents of the hyperclarity
of linguistic philosophy. For upon what basis can a philosophy of
order assert anything at all about the foundations of society? If no
absolute propositions[11] can be articulated by a theory of consciousness, does this not undermine the remarkable confidence with which
Voegelin dismisses so significant a part of the history of Western speculation? His exposition of the fundamental experiences which he contends must be presupposed by philosophical reflection are highly
condensed. Yet the brief discussion in his 1943 letter to Alfred Schütz
does make some contribution toward elaborating these experiences.[12]
His article "On Debate and Existence" (1967), with the explication of
the "experience of existence," also makes a contribution in this regard.[13]

Voegelin conceives of political theory not as an ideology, utopia, or
scientific methodology, but as an experiential discipline of right order
in the person and society. Since experience is the control for the propositions elucidated in the course of this theoretical analysis, it would
be well to preface an exposition of those propositions with a reflection
on Voegelin's analysis of the structure of experience itself. This "experience" is multi-dimensional in nature and incapable of being contracted, in the Comtean or logical positivist fashion, to the single
plane of physical sensation.

The "Experience of Existence"

The Archimedean point of Voegelin's inquiry is the empirical reality of
the human person in an awareness of the finiteness of life. The person

> discovers his existence as illuminated from within by Intellect
> or Nous. Intellect is the instrument of self-interpretation as
> much as it is a part of the structure of his existence . . . man
> discovers himself as being not a world unto himself, but an ex-

11. Ibid., 57.
12. "Brief an Alfred Schütz über Edmund Husserl," *Anamnesis*, 21–36.
13. "On Debate and Existence," *The Intercollegiate Review* 3 (March-April 1967),
143–52.

istent among others: he experiences a world of existents of which he is a part.[14]

In his paper "Debate and Existence," the point is made that "The logical operations of Intellect *qua* Reason will arrive at widely different results if Reason has cut loose from the *condicio humana*.[15] A fragile bond keeps reason tied to this condition, which is to say, to reality. The rejection of the fragile bond and the pursuit of massively possessive "knowledge" based on an illusory simplification of life have produced the imaginative Gnostic ideological speculations of the modern era. These speculations, although occasionally possessing an internal rational coherence, are actually the repudiation of a rational theory of politics because they are grounded on an imagined "second reality." They proclaim an illusory self-salvation and self-perfection for the race within history. The thinkers of the second reality reject the

> experience of finiteness and creatureliness in our existence, of being creatures of a day as the poets call man, of being born and bound to die, of dissatisfaction with the state experienced as imperfect, of apprehension of a perfection that is not of this world but is a privilege of the gods, or possible fulfillment in a state beyond this world.[16]

They renounce existence in uncertain truth for existence in certain untruth. With such people it is impossible to engage in rational communication, for "edifices of reason enacted on the experiential basis of existence in truth" are "useless in a meeting with edifices of reason erected on a different experiential basis."[17]

Voegelin is one of a number of contemporary thinkers such as Alois Dempf[18] and Hans Urs von Balthasar who are critical of system-building in modern philosophy. The term "system" is frequently used today to refer to any orderly body of philosophical speculation, and the analogue from the history of philosophy usually referred to is that

14. Ibid., 149.
15. Ibid., 151–52.
16. Ibid., 146.
17. Ibid., 152.
18. Voegelin first published his essay on "Historiogenesis" in the *Festschrift für Alois Dempf*, ed. Max Müller and Michael Schmaus (Freiburg/Munich: Albert, 1960), 419–46. It was later published as a chapter in *Anamnesis* (1966) and also as ch. I of vol. IV of *Order and History*.

of Thomistic and Aristotelian "systems." One could maintain, however, that systems are a modern invention, and doubt that it is possible to properly speak of a system before Descartes. Whereas a work such as the *Summa Theologiae* employs analogical reasoning and remains heuristic, moving in the tension between reason and faith, a systematic construction of a Spinoza or a Hegel derives its propositions from axioms. In its enclosed conversation with itself, it becomes further and further removed from the reality which it is supposed to be explicating. The system is founded on the assumption that all areas of life are susceptible to being compressed to the point where the finite human intellect can adequately comprehend and conceptualize them. System-constructors misconstrue the fundamental experience of life, which teaches that some dimensions of reality cannot adequately be conceptualized within the framework of intellectual systems.

One of the modern thinkers to whom Voegelin consistently refers with respect is Bergson,[19] and he has sought to follow Bergson in fashioning a philosophy that passes "from reality to concepts and no longer from concepts to reality."[20] Voegelin is a philosophical realist rather than an idealist since he maintains that the structure of reality exists independently of thought. The task is to attune one's thinking to that reality (or, more precisely, to recognize one's thought as *participating* in the noetic structure of existence), rather than attempt to force reality to conform to one's concepts. The nature of truth is that it exists "concealed" and that its presence is disclosed, not coerced in the manner of Bacon's "rack" for nature. In this sense, Voegelin is an empiricist, although it is the panoply of human experience and not an arbitrarily abstracted segment of it that he takes for his field of observation.

Knowledge and Politics

Given continued emphasis upon the inevitable limitations of human understanding, the criticism of system-building, and concern about

19. See, for example, *Anamnesis*, 42. See also "Reason: The Classic Experience," *Southern Review*, n.s. 10, 2 (Spring 1974), 246. The work of Bergson which bears most directly on the present study is *Essai sur les données immédiates de la conscience* (Paris: Alcan, 1889).

20. Henri Bergson, *An Introduction to Metaphysics*, trans. T. E. Hulme (London: Macmillan, 1912), 40.

inappropriate philosophical symbolization,[21] one might think that Voegelin would attempt no political theory at all but content himself with admonitions to those who adopt ideologies and intimations of inexpressible mysteries. He also could have retreated into skepticism. Yet he has moved beyond this tenable but ultimately inadequate position and driven himself to explicate the vital distinction between ideology and authentic knowledge of the human situation.

Political philosophy has to include a theory of knowledge as well as insight into the dynamics of society. Political theory should also take cognizance of the limits of knowledge. Included in this category is the understanding—invaluable for a concept of order in political society—of the fantasy permeating those speculations on politics which assume that life is something other than it is and that a realm of perfect human fulfillment is obtainable by virtue of the proper manipulation of the institutional environment. The constructive aspect of Voegelin's work consists of an attempt to elaborate, after the manner of the classical political theorists, the principles of political realism.

Voegelin is committed to the recovery of classical theorizing regarding the interpenetration of mind and society. In a critical exegesis of Plato in the third volume of *Order and History*, he renders an account of Plato's discovery (intimated but not fully articulated in Heraclitus) of the "macro-anthropological" principle. In contrast with the "micro-anthropological" principle enunciated in the Egyptian and Babylonian symbolizations, which conceived of society as a miniature analogue of cosmic rhythms, the macro-anthropological principle describes society as the reflection of the order of the psyche in the regnant character type. This anthropology is derived from the Platonic-Aristotelian heritage.

Voegelin accepts in its essentials the portrait of the *spoudaios* sketched by Aristotle (especially in Books I, IV, and X of the *Nicomachean Ethics*).[22] The *spoudaios* is the person who has his or her priorities in order, who pursues as the highest good that which actually is the highest good and not one that is only instrumental for attaining some further end (and is therefore inherently insufficient). *Eudaimonia* can result only from the *bios theoretikos*, the life of reason. Such a life is the fulfillment of the capacities and powers that are most distinc-

---

21. For some expression of this concern, see *Israel and Revelation*, 9–11; *The World of the Polis*, 171–74.
22. Cf. ch. 10 of *Plato and Aristotle*.

tively human.[23] Individual changes in a great number of people in a community may have the effect of changing the mores, and ultimately the institutions, of a society because the hierarchy of purposes for individual action has changed.[24]

It might be inferred from the nature of the foregoing sketch that Voegelin has been too concerned with other problems of philosophy to offer the kind of minute and explicit analysis of fundamental experiences provided by the late phenomenological philosopher Alfred Schütz. Yet in *Anamnesis* Voegelin acknowledges Schütz as the "silent partner" of all his work, and thus indicates the esteem in which he holds such investigations.[25]

23. *Nichomachean Ethics*, trans. H. Rockam (Cambridge: Harvard University Press, 1956), bk. X, 7.

24. *The World of the Polis*, 283.

25. "In Memoriam Alfred Schütz," *Anamnesis*, 17–20. For Schütz's work, see *Alfred Schütz: Collected Papers*, ed. H. L. van Breda, 3 vols. (The Hague: Martinus Nijhoff, 1967).

9

Israel and Revelation:
The Tension of Biblical Existence

Some of the considerations of historical form in chapter 7 had particular reference to the first volume of *Order and History*. I would now like to consider *Israel and Revelation* in more detail.[1] In his study of the theme of order and history, Eric Voegelin undertakes a renewal of the perennial investigation into the source of order. Philosophical inquiry, he maintains, is a way of diagnosing "modes of existence in untruth" and, as in the instance of Plato, is "the means of establishing islands of order in the disorder of the age." He states at the commencement that his work does not represent an effort to explore curiosities of a dead past, but is, rather, an investigation into the nature of the order in which we live presently.

Accordingly, *Israel and Revelation* (1956), the inaugural volume of *Order and History,* articulates a theory of history informed by a sustained reflection on the "drama of humanity" and an analysis of the symbols that the human race has fashioned to probe the meaning of its existence. In its synthesis of biblical theology with classical philosophy, and in its viewing of the struggle for meaningful order *sub specie aeternitatis,* this study displays a rare scope and penetration.

This chapter concentrates on the main outline and thrust of *Israel and Revelation.* As the *History* developed over the years, Voegelin modified his original orientation. In the introduction to the fourth volume, *The Ecumenic Age* (1974), he enunciates the reasons for the alteration in perspective. Nevertheless, *Israel and Revelation* remains foundational for the enterprise of *Order and History,* which has devel-

---

1. I have developed a number of the central notions in this chapter more fully in "The Tension of Consciousness: The Pneumatic Differentiation," in *Voegelin and the Theologian: Ten Studies in Interpretation,* ed. John Kirby and William M. Thompson (New York: Edwin Mellen Press, 1983).

oped into an intricate analysis of the amalgam of philosophical understanding and biblical faith that is the bedrock of Western civilization.

Since *Israel and Revelation* was published more than thirty years
ago, it is appropriate, first, to recollect its central theme. I then want
to elaborate on the fundamental principles according to which the
analysis of revelation in volume 1 proceeds, and subsequently consider
what bearing revelation has on historical, political existence. The context for this consideration is the tension that exists between the sacred
order (the kingdom of God) and Israel's life as a people in political
history. It will also be necessary at least to describe the dilemma that
the problem of evil poses for Voegelin's philosophical perspective.

The Emergence of Historical Consciousness in Israel

The premises of this inquiry are developed in an introductory section
entitled "The Symbolization of Order." These reflections provide the
theoretical framework that informs this study of the Israelite experience in the context of the civilizations of the ancient Near East. History is to be understood as a drama in which the human race takes
part as an actor—not a spectator. The meaning of the drama is uncertain, but the uncertainty is partially diminished when the fundamental
symbols of humanity's participation in existence are differentiated—
that is, when some aspect of the total experience of reality becomes
more acutely pronounced in consciousness. The sharpened consciousness of one aspect of reality does not completely invalidate the other
elements of the fundamental experience; rather, it provides the vantage
point for a clearer awareness of participation in the life of the world.
When this occurred in Israel, a new type of person appeared on the
world-political scene, a person who stood forth as an individual and
who lived and acted politically *vis-à-vis* God. The main outlines for
the emergence of this new historical consciousness are as follows:

In the ancient Near East, the human race existed within a cosmological civilization, one whose symbolization expressed the mythical
participation of society in the Creator who orders the cosmos. In Mesopotamia the empire's spatial organization was regarded as the archetype of the order of the cosmos on the principle of the correspondence
between macrocosm and micrososm. At the *omphalos*, or sacred

center where heaven and earth meet, the social order was periodically regenerated. During the New Year celebration, the king, as the analogue of the deity, participated in the annual victory over the powers of chaos.

Egyptian culture was also grounded in the consubstantiality of the sacred order with the pharaonic order, Pharaoh being the mediator through whom the divine *Maat* (order, justice, truth) emanated into society. Pharaonic order was a continuous renewal and reenactment of the cosmic order from eternity. Through Pharaoh, in whom the presence of deity was manifest, the most humble subject participated in the timeless serenity of cosmic order. The Egyptian style of social and sacred consonance fashioned a static and stable civilization that survived without fundamental alteration for more than three thousand years.

These civilizations had tendencies toward a breakthrough into the radical transcendence of sacred reality over against the ordinary life of society. This was especially true in Egypt, as evidenced in the Memphite theology and the reform of Akhenaton. But proclivities toward the differentiation of fundamental experience and symbolization never achieved a status that could become the ordering force of a religious personality who, in turn, could become the center of a new type of community. Rather, gods and people, heaven and earth, nature and history, the rhythms of fertility and the realities of politics were bound up in one unified whole; and the primary experience of the unitary nature of life and order was expressed in a mythical pattern of symbolism, each element of which was an integral part of the whole.[2]

It was in Israel that the search for authentic order was carried forward. Under Dynasty XIX, which struggled in vain to break the limits of imperial symbolization, Moses led an "exodus from cosmological civilization" in the thirteenth century B.C.E. The Exodus was not merely another occurrence in secular history but, according to the witness of the Hebrew Bible, an event of liberation by Yahweh. Israel was liberated from the *Sheol* (realm of the dead) of Egypt for existence in historical form. The Exodus resulted in a development of the formerly elemental experience through an intensified awareness of the chasm between ordinary life, in which gods and human beings coexist in a consubstantial community, and the transcendent deity beyond the order of society regarded as an integral part of the cosmic order. The

2. *Israel and Revelation*, 111–12.

movement toward more consonance with the sacred, however, was primarily an event experienced in the person of Moses,[3] though anticipated in the life of Abraham. This event fashioned a new order of the person and, through the agency of Moses, a new type of society living in immediacy under the kingdom of God. History was the inner form of Israel's life under God, in contrast to contemporary civilizations that existed in the form of cosmological myth. Without Israel there would be no history—only the recurring rhythms of cosmological civilization.[4]

From the very beginning, however, this way of life was difficult to maintain, owing both to internal pressures and those exerted by surrounding societies. Tradition portrays the history of Israel in the pre-state period as an undulating movement toward and away from the covenantal order given in the Mosaic revelation. The greater apostasy came when, under the duress of political necessity, the people demanded a monarchy like the surrounding nations. This fateful development brought about a reversal of the Exodus and a reentry into the *Sheol* of cosmological civilization—that is, a fall from true existence to the inauthentic existence of cosmological empire. From this point on, the perpetual task of history was to regain the order that had been eroded or eclipsed.

The history of Israel would have been an indefinite undulatory movement of defections and returns to the order of the covenant had it not been for the prophets. These new bearers of meaning rejected the institution of the monarchy and awakened the universalist potentialities of Yahweh's revelation to Moses that lay dormant in the tradition. To them, the existence or nonexistence of the kingdom was irrelevant to leading a just life. Their mission was to recall Israel to the covenant. The prophets were spokesmen of the new Israel in search of its identity—the new order, or one might even say the "new creation."

Since, however, the prophetic call to return to the authentic way of life proved ineffectual, the *omphalos* shifted from the Chosen People to the prophet himself (for example Jeremiah) who lived in resistance to his society. The climax of prophecy in the Hebrew Bible was Second Isaiah's portrayal of the Suffering Servant, said to be the Prophet himself, and subsequent individuals of this type. The keynote of Second Isaiah's message is Israel's exodus from itself in order to announce to all people the revelation it had received. Thus the Servant represents a

3. Ibid., 388.
4. Ibid., 126.

new community, one that no longer has to reside in Canaan but, with a universal outreach, includes each individual whose very personality is "the sensorium of transcendence" and becomes the center of an ecumenical humanity.[5]

The final result was a differentiation of *theologia supranaturalis* from *theologia civilis,* both of which were united in primitive societies. History was punctuated by other irruptions of transcendent reality, such as the enlightenment of a Buddha or the opsis of Plato, but, from Voegelin's perspective, the inbreaking of sacred reality found its optimum clarity in the Hebrew Bible and the New Testament, where history is structured by crucial events such as the Exodus or the Incarnation.[6] From this perspective, history is viewed as a drama in which every society, in its allotted time and space, struggles to give shape to its own truth.

The Quest for Authorization

With this sketch of the volume in mind, we might consider an interpretation of what is traditionally called "revelation." Revelation obviously plays a central role in cultural and historical studies that focus on religious experience. Religious symbols serve to synthesize a people's ethos—the tone, character, and quality of their life, its ethical and aesthetic form and mood—and their worldview—the image they retain of the way things are, their most comprehensive notions of order. In religious belief and practice, a community's ethos is rendered intellectually reasonable by being shown to represent a way of life ideally adapted to the actual state of affairs the worldview describes, while the worldview is rendered affectively credible by being presented as an image of an actual state of affairs peculiarly well-arranged to accommodate such a way of life. This confrontation and mutual confirmation objectivizes moral and aesthetic preferences by depicting them as the imposed conditions of life implicit in a world with a par-

5. Voegelin highlights Second Isaiah's vision of the universality of the "spiritual exodus" and its relation to the conquest of Cyrus, whom the prophet hailed as Yahweh's "Anointed" (Isa. 45:1) in *The Ecumenic Age.*

6. Voegelin's understanding of the encounter with the Incarnation as a "structuring event" in human history is presented succinctly in his essay on "History and Gnosis," in *The Old Testament and Christian Faith,* ed. B. W. Anderson (New York: Herder and Herder, 1969), 64–89, especially 82ff.

ticular structure, as mere common sense given the unalterable shape of reality. It also supports these received beliefs about the world by invoking moral and aesthetic sentiments as experiential evidence for their veracity. Religious symbols formulate a basic congruence between a particular way of life and a specific (if, most frequently, implicit) metaphysic, and in so doing sustain each with the borrowed authority of the other.[7]

The conviction that religion tunes human activity to an envisaged cosmic order on the plane of human experience is hardly novel, but scarcely investigated either. Thus we possess only limited empirical knowledge of the way in which this is accomplished. An extensive ethnographic literature to demonstrate that this takes place does exist. But the theoretical framework that provides an analytic account of it does not.[8] Theoretical understanding is thus one of the significant attempts made in *Order and History.*

It is obviously important to grasp the fundamental principles according to which the analysis of revelation in volume 1 proceeds. In order to understand the full range and subtlety of this thought, it would be worthwhile to consider briefly the theoretical foundations from which the broader structure of this interpretation unfolds.

The concern here is with the development of human consciousness as it differentiates historically by treating the history of experiences and their symbolization. In *The New Science of Politics,* which offered a preliminary sketch of the enterprise he subsequently developed into *Order and History,* Voegelin indicated that his aim was to contribute to the social sciences on the level of genuine theory. What was expressed by theory he took to be an attempt at articulating the meaning of life by explicating the content of a definite class of experiences. Theory " . . . derives its validity from the aggregate of experiences to which it must permanently refer for empirical control."[9] These experiences are constitutive of the inner life of one whose character is formed by them, a person such as Aristotle called the *spoudaios,* the mature individual.

The range of experience is always present in the fullness of its dimensions, though the structure of the range varies from the elemental to the complex. Experience may become more or less conscious and

7. Cf. Geertz, *The Interpretation of Cultures,* 89–90.
8. Ibid., 90.
9. *The New Science of Politics,* 64.

articulate, depending on one's ability—and willingness—to become aware of its full range of implicit contents. The process of development does not take place in the lifetime of a single individual or even a society or civilization, but extends through a myriad of societies. This process of increasingly complex insight constitutes what is meant by history.[10]

The most significant differentiations indicate advances in consciousness. The continuity of the fundamental substratum of experience, however, remains constant; whatever becomes differentiated out of it was always contained within it. It is therefore useful to consider the unchanging contents of this core of experience.

The most fundamental element of this core of experience is tension, and classical philosophers were the first to give it expression. Tension of existence may express itself in various ways—not only as an awareness of mortality, but also as a questioning unrest,[11] as the "omnidimensional 'desire to know.' "[12] Voegelin believes that the foundational element ultimately motivating this experience of tension is characterized by an attraction toward the sacred.[13] Thus life has an "in between" or *metaxy* character. The individual is characterized by a fundamental *eros* or tension toward the unlimited, but can never attain it without ceasing to be finite. The tension may tempt man to exceed the limits of the human condition through some form of gnosis, the pretension to a certain and definitive understanding of life itself through knowledge. To live authentically within this tension is itself the human condition, and the concept of *metaxy* symbolizes the fundamental tension that is a constant feature of life. Tension is the central experience from which searching and striving proceed. It can never be left behind and must always be represented and communicated through symbols.

In the drive to understand, the contents of the experiential ground of thought are differentiated and raised into consciousness, thereby constituting reflective existence as perpetually moving toward a more penetrating understanding of reality. The process of differentiation is consequently marked by a revelatory character, whether it emphasizes the noetic (in the instance of philosophy) or the religious.

10. IV. 1; see also I. 130; II. 2; IV. 6, 226, 303, 332–35.
11. "Reason: The Classic Experience," *Southern Review,* n.s. 10, no. 2 (Spring 1974), 237–64.
12. *The Ecumenic Age,* 237.
13. *Israel and Revelation,* 2; *The Ecumenic Age,* 330.

It is in this sense that we can speak of the constitution of reason through revelation: The life of reason is firmly embedded in a revelation because " . . . the God who appeared to the philosophers, and who elicited from Parmenides the exclamation 'Is!,' was the same God who revealed himself to Moses as the 'I am who (or: what) I am,' as the God who is what he is in the concrete theophany to which man responds."[14]

In the earlier volumes of *Order and History*, Voegelin tended to employ the terms "reason" and "revelation" for disclosures of being to Greek philosophers and Israelite religious thinkers respectively.[15] In *The Ecumenic Age*, however, a shift to different terms makes clearer that both experiences are events that have the character of disclosure: "noetic" and "pneumatic" differentiation. In the instance of noetic differentiation, the discovery of reason, both Plato and Aristotle were aware, he maintains, that *noesis* was not an autonomous human project (as the later concept of "natural reason" would have it):

> Participation in the noetic movement is not an autonomous project of action but the response to a theophanic event (the Promethean light exceeding bright, the Socratic *daimonion*) or its persuasive communication (the Platonic Peitho). To this revelatory movement (*kinesis*) from the divine ground, man can respond by his questioning and searching, but the theophanic event itself is not at his command.[16]

Although the process of noetic differentiation was complex and required the contributions of several generations of Hellenic "mystic-philosophers,"[17] it may be described concisely as "the adequate articulation and symbolization of the questioning consciousness."[18]

A revelatory event, according to this analysis, never provides information about the world; rather, it renders explicit what was always implicit in the substratum of experience.[19] For this reason, revelation

14. *The Ecumenic Age*, 229.
15. *Plato and Aristotle*, 204.
16. *The Ecumenic Age*, 217.
17. For a summary of the process and its results, see *The Ecumenic Age*, 177–78.
18. "Reason: The Classic Experience," 241.
19. Cf. *The World of the Polis*, 283: "The mystic-philosopher has no information to tender; he can only communicate the discovery which he has made in his own soul, hoping that such communication will stir up parallel discoveries in the souls of others." Cf. also *Plato*

cannot be something arbitrary or subjective in the pejorative sense; the test of the validity of its content always remains its grounding in experienced reality. If a person claims to have received through revelation any type of informational knowledge, whether rational truths, miraculous occurrences (past, present, or future), or political or military policies preferred by God, he or she is simply misconstruing the nature of revelation. Informational understanding can be obtained only through the necessary procedures of rational inquiry, the patient activity of the questioning self as it carefully and critically raises its questions and considers the data of experience in light of them. Any attempt to bypass this necessary process is to deviate into some form of gnosis—intellectual, emotional, or volitional.[20] Because the Israelite revelation was focused on the pneumatic center rather than the noetic periphery, the tradition deriving from it was always susceptible to such deviations; reason was not adequately articulated to serve as a consistently adequate critical control on thought.[21]

This brings us to the subject of this volume's interpretation of revelation, in the traditional sense, as constituted by the Israelite experience of the sacred and its subsequent history in the Christian tradition. It is worth briefly tracing this development historically since it took place over a far longer period than the philosophical one. Although Voegelin acknowledges that Moses, in the symbol of "I am who I am," was the first to articulate the human experience of the sacred presence in order to express the essential omnipresence of a substantially hidden God,[22] he accepts the tradition that the first movements of revelation occurred in Abraham, movements which gave rise to an expectation of future fulfillment:

---

and Aristotle, 84, on Plato's conception of inquiry (*zetema*) as exegesis of the depths of the soul. For some modern interpretations of the nature of revelation that are fundamentally in accord with this position, see H. Richard Niebuhr, *The Meaning of Revelation* (New York: Macmillan, 1941) and John Macquarrie, *Principles of Christian Theology* (New York: Scribner's, 1966).

20. For a discussion of Isaiah's speculation on the divine plan of history as a form of incipient gnosis, see *Israel and Revelation*, 451. For the nature of the Gnostic temptation as a general human problem ("The temptation to fall from a spiritual height that brings the element of uncertainty into final clarity down into the more solid certainty of world-immanent, sensible, fulfillment . . . "), see *Science, Politics, and Gnosticism* (Chicago: Regnery Gateway, 1968), 107–9, 114. For a reflection of the range of possible varieties of gnosis—intellectual, emotional, volitional—see *The New Science of Politics*, 124.

21. *Israel and Revelation*, 240, 237.

22. Ibid., 411.

In the case of Abram's experience this 'future' is not yet understood as the eternity under whose judgment man exists in his
present. To be sure, Yahweh's *berith* is already the flash of eternity into time; but the true nature of this 'future' as transcendence is still veiled by the sensuous analogues of a glorious
future in historical time.[23]

This futuristic component in the early experience remained a continuing influence, perduring through Israelite and later Judaic history
and issuing into the apocalyptic literature. At the time, however, it led
to comparatively little because it did not become socially effective: The
new domain of Yahweh is not yet the political order of a people in Canaan; for the present it does not extend beyond the soul of Abraham.[24]

The identity of Israel as a people originated from Moses, and the identity of the person of Moses originated from his response to a further
revelation. This became a collective—compared to strictly individual—reality when Moses communicated the substance of his experience to the Israelites and thereby constituted them as a people: "To
the skeptical sons of Israel Moses will have to say: '*Ehyeh* [I am] has
sent me to you' (Exod. 3:14). The people thus will break the bondage
of Egypt and enter the present under God, once they have responded
to the revelation of God's presence with them."[25]

The social order subsequently founded exhibited its well-known un-
dulations, and the difficulties took three principal forms. One was an
inclination to equate the goal of Israel's existence with some form of
worldly success, such as a kingdom of Solomonic grandeur in Canaan.
Another was a tendency to retreat from conscious existence in the immediate presence of Yahweh by reintroducing mediating existences:
The Davidic king conceived of as "Son of God," the reconceiving of
the living Word of God as sacred scripture, and the fictional invention
of the Deuteronomic Moses as Lawgiver and author of scripture. Finally, there was a recurrent temptation among the prophets to escape
from the tension created by this situation, as manifested in various
expectations of a coming age in which the lion lies down with the
lamb and holy men and women have direct insight into the intentions
of Yahweh.

23. Ibid., 194.
24. Ibid.
25. Ibid., 27.

On the other hand, the one genuinely significant advance made later in the history of Israel was intimately related to this last pattern. The advance resulted from the outgrowth of an inchoate further step in the process of development—the realization that questions of order extend beyond the life of a concrete society and its institution. Voegelin speaks of this "Exodus of Israel from itself," and he sees it as culminating in the representative suffering of Deutero-Isaiah.[26] This was the zenith of development in Israel, but it occurred almost simultaneously with the major defection into Deuteronomist legalism and scripturalism, which some consider the principal point of demarcation between the history of Israel and that of Judaism. This situation is significant because it indicates the character of the crucial problem of religion as such, a problem that Christianity had to confront centuries later, especially after the Council of Nicaea: ". . . it looks as if in Deuteronomy we were touching the genesis of 'religion,' defined as the transformation of existence in historical form into the secondary possession of a 'creed' concerning the relation between God and man."[27] That this should have happened is comprehensible, almost inevitable.

> The prophets, philosophers, and saints, who can translate the order of the spirit into the practice of conduct without institutional support and pressure, are rare. For its survival in the world, therefore, the order of the spirit has to rely on a fanatical belief in the symbols of a creed more often than on the *fides caritate formata*—though such reliance, if it becomes socially predominant, is apt to kill the order it is supposed to preserve.[28]

It is worth noting here that this approach throws new light on discussions about "historical revelation." Much attention focuses on the semantic field, or the pattern of symbolization within which the various textual statements are made. Israel's experience fashioned a sense of history that was novel in a cultural environment dominated by a mythical view of reality. History was, in fact, the "inner form" of Israel's existence before Yahweh. *The Ecumenic Age* does not speak of a *Heilsgeschichte*, or a history of salvation distinguished from secular history. In fact, the volume abandons the view that history as a linear

26. Ibid., 491–515.
27. Ibid., 376.
28. Ibid., 376–77.

course of events was an Israelite discovery since historiogenesis had its inception, at least in mythopoeic form, by the end of the third millennium B.C.E. as evidenced, for instance, by the Sumerian King List.[29] The concern here is to stress the experience that initiated a new historical *consciousness*.

Israel's breakthrough into a new historical consciousness poses a problem within the framework of this hermeneutic. The fundamental dilemma of Israel's existence, according to this interpretation, is the relationship between the life of the spirit and life in the world. The Hebrew Bible witnesses in various ways the striving of the individual to escape confinement in a particular form of social organization and to separate the sacred from the collective life and institutions of a people. The degree of success of this project continues to be a matter of historical debate.

Having given some consideration to an outline of the stages in the emergence of historical consciousness in Israel, and to the principal features of one possible interpretation of revelation, our task now is to consider what bearing revelation has on historical existence, which is ineluctably political. It is not accidental that the first volume of a projected study of *Order and History* is devoted to ancient Israel. Since apocalyptic expectations stand on the periphery of the Hebrew Bible, the dominant concern is with the issue of what revelation means for this world. The two principal Hebrew Bible motifs—the covenant (treaty) between two parties and the reign of God—are evoked from political experience, and thus are resonant with a search for authorization. According to the Hebrew Bible, revelation touches human life in a society whose symbols provide the form of self-understanding. Yet to say this is not to maintain that the state is a theocratic order. On the contrary, because of the gulf between the sacred and the secular, the sacred order can never be incarnate in a particular form of government or in any ethnic community. No "chosen people" can be the *omphalos* of history. There was seemingly nothing in original Yahwism that would have imposed a particular political form on the people. *Israel and Revelation* seems to press the point to the conclusion that Israel's attempt to adapt to any political organization was from the outset doomed to failure. The failure of the Israelite experiment was not just a historical failure—the fate of an insignificant nation

---

29. See Altizer, "A New History and a New but Ancient God?" 757–64, who asks if Voegelin has surrendered "a unilinear conception of history even while conceiving the process of history as an eschatological movement in time" (763).

overwhelmed by the imperial power of Assyria and Babylonia. Rather, owing to the very character of the sacred order, Israel's history in the world—that is, in the realm of political struggle and political organization—was intrinsically a history of failure.[30]

Voegelin has directed a penetrating criticism against the existentialist view represented by Bultmann, which attenuated the impact of the world and history by seizing a fragmentary truth out of the whole and eliminating or omitting other aspects of experience and symbolization. The experience of eschatological existence, he maintains, is not in itself illusory; for "we have indeed experiences of alienation; of being strangers in a world that is not ours . . . "[31] But the significance of one element of experience does not justify dismissing other aspects of life.

Nevertheless, for revelation to reach its optimum clarity it was necessary for Israel to go beyond itself and become the light of salvation to the entire human race. The Mosaic experience had to be disengaged from the collective symbolism of Israel's self-understanding so that the individual personality might emerge as the locus of the new order.[32] It was the prophets who struggled to emancipate the psyche from the collectivism of the Chosen People. This achievement, however, was nonetheless a limited one.

The Symmetry of Biblical Reality

Once we begin from the premise of a biblical people, a historical community within which individuals lived out their days, the question

30. This evaluation of Israel's existence as a people should not be confused with that of Rudolf Bultmann, who, from existentialist premises, regards Israel's history as a *Geschichte des Scheiterns*. See Bultmann, "Prophecy and Fulfillment," in Claus Westermann, *Essays on Old Testament Hermeneutics*, ed. J. L. Mays (Richmond: John Knox Press, 1963), 50–75.

31. See Voegelin's "History and Gnosis," in *The Old Testament and Christian Faith*, ed. Bernhard Anderson (New York: Association Press, 1962), 83 and *passim*, wherein Voegelin responds to Bultmann's essay, "The Significance of the Old Testament for Christian Faith" and other writings.

32. Biblically: "the new order of the soul." Regarding the use of the word "soul" within the context of the Hebrew Bible, Voegelin writes: "For a further explanation of the injunction to abstain from blood, see Leviticus 17:11: 'For the life [*nephesh*] of the flesh is in the blood; and I have given it to you to be placed on the altar to expiate your souls [*nephesh*]; for blood expiates because of the life [*nephesh*] in it.' The difficulties of translation are the same as in the case of the Greek *psyche* in Homeric usage. The life-soul, seated in the blood, is supposed to be ontologically of the same substance as the life-soul that was breathed into man by the animating breath of God" (Gen. 2:7); *Israel and Revelation*, 173, n. 22.

arises as to what bearing revelation has upon life in a society where one must act politically and assume social responsibility. It is important to begin by recognizing that revelation induces a tension between the sacred and temporal orders. This tension is inescapable, if, as Micah's prophetic exhortation suggests, the standard by which human actions are judged is derived from the experience of the sacred, not from the realm of politics. Chapter 9 reflects on the tension that existed in Israelite tradition between the reign of God and the kingdom of David.

We now come to the heart of the matter—namely, the tension that characterized Israel's life in the zone between the secular and the sacred. Moses experienced a breakthrough that went beyond the dim apprehensions of the sacred in Egypt or Mesopotamia, but the reality he experienced was couched in the sensuous, collective symbols of the Exodus and the conquest of Canaan. The question was whether, in the course of Israelite tradition, the mortgage of the historical circumstances that enabled Israel to achieve its unique self-understanding could be gradually reduced so that people in the present could acknowledge its universal implications.

Israel and Revelation maintains that the book of Deuteronomy, which codified the Torah, made the tension permanent, thereby ossifying the historical revelation and bequeathing to the future the legalism based on a canonical book.[33] The great prophets, however, sought to abolish the tension, and their struggle passed through three stages. First, Amos and Hosea anticipated the political restoration of Israel under the conditions of pragmatic history. Second, Isaiah's awareness of the gulf between society and the sacred order prompted a faith in the rule of a future king under completely changed social conditions. Finally, Jeremiah turned the futuristic faith back to the present and the prophet *himself* as one who enacted the fate of his people and became the *omphalos* of order in history. Thus the messianic hope moved toward separating the eternal from the temporal, the spiritual from the political, the universal from Israelite collectivism. The end of the tension, which occurred with Christianity, was anticipated by Second Isaiah's message of Israel's exodus from itself to communicate revelation to all people. From Voegelin's perspective, the Israelite decision to establish a kingdom like that of other nations was the great aberration from the Mosaic revelation.[34]

33. Ibid., 173.
34. *The Ecumenic Age*, 418.

At one point, Voegelin's reflections prompt the question of whether the word of Yahweh, spoken by the prophet, may exert a power for social reform. In the context of a comparison of Isaiah and Jeremiah, he remarks:

> The order of society in history is reconstituted in fact through the men who challenge the disorder of the surrounding society with the order they experience as living in themselves. The word of the prophet is not spoken to the wind, it is not futile or impotent, if it does not reform the society which he loves because it has given him birth.[35]

There was a profound difference, he maintains, between Isaiah and Jeremiah. Isaiah envisioned reform through change in the constitution of reality. Later, in a virtual *tour de force,* Jeremiah returned the prophetic word to "the untransfigured present," the world in which we live. This achievement, however, made an impact not in the reform of society, but in the formation of a new community: the "remnant" of Israel which is a continuation of order in history when its realization in the life of a people is in crisis. In Jeremiah, the human personality had broken the elemental nature of collective life and recognized itself as the authoritative source of order in society. Despite the visions of prophets such as Isaiah, the Israel organized as kingdom "went the way of all organizations, their governments, and kings in history."[36] What remains, however, is a residue of individuals, like Jeremiah, who exemplify authenticity of life.

In his understanding of the prophets, Voegelin consequently wants to correct what he considers the delusion that the promised land or the perfect social order can be achieved through evolution or revolution. His concern about this matter is voiced in the preface to this volume, where he states that "the prophetic conception of a change in the constitution of being lies at the root of our contemporary beliefs in the perfection of society, either through progress or through a communist revolution." He goes on to say, "Metastatic faith is one of the great sources of disorder, if not the principal one, in the contemporary world; and it is a matter of life and death for all of us to understand the phenomenon and to find remedies against it before it destroys

---

35. *Israel and Revelation,* 483.
36. Ibid., 483.

us."[37] He insists that the dilemmas of history cannot be resolved by "Canaans or Utopias."

Finally, any theory that attempts to reflect on order and disorder in history must come to terms with the problem of evil. The dilemma is peculiarly inescapable in any attempt to understand the tragic dimension of Israel's history. The problem of the evil that mars creation is portrayed in dramatic form in the biblical narratives of primeval history (Gen. 1:11). The Flood story, for instance, is introduced by the announcement of Yahweh's decision to destroy the earth owing to the *hamas* (violence, lawlessness) that had corrupted it (Gen. 11:13). In the present narration, the judgment of Yahweh takes the form of a cosmic catastrophe in which the earth almost returned to precreation chaos, the watery abyss of Genesis 1:2. The story is prehistorical in the sense that it preserves the elemental experience, common to all peoples at all times, of the threat to human life— life that is suspended, so to speak, over the abyss of chaos. It portrays an *Urgeschehen*,[38] in which instance *Ur-* refers to a primal occurrence in mythical consciousness. This primal experience survives even when the transition is made from mythical to historical consciousness. The irruption of the spirit that occurred in Israel did not cancel out the experience but raised it to articulation, resulting in a polarity of creation versus chaos, order versus disorder, existence versus nonexistence.[39]

In the story of the Flood, the violence that corrupts the earth is traced to the human heart (mind, will), for "Yahweh saw ... that every imagination of the thoughts of [man's] heart was only evil continually." This mystery of evil poses problems for Voegelin's philosophical perspective. Why is it that rational people everywhere do not share the noetic vision of reality? Why is it that only certain people at certain times are given the insight? And why is it that, once the vision is gained by prophets, philosophers, and saints, it is rejected, deformed, or eclipsed and must be rediscovered once again?

While these questions remain, it is still possible to assert that a philosophical interpretation of the Bible challenges us to rethink the

37. Ibid., xiii.
38. This view of the *Urgeschichte* is advanced by Claus Westermann, whose commentary, *Genesis 1-11* (Darmstadt: Wissenschaftliche Buchgesellschaft, 1972), is illuminated by the phenomenological study of religion.
39. For a treatment of the biblical theme, see Bernhard Anderson, *Creation versus Chaos* (New York: Association Press, 1962).

relation between prophecy and apocalypse and, in particular, to reconsider how these biblical perspectives converge in the New Testament. This interpretation raises questions of meaning to prominence, questions nascent in mythical consciousness and brought to articulate expression through the historical experience of ancient Israel and Christianity.[40]

40. The biblical analysis in this chapter mainly follows that of B. Anderson's *Creation versus Chaos*; *The Eighth Century Prophets* (Philadelphia: Fortress Press, 1978); and *Understanding the Old Testament* (Englewood Cliffs, NJ: Prentice-Hall, 1975).

10

The Ecumenic Age: Prospectus
and Modification

As we have already seen, more than three decades ago Eric Voegelin published the first in a projected series of six volumes designed as an inquiry into the nature of order in history and society. Under the rubric *Order and History,* he intended this project to elaborate the history of the symbolization of order extending from the empires of the ancient Near East, characterized by cosmological myths, to the modern nation-state, with its proper symbolism. The first volume, *Israel and Revelation* (1956), treated Mesopotamia, Egypt, and especially Israel. Two additional volumes followed soon afterwards: *The World of the Polis* and *Plato and Aristotle* (1957).

Seventeen years elapsed before the fourth volume was published, and once it eventually appeared, it was clear that the project was not going to proceed as originally intended. In both style and substance, *The Ecumenic Age* differs from the previous volumes, and the author himself states that he found it necessary to break with the original prospectus. There would not be six volumes. Only one more was published, posthumously, in the form of a collection of essays (some previously published) on contemporary problems that have motivated the search for order in history. The projected volume on "The Protestant Centuries" was abandoned, and volume 5 presents reflections on the present in a form rather different from what was originally planned.

Voegelin's characterization of the magnitude of the change is ambiguous. He speaks of a "break" in the program of the *History,* and suggests an inadequacy in the principles governing the earlier volumes—which was that "the order of history emerges from the history of order." And in fact he does report that the previous conception was no longer viable since it had not taken adequate account of significant lines of meaning in history that did not run along lines of time. The unfolding of the history of order did not conform, consequently, to the clearly delineated pattern or course that was originally anticipated. Yet Voegelin did not draw the conclusion that the original principle was misconceived or that it should be abandoned. On the contrary, he reasserted its essential validity, and found no need to revise it. One is confronted, consequently, with the anomaly of a break in program that requires no significant revision of the original thesis.

In explaining the change, Voegelin notes that one of the dilemmas he encountered came into perspective as he examined the dynamics of the Ecumenic Age. What was clear about this period, in addition to its unique fecundity, was the complex diversity of experience. A variety of significant movements appear, in diverse places, manifesting little apparent connection with one another; simultaneously they penetrate and shape the cultural fields of East and West. Each, moreover, bears the mark of a particular cultural and ethnic identity. In Persia, there is Zoroaster; in Greece the philosophers, in Israel the prophets and then the Christ, in China Confucius and Lao-tzu, in India the Buddha. Unless one engages in philosophical a prioris, it is difficult to maintain that a profound insight into the nature of life emerged from one single event, and there is no sound empirical basis (that is, in the awareness of the participants) for interpreting these events as a linear progression. The most plausible approach would seem to be that of Karl Jaspers—namely, to draw together the entire period as an "axis-time" in the development of the human race. But even that may be criticized because no such common experience existed in the awareness of the participants. None of them thought of themselves as being involved in an epoch in Jasper's sense, so the characterization had to be imposed from outside. Aesthetically deficient as it may have been, it seems that there was no alternative, consequently, to accepting the unconnected plurality of historical events as an a priori.

The Process of Differentiating Consciousness

The fourth volume departs from a unilinear pattern in order to accommodate synchronic patterns and configurations. In the fifth and final volume, Voegelin apparently intended to break completely with a single line of time and trace topics and issues both diachronically and synchronically.

The introduction to volume 4 details the extension of ideas that had taken place between 1957 and 1974, between the publication of *Plato and Aristotle* and *The Ecumenic Age*. And the most significant new expression—possibly the central reason for the revision of the program—is revealed in a series of statements here: "The truth of existence discovered by the prophets of Israel and the philosophers of Hellas, though it appears later in time than the truth of the cosmos, cannot simply replace it, because the new insights, while indirectly affecting the image of reality as a whole, pertain directly only to man's consciousness of his existential tension."[1] The meaning of insight has nowhere in the earlier volumes been suggested with such precision. Nor had the source of those insights been so exactly located before. In the previous volumes terms such as "human nature" had demanded that the reader presume a kind of interior topography of humanity along the lines established through the evolution of Christian thought, incorporating the nascent insights of Israel and Greece. The term "consciousness" had rarely appeared in the first three volumes; and when it did appear, there was no indication that it bore any extraordinary burden of meaning. There had been no previous indication that the central *locus* of our humanity was consciousness.[2] In the earlier volumes, the term most often used to suggest the core of our humanity was "human nature." In *The Ecumenic Age*, it is noted, in passing, that human nature is simply "classical language" for "the structure of consciousness."[3]

Although *The Ecumenic Age* represents a considerable departure from the format of the earlier volumes, nothing in the new volume is as significant as this placement of the sense of our humanity specifically in "consciousness." This change of terminology, along with the shift of emphasis it contains, removes the ambiguity of such terms as "human nature" and "experiences of transcendence." It constricts the area affected by the process of differentiation from elemental to elaborated symbolisms, while at the same time broadening the context in which those symbolisms may be understood to operate through time. In volume 4, *Order and History* has become, explicitly, a de-

1. *The Ecumenic Age*, 8.
2. Discussion of Voegelin's understanding of consciousness in this chapter is limited to its meaning within *The Ecumenic Age*, and thus does not consider the essays which are concerned with consciousness in *Anamnesis*.
3. *The Ecumenic Age*, 252.

scription of the process of evolving consciousness—an actual theory of consciousness.

But consciousness cannot be understood as an object freestanding in the world. Rather, in the manner of field-theory, there exist intertwining strata, spatially and temporally manifested, which are interdependent not only for their reality but for their meaning within reality. Among the elements we perceive as distinct from the process of consciousness is the cosmos itself. But this cosmos is not an object among others; it is the background against which all else exists.[4] Consciousness evolves within a cosmos that preexists, and it is principally for this reason that this new work begins with reflection on the limitations that awareness must impose on the meaning of events that occur within the field of consciousness.[5]

In the early pages of the introduction to *The Ecumenic Age*, then, and with a minimum of comment distinguishing the new ideational content of this volume from that of the preceding volumes, the area of meaning is shifted from the "soul" of *The New Science of Politics, Israel and Revelation, The World of the Polis,* and *Plato and Aristotle* to the "consciousness" of *The Ecumenic Age*. Having made this change of terminology and position, Voegelin then proceeds to define sharply the degree to which insights arising within consciousness can be said to condition those aspects of reality that lie beyond consciousness, or beyond what may be called a "transformation boundary" that interfaces consciousness with that intelligible congeries of entities that lie outside consciousness.

There is, then, an important shift from the elemental symbols of "soul" and "human nature" to the highly specific and differentiated symbolism of "consciousness," inexorably carrying, as it does, not only the venerable weight of the classical "psyche," but to some extent that of the Pauline "pneuma" as well. Voegelin himself does not depreciate the seriousness of the shift. In fact, he has explicitly noted in another essay that he would no longer distinguish between *psyche* and *pneuma:*

> One can no longer use the medieval distinction between the theologian's supernatural revelation and the philosopher's natural reason, when any number of texts will attest the revelatory

4. Ibid., 72.
5. Ibid., 8.

consciousness of the Greek poets and philosophers, nor can one let revelation begin with the Israelite and Christian experiences, when the mystery of divine presence in reality is attested as experienced by man, as far back as ca. 20,000 B.C., by the petroglyphic symbols of the Palaeolithicum.[6]

In the early volumes, no sharp distinction exists between noetic insights and the context in which they appear. The new insights, and those who came to possess and transmit them, moved from the *pseudos* of the old mythical order into the *aletheia* of life in authenticity in the presence of the new vision. In some certain sense, the cosmos itself becomes a new reality by virtue of the prophet or philosopher's entrance into Pauline truth (2 Corinthians 5:17).

Present in the previous volumes was the kind of language that required the reader to understand that the subject of *Order and History* was, in fact, primarily the history of order as it emerged in human awareness. The emphasis was on history as, in some sense, the collective record of experience in the form of societies capable of representation and action, subject to interpretation, but nonetheless possessed of a certain irreducibility, a certain linear character relatively independent of the workings of the mind itself. But *The Ecumenic Age* denies this view of history. In fact, as Thomas Altizer has observed, the breaking of the original program of *Order and History* "may well signify the end of what we have known as history."[7] History, as the term is now employed, has become not a record of events and their consequences, but a record of the evolution of consciousness from compactness to differentiation. Its epochs become the disequilibrium of consciousness, the search for a new equilibrium and the deformation through which disoriented consciousness may derail in its search for a new balance. The points of disequilibrium become identified with those occasions when a mythopoetic order begins to lose its power of shaping the motion of consciousness forward along the vector from "the Apeirontic depth" to the heights of rational insight. The search becomes identified with the symbol of exodus, whereby consciousness moves from the newly discovered untruth of an existence within the old traditional desiccated symbolisms and forms to seek out the new truth.

6. Voegelin, "Response to Professor Altizer's 'A New History and a New but Ancient God?' " 766.

7. Altizer, "A New History and a New but Ancient God?" 757–58.

What becomes more articulate in *The Ecumenic Age* is a far more drastic cleavage between the "interior" of consciousness and the "exterior" of the cosmos and all it contains than previously supposed. Thus, in volume 4, a sharp distinction is made between the altered reality of consciousness through a sacred event and the unaltered reality of the world, to which, in fact, the new insights cannot be said to apply. It is certainly true that the differentiation of insight does not abolish the cosmos in which the event takes place,[8] and equally true that the process of the evolution of consciousness does not alter the fabric of the cosmos. Moreover, few will wish to dissent from the assertion that serious disturbances in the understanding of reality are inevitable if and when awareness of the contextual wholeness is lost.[9] This contextual wholeness included the entirety of reality beyond the transformation boundary of the individual human consciousness; most specifically, it refers to the world and that enduring order of reality within it that are not subject to the modalities of differentiating consciousness. But that very intransigence of reality beyond human consciousness serves to index the more frenetic "exuberant differentiations" even as it diminishes the empirical accuracy of the Pauline vision referred to earlier. "That any one of the things that come into being could stop the process and master it forever after is an absurdity, not to be entertained as long as a man's apperception of reality is not badly disturbed."[10] It is possible to resolve the difficulties presented to a theory of consciousness by realities such as Gnostic thought by disestablishing the implicit monism, both spatial and temporal, which is as implicit in every variation of gnosticism.

In a general way, these remarks attempt to formulate the bases of a theory of consciousness that is firmly grounded in, and insists upon a return to, original experience. The emergent problems associated with such a theory are obvious, but their successful analysis is not foreclosed. Still, some of the more insistent questions that arise may be set out in this manner:

1. If we are to divide reality sharply between evolving consciousness and the world in which that consciousness clearly arises, from where do the insights come that cause the process of differentiating consciousness to begin and continue?

8. *The Ecumenic Age*, 8–9.
9. Ibid., 176.
10. Ibid.

2. If this division amounts to a given condition in which consciousness resides on one side of a transformation boundary (formed by the physiological character of the nervous system) and the rest of the world on the other, exactly what is the mode and the meaning of communication between them?

3. Since historically differentiating experience is founded in the consciousness of actual human beings in real bodies,[11] how do these various human beings unify the meaning of their equally various experiences, both that of their own internal experience and that of the rest of the world, into the representational structures that begin with symbolisms at the elemental level and proceed to those immense symbolic structures that we call "institutions," "religions," "states"?

Before the first question can be answered properly, it would be helpful to describe briefly the figure Voegelin adopts to characterize the structure of consciousness. He refers to the situation of consciousness as existing in the "Metaxy," Plato's "In-Between." The figure is well chosen. While it refers specifically to the state between Anaximander's Apeirontic depth and the noetic height of the later philosophers, it connotes, in *The Ecumenic Age,* much more. It is not simply the "In-Between," the present moment that divides the symbolisms of the Beginning from those of the Beyond, though it is certainly and decisively that.

The initial question can be answered by pointing out that the insights which extend the field of awareness derive from the "motion" of the psyche itself. Like the photon, consciousness possesses no "rest mass." Consciousness is a processive, not an objective, reality; and like a wave, it cannot be said to possess a "place" or a "time" or to exist without motion. The insights flow not from "outside" or "inside," but from the movement of the process itself. Even given the nonpredictability of their occurrence in any given situation, the occurrence of such insights is certainly predictable since they are fundamental to the process of developing consciousness.

Thus the division between consciousness and the cosmos ceases to be relevant only when we speak of the entire process, the reality of which both consciousness and cosmos are constituents. In fact, the very differentiation of reality within the process is dependent upon the

11. Ibid., 333.

bipolar "inside-outside" of the individual transformation boundary since that differentiation occurs as the psyche "moves" through perceptions of both consciousness and cosmos.

The second question must be answered in reference to the answer to the first. The field through which the development of consciousness takes place extends in relation to a vast and varied pattern of experience. The transformation boundary, which limits and controls the passage of information into concrete individual psyches and the flow of communication outward from them into the world inhabited by others (to whom the communication presents itself as experience), establishes another aspect of reality in that no exterior experience can be unequivocal because it must be transformed by the very act of perception into an intelligible symbolism that relates in some way to the field of individual awareness. Similarly, no internal experience, when transformed into a symbolic communication, can avoid what Cassirer has called "the curse of mediacy" in that the symbol cannot be congruent and equal to the experience as it passes from the psyche into the cosmos.

Question three resolves itself in terms of the symbolisms dealt with extensively in the previous volumes of *Order and History*. The shape of reality, inevitably different in detail for every person, is nonetheless generally similar among everyone because of the generic identity of the physiological species, and, even more significantly, because the components of consciousness—what we call symbols—through which reality is discerned, and by which that "motion" is continued, are themselves, for all their variety, generally determinate and empirically proven so.[12]

A further answer to the third question, regarding communication as an intelligible part of the development of the mind, may be resolved by referring to a discussion of Aristotle's *theoria*. In *The New Science of Politics, theoria* is described as that type of rational construction and communication among mature individuals who are "capable of imaginative reenactment of the experiences of which theory is an explication . . . Theory as an explication of certain experiences is intelligible only to those in whom the explication will stir up parallel experiences as the empirical basis for testing the truth of theory."[13] Theory, in this

12. See Eric Neumann, *The Origins and History of Consciousness* (Princeton: Princeton University Press, 1954).
13. *The New Science of Politics*, 64.

context, seems not so much a technical term as a description of meaningful communication as opposed to mere opinion. Simultaneously, it exemplifies the highest form of communicative consciousness. But unless a theoretical explanation awakens a similar experience in another, it will create the impression of empty talk or possibly be repudiated as an irrelevant expression of subjective opinions.[14]

The Ionian Truth

Any description of consciousness immediately calls for a concomitant description of its context, insofar as such a description is possible. The dilemma is that the analytical language by which the context must be evoked is itself no more than a product of consciousness. Thus the distinction between the process of consciousness and the process of reality as analytically opposed to or discrete from consciousness is rendered equivocal. That is to say, the context cannot be said to be observed as distinct from its presence in awareness; in fact, all that can be said of the context unequivocally is that it appears within consciousness as elementarily distinct, though it must be symbolically absorbed and theoretically represented in a manner indistinguishable from the presentation of internal contents unique to the consciousness.

Given this limitation inherent in the relation of symbols to the experience underlying them, an analysis of the context of consciousness is still possible. The mature person capable of contemplative insight stands in opposition to those whose horizons extend no farther than the will to power and who invent chimera for the purpose of obscur-

---

14. Ibid., 64–65. For more on this general topic, see Voegelin's essay "On Debate and Existence," *Intercollegiate Review* 3 (1967), 143–52.

> Rational argument could not prevail because the partner to the discussion did not accept as binding for himself the matrix of reality in which all specific questions concerning our existence as human beings are ultimately rooted; he has overlaid the reality of existence with another mode of existence that Robert Musil has called the Second Reality. Behind the appearance of a rational debate there lurked the difference of two modes of existence, of existence in truth and existence in untruth. The universe of rational discourse collapses, we may say, when the common ground of existence in reality has disappeared (143).

ing reality as it is.[15] In such individuals, the context of consciousness is contracted into consciousness itself, as in the Hegel-Feuerbach-Marx ideational vector. The closed individual falls into the delusion that mind and external world are entirely congruent; that one's "idea" exhausts the possibilities and meanings of life; that the only unexplored territory must be the thoughts not yet conceived. In such a case, the context of consciousness is reduced to no more than "areas" or "zones" of awareness not yet explored but nonetheless present in some sense since humanity, self-created as Marx would have us believe in the 1844 *Manuscripts,* on principle cannot admit the existence of something outside the range of its totally dominating consciousness.

A discussion of the logical fallacies involved in this position would be too lengthy to attempt here.[16] It is a falsification of experience to purport that the life process is "nothing more than" the motion of consciousness through reality. The semirational basis of the disorder is explained by reference to the irreducible difficulties of symbolic and theoretic communication set out earlier—and by noting that an immature consciousness, unable to bear the tension of partial communication any more than it can bear the interior uncertainties and exterior ambiguities of life, is bound to find itself alienated. The term, popular among German idealists and romantics long before it was appropriated by Marx—*Selbstentfremdung,* in the vocabulary of Hegel—refers to that condition of interior emptiness that perceives itself as split off from the wholeness of which it is properly a part. The phenomenon, at least as old as the original Gnostic writers, and as immediate as certain varieties of schizophrenia, has generally resolved itself in contemporary times through the formula of Feuerbach—that is, by denying the reality of those aspects of life that lie outside the alienated consciousness and by drawing them into awareness through construction of an illusion of "self-godhood." The purpose of the magical act is to allay anxiety, which the disordered consciousness will not or cannot control through an imaginative annihilation of everything beyond the self and a recreation of it within, stripped of all meaning and possibility that threatens the disordered mind itself. The "second reality" thus created is the projection of the contracted consciousness, itself as deformed, partial, illogical, and unintelligible as the consciousness which, in its desperation, has produced it.

15. *The Ecumenic Age,* 184.
16. Cf. "Marx: Inverted Dialectics," in *From Enlightenment to Revolution,* 240–72.

Consciousness and the context in which it becomes intelligible to itself as life moves on—which it experiences as present both within and outside itself—arise from somewhere. But where? One answer returns for its substance to those who possessed the experience of their own consciousness emerging without a vast social and philosophical mechanism already in existence to "explain" the significance of the experience in mythopoetic terms.

> Reality was experienced by Anaximander (fl. 560 B.C.) as a cosmic process in which things emerge from, and disappear into, the non-existence of the Apeiron. Things do not exist out of themselves, all at once and forever; they exist out of the ground to which they return. Hence, to exist means to participate in two modes of reality: (1) In the Apeiron as the timeless arche of things and (2) in the ordered succession of things as the manifestation of the Apeiron in time.[17]

The motion from the darkness of nonexistence into the light of existence is the primary cycle that dominates all lesser cycles. This is brought out in Anaximander's statement: " 'The origin (arche) of things is the Apeiron. . . . It is necessary for things to perish into that from which they were born; for they pay one another penalty for their injustice (adikia) according to the ordinance of Time.' "[18]

Voegelin contends that the Anaximandrian Apeiron—which he calls the "Ionian truth of the process"—is "present in the background of consciousness when the later thinkers explore specific structures for the case of societies in history."[19] The symbol of the Apeiron as the Boundless, the Depth, serves as a polarity both of the cosmos and the psyche. The opposite polarity, the One of Plato, stands as the noetically discoverable antipode of the Apeiron. It is the height as the Apeiron is the depth.[20]

Summarizing briefly, the process of consciousness makes reality intelligible by both its experiences and the symbolizing act of differentiation from original compactness. Through its interaction with the

17. The Ecumenic Age, 174.
18. A_9B_1.
19. The Ecumenic Age, 175.
20. "Once the truth of existence had been understood as the In-Between reality of noetic consciousness, the truth of the entire process could be reformulated as the existence of all things in the In-Between of the One and the Apeiron." The Ecumenic Age, 185.

process of reality and the events it encounters, this process of differentiating consciousness in turn produces its own attempt at intelligibility through time, and this process is called history.

Consciousness thus "moves" through an additional dimension in that it stands between the process of reality from which it arises and the process of history that arises from it. What happens "in" history is the very process of evolving consciousness that constitutes history. History is not a finite collection of events given once for all, but a process that continues to generate itself through the individuals who participate in it.[21]

As consciousness renders intelligible and establishes the nature of the reality of the cosmos as process, so history, differentiated from consciousness, makes intelligible and establishes the nature of consciousness—and not for one person, a visionary, seer, or saint alone, but for all individuals who can participate in the process. History, then, becomes an element in the context of consciousness, bearing as much meaning and reality as the world itself does. The field of consciousness, in its noetic development, is thus expanded by the addition of an extensive constellation of symbolisms that are no longer yoked to the cyclical cosmological order.

We have seen a significant complication in Voegelin's former understanding of the development of consciousness. Much of the analysis of the preceding volumes was concerned with the movement beyond what was characterized as the "cosmological" mentality, and it was designed to make the point that historical consciousness is a result of the experiences represented by Israelite prophetism and classical Greek philosophy, especially the former. The thesis was that meaning in history was so intimately connected with these differentiations of consciousness that it was constituted by them.

The Ecumenic Age reports that the matter must be perceived in a new light. The problem in the first instance is that the author has discovered evidence of historical consciousness antedating the Israelites and Greeks by centuries, and that, furthermore, this consciousness finds expression in a symbolic form that is cosmological. In "historiogenesis," the name given to this newly discovered form,[22] historical consciousness is unmistakable in events placed on an irreversible time line; at the same time, however, cosmological thinking is equally ap-

21. Ibid., 332.
22. Ibid., 7.

parent in shaping the line in terms of myths involving intramundane deities. Historical consciousness and cosmological thinking are not, consequently, nearly so alien as one might think. To complicate the picture further, it also turns out that this blend of history and cosmology is a "millennial constant" that does not disappear as consciousness develops but, on the contrary, persists until the present. In fact, most philosophy of history has taken this form, including even the Pauline and Augustinian versions. The unilinear history that supposedly was engendered by the differentiating events, together with the punctuations of meaning on it, is in reality a cosmological symbolism. The obvious implication is that it is no longer possible to speak of "settled topical blocks" in the manner that *Order and History* itself had accustomed its readers. The actual history of consciousness is too complex and unilinear.

Rituals of Power

The theme of *Order and History* has been the relationship between personal and political order. The first three volumes documented an increasing alienation between the two: The order of the person became increasingly separated from the order of society. The basis for order in the articulated life of the person, once in Israel and Greece, was not accepted as the basis for political order in either society. The question for *The Ecumenic Age,* then, is how this relationship subsequently evolved as these societies, which had been the context for the emergence of the new consciousness, together with their cosmological neighbors, succumbed to new forces and a new era.

The answer, in brief, is that the alienation became more severe over an extensive period before amelioration was found, and when it was found, it bore the marks of the struggle. Eventually, a reconciliation of sorts was effected through the civilizational triumph of the ecumenic religions. But this was preceded by several centuries of turmoil, in which the alienation between psyche and power became much more acute and what were by now traditional insights into human nature were threatened with obliteration. In turn, the measures taken in philosophy and the ecumenic religions to protect these insights against loss determined the form in which they eventually became effective as a civilizational influence. This form was highly vulnerable to deformation, thus paving the way for later personal and political dilemmas that still beset us.

According to the periodization of *Order and History*, the new era commences with the conquest of Media by the Persian Cyrus in 550 B.C.E. and extends to the disintegration of the Roman Empire in the sixth century C.E. The era thus begins and ends with imperialism, and empire-building is the central theme of its history. One after another, a succession of empires rise and fall, transforming the political landscape almost beyond recognition. In each instance, the imperial impulse appears, and a small, previously inconsequential society expands, mainly by force, into a huge multicivilizational structure. In the process, the traditional forms of political order are shattered. Ethnic societies such as Israel and Greece, as well as the old cosmological empires, are broken: they lose not only the capacity for self-government but often cultural identity as well. They become objects of conquest.

The perplexing factor about these empires was not merely their destructiveness; they also possessed little of an affirmative character to substitute for the societies they annihilated. In this sense, they were not societies at all. They lacked ethical substance because they had no coherent cultural basis. They were mere organizational shells, bound together by little more than the conqueror's will to power. They did not organize themselves, and whatever order they experienced was imposed on them. The only authentic purpose that was to be found in them was expansion, but expansion per se is hardly an adequate basis for a society. A certain dynamic in imperial expansion provided an answer of sorts to the problem of meaning, but it was not actually satisfactory. In every instance the expansion eventually came up against insurmountable natural limits, fell short of unifying the known world, and retracted. Eventually, therefore, the problem of meaning had to be confronted.[23]

The impact of this confrontation was profound. Entire societies were cast into the void. Not only did individual empires have little clearly defined identity and purpose, but the process of imperialism, the longer it continued, seemed pointless. The victims were increasingly left with a sense that history is a succession of events that lead nowhere. The result, typically, was that the realm in which order was sought contracted sharply. Since it could not be discovered in society,

23. For Voegelin's remarks on "Expansion during the Ecumenic Age," see vol. IV, 197–211.

it was pursued independently of politics in personal life.[24] This provided a fertile soil for the growth of religion, and explains why the Ecumenic Age was so extraordinarily fertile as the birthplace of religions. But it also promoted the alienation of many from reality, as exemplified by gnosticism and apocalypticism. From the meaninglessness of history it was not a major step to the conclusion that life itself is evil and must be overcome, and this was a step that more than a few were inclined to take.

Such a loss of balance, however, was not inevitable. Not everyone fell victim to it, and gradually devices were developed to protect against it. But in order for these to be effective, they themselves had to be protected. Israel and Greece were both victims of imperialism, and in both societies the cultural heritage was threatened. The process of creating such protection was central to the development of the ecumenic religions, especially Judaism and Christianity. It entailed, on the one hand, the creation of scripture as a fixed corpus of sacred literature and, on the other, the elaboration of dogma as the authoritative interpretation of religious truth. The assumption was that, together, scripture and dogma would stabilize the truth revealed in the unique events of revelation, and that it could be passed on in a relatively integral form to persons well removed from the original revelation.[25] A similar process took place in philosophy, as the Stoics "demythologized" the teaching of Plato and Aristotle and converted it into literal, propositional form. Philosophy as well became doctrine,[26] and the doctrinalization of philosophy contributed significantly to the development of doctrine in religion as philosophy was absorbed into religious thought.[27]

Moreover, as philosophy and the ecumenic religions evolved, they manifested a tendency to accommodate themselves to the course of history. These events, which otherwise seemed so devoid of significance, took on a new meaning when viewed in the light of the religious his-

24. Ibid., 21–22.

25. Voegelin has written in another context: "[mysticism] did not solve the problem with which the Church was faced at the time, that is the problem of developing Christian doctrine further through a differentiation of mystical culture from the symbolism of the dogma as well as the problem of reinterpreting the meaning of dogmatic symbols in the light of active religious experience. The year 1300 may be said to mark the epoch from which the decline of the Church begins—decline defined in terms of decreasing absorptiveness for the movement of the spirit." "The People of God," unpublished manuscript, 9.

26. *The Ecumenic Age*, 36–43.

27. Ibid., 43–48.

tory of the age. An ecumenical self-understanding developed among both philosophers and religious leaders: They perceived themselves as representatives of a truth valid for all, and acquired a missionary impulse. As this developed, they became sensitive to the parallel between their aspirations and those of the empire-builders, and they were led to the conclusion that this convergence was more than a coincidence. It was providential: The purpose of empire had been to prepare the ground for the spread of religious and philosophical truth.[28] The most obvious examples are, of course, the Stoic and Christian attitude toward the Roman Empire, but there is ample evidence that this was in fact a much more generalized phenomenon in the Ecumenic Age.

This linkage of pragmatic and religious history, in turn, facilitated the embrace of philosophy and the ecumenic religions by the empires. The eventual result of the marriage was ecumenic society—an entirely new social form that represented at least a measure of reconciliation between secular and religious order. This achievement was won, however, at a price, as has been indicated. The devices developed in the Ecumenic Age to safeguard an understanding of the meaning of human nature had the capacity to play another role. Because they tended to objectify this understanding, they were liable to cut it off from its experiential foundations. This entailed the risk of reducing the understanding to the status of a mere opinion that could be accepted or rejected as a matter of personal preference.[29]

This risk has been fully realized in recent history, and goes a long way toward accounting for the intellectual confusion of modernity. Much of the history of the modern period consists of a revolt against the symbols inherited from the Ecumenic Age. The meaning of these symbols was deformed through theological and metaphysical dogmatism. By adding more doctrine, however, the modern revolt only succeeded in compounding the problem, so that contemporary errors were stacked on top of medieval ones. The net result is a great block of accumulated symbols that serve only to eclipse reality.[30] The problems of the present age are therefore connected with the events of the Ecumenic Age, and the implication of volume 4 is that the forms used to transmit the insights discovered in that age to posterity must be viewed with tempered skepticism.

28. Ibid., 134–37.
29. Ibid., 43–44.
30. Ibid., 58.

Oikoumene

As a philosophical work, *The Ecumenic Age* has two principal themes—history and the unity of the human race. Both are presented as central to the progress of events and consciousness in the Ecumenic Age.

1. The question of the nature of the meaning to be discerned in history is central to the entire project of *Order and History*, and the position it takes is consistently maintained. Voegelin has held, on the one hand, that the answers given to the questions about the philosophy of history by Plato, Aristotle, and the early Christians are essentially correct and, on the other hand, that the central problems of modernity can be traced to a revolt against these answers in favor of a progressivist immanentization of Christian eschatology.[31] Volume 4 focuses attention on the details and philosophical logic of the classical Greek and Christian answers.

The argument begins with the proposition that history has its origin in the differentiation of consciousness that took place in the Ecumenic Age. Voegelin discourages isolating the religious events of the era from the secular, maintaining that religious manifestations and ecumenic empires are fused together as two aspects of one integral unit. Both actually contribute to the emergence of historical consciousness. Nonetheless, the primary accent falls on philosophical and religious experiences. Imperial expansion contributed to the preparation of the social and cultural ground, but by itself, as we have seen, it was not conducive to the discernment of history as a source of meaning. Rather, expansion was considered senseless until pragmatic events were related to the experiences that emerged through religious advances.

Consequently, there is meaning in history primarily because consciousness has a history. The basis of the distinction between before and after on an irreversible line is the development of consciousness in the differentiating events. Plato, Aristotle, the early Christians, and before them the prophets of Israel were aware that something fundamentally new was occurring in what they experienced, and they distinguished the Before and After of these experiences. They thereby differentiated history as the distinctive mode of human time. Natural

---

31. The nature of this revolt is spelled out in *From Enlightenment to Revolution*.

events might have their cyclical rhythms, but the human mode of being, because it involved consciousness, was different.[32]

This original conception of history was, however, complex. The emergence of a more profound understanding of life was interpreted as evidence of the processual character of reality. Reality in the comprehensive sense was in motion, and the movement was experienced as having direction.[33] The direction of the process was discovered, moreover, to be eschatological. Both the Greek and the Christian theophanies included an experience of transfiguration, as Paul speaks of it. Plato, Aristotle, Paul, and others were led to encounter a depth of reality transcending finitude; and they came away from this experience with a sense that reality as a whole was moving in that direction. Beyond the cosmos, where order is always limited and compromised by disorder, a reality free of disorder became visible to them; this they perceived as the *telos* of the movement of life.

At the same time, however, the movement did not in fact come to its conclusion, nor was there actually any sufficient reason for believing that it would. Alongside the experience of theophany was the equally significant experience of the duration of the cosmos. Though consciousness developed, human beings continued to be subject to the biological rhythms of nature and death. Life revealed itself, therefore, to be paradoxical. It remained constant even though it was changing, it remained within itself even though it recognizably moved beyond itself. Human existence was simultaneously both mortal and immortal.

This paradox is at the center of life itself, and it must be respected if consciousness is not to lose its balance. The force of religious experiences is such that unbalancing is very likely. The subject can be swept away by visions of a transfigured reality, and only the greatest care prevents this from degenerating into apocalypticism or some form of world alienation. Plato and Aristotle in particular succeeded in resolving this dilemma through their use of reason, and this is one of the most significant events in history. It has set the pattern for the life of reason in Western civilization even until the present.

Equally important is the maintenance of openness toward the historical process itself. The natural tendency, as lines of meaning begin to appear in history, is to convert them into a meaning *of* history that is purported to be final and complete. Unfortunately, however, the flow

32. Cf. "The Beginning and the Beyond," vol. IV, 7–11.
33. See the section entitled: "The Process of Reality," vol. IV, 171–78.

of events refuses to cease, and very soon each such effort is revealed to be (in Jacob Burckhardt's apt phrase) an "impertinent anticipation." Furthermore, the proferred answers conflict, and after a time the contradictions among them suggest the obvious conclusion that they aim to accomplish the impossible. Plato and Aristotle were wiser. They recognized that the process is beyond human control, that its length is indeterminate, and that it will therefore ineluctably be unpredictable. Unlike Hegel, they recognized that certain questions simply cannot be answered, and they make no attempt to elevate their thought to the position of being the *telos* toward which history moves.

2. The unity of the human race became a central issue in the Ecumenic Age because, as we have seen, ecumenism played a significant role in the self-definition of both the new empires and the new religions. They aspired to represent the unity of the human race visibly and in fact even to encompass all of humanity. The basis and meaning of this unity, however, was not a simple matter to establish. It was subject to conflicting interpretations as various empires and religions pursued their programs of expansion, and it took much of the duration of the age to work through the resulting complications.

The "ecumene" may be seen as a cosmological symbol that was redefined under the impact of the changes that occurred in the Ecumenic Age. The original term *oikoumene,* found in the Homeric epics, was part of a symbolism that linked it as a twin to the term *okeanos. Oikoumene* meant the inhabited world, the earth on which humanity dwells and from which it draws sustenance, while *okeanos* referred to a "horizon" marking the boundary between human habitation and the world beyond. *Okeanos* symbolized the penumbra of mystery separating life on earth from death and the gods. As the presuppositions on which this symbolism rested were destroyed, the concept of the ecumene was retained, but its meaning altered; a fragmentation of symbolism corresponded to the alienation of power and spirit we have previously seen. To Polybius, for example, writing in the second century B.C.E., the ecumene is the power field that is the scene of imperial conquest. It is simply a territory, the known inhabited area that can be made the object of imperial organization. In this pragmatic conception, what *okeanos* symbolized is completely eliminated, and the ecumene is reduced to a geographical expanse. The ecumenic religions, however, also possessed a concept of the ecumene, which reinvested it with a transcendent horizon. The religious ecumene was the potential range of converts (all of those currently living), and the assumption was that conversion would unify the ecumene regardless of what other differences remained.[34]

Both concepts had their deficiencies, but the pragmatic ecumene was particularly defective. The unity provided by conquest was, as we have seen, only a spurious one, and the conquest never succeeded in attaining its goal. The more it was explored, the more the ecumene expanded; the farther conquest proceeded from its center, the more difficult the obstacles became. In establishing an order transcending empire, the ecumenic religions solved this dilemma in principle, but the solution was compromised by their own ecumenic ambitions, which also were frustrated. They, too, found the ecumene a larger field than any one of them was able successfully to penetrate, and they encountered the further problem that ecumenicity is not identical with universality. Those men and women who inhabit the earth at any one time do not comprise the entirety of the human race; their predecessors and successors must also be taken into account.

The picture has become even more complex subsequently as historical knowledge has expanded. In what may be called the "Chinese ecumene," an ecumenical consciousness developed concurrently with the imperial unification of China at precisely the same time as the Western Ecumenic Age. The symbolism created to characterize the resulting society—*t'ien-hsia*—is the exact equivalent of the Greek *oikoumene*. This cannot be attributed to cultural diffusion or stimulation since there is no evidence of contact between China and the West during this period. Thus the obvious question is how to relate these two concurrent ecumenisms in East and West. The question can be broadened, moreover, when one takes into account societies not involved in the Ecumenic Age but eventually affected by similar processes of change. What about non-Mediterranean Africa, Europe, the Americas, and the rest of Asia?

A plausible answer is that the human race is in fact one, but this must be understood as an eschatological symbol. The symbol emerges and evolves, and indicates something about its direction. Ultimately, the development of the ecumenical symbolism converges with historical consciousness. History becomes the substitute to take the place of *okeanos*. The combination of universal humanity and the process of reality become an equivalent to the obsolete *oikoumene/okeanos*.[35]

34. *The Ecumenic Age*, 207–9.
35. Ibid., 308.

Meaning in History:
An Ethic for a
Theory of Consciousness

The Ecumenic Age, like the preceding volumes of *Order and History,* invites attention from a variety of perspectives, and a comprehensive appraisal would encompass all of these. Questions must be raised, for instance, concerning the concepts that are introduced. Is the "Ecumenic Age" a preferable alternative to Jaspers's "axis-time"? What does "ecumenic society" actually mean? And does it apply equally well in all of the cases to which it is intended to apply? Other questions concern the appraisal of the pragmatic history of the period in question. Was the process of empire-building and maintenance actually as unconstructive and meaningless as suggested? Authoritative sources from the period are cited as evidence, but the list is selective. Certainly not all of the evidence points to this conclusion. Why, for example, is the self-interpretation of the Roman empire so neglected? Still other questions could be posed about the exegesis. I have already noted some of the difficulties with the interpretation of Christian sources, and similar questions are in order with respect to the reflections on Plato, Hegel, and others. In particular, it is important that the innovative interpretation of Plato as a philosopher of history be subjected to critical scrutiny.

The main theme that must be addressed is the underlying intellectual position. It is especially necessary to come to terms with the issue of philosophy of history since this is the ostensible subject of *Order and History.* Voegelin's principal achievement in this area lies in his formulation of the modern problem. This formulation provides the terms for defining the task of the philosophy of history in the current situation; that is to say, philosophy of history as practiced earlier in the modern period—especially in the nineteenth century—is no longer possible, yet the quest for meaning goes on and can be divorced from history with only the most strenuous effort. Consequently, theories of history continue to make sense—to be significant—even if claims to final knowledge do not. The pretensions of Hegel and Marx may appear slightly ludicrous today, but the concern that motivated their work is still very much present.

We continue to seek meaning *in* history even if it is not possible to attain the meaning *of* history. And that is precisely as it should be.

Ever since the emergence of historical consciousness, we naturally seek meaning in the processes of history, but that need not result in or be dependent on establishing the meaning of the whole. It is impossible to know the meaning of the whole, and the attempt to do so should be abandoned as mistaken in principle. But from our inability to know the whole, it does not follow that we can know nothing. Meaning can be found *in* history even though the overall course remains obscure.

The question, however, is how to accomplish this. The notion of meaningful history is so closely related to the idea of *telos* in modern thinking that it is difficult, initially at least, even to comprehend how there can be meaning in historical events without an ultimate end to which they can be related. One answer, as we have seen, focuses on the events in which the development of consciousness occurred. A basis for meaning in history emerged when consciousness took its great leap forward. The break away from cosmological thinking was an epochal moment in the history of the human race that altered existence in a fundamental way. Its effects continue to be experienced to the present moment. This change occurred, moreover, and established its line of meaning in history without any necessary connection with an end of history. As Plato in particular was aware, even though the dynamics of existence had altered, the ambiguities of history were not eliminated. If anything, they were deepened.

As a partial answer, this has a great deal to commend it. Yet particular aspects of the argument are open to question—whether, for example, Plato and Aristotle actually achieved the degree of historical consciousness one may want to claim for them; or whether teleology is in fact as unessential to Christian thought as this analysis suggests. The only serious criticism is that possibly this is not all that can be said, and that other legitimate sources of meaning may exist as well. In this analysis the experience that makes advances in consciousness possible appears to be the *sole* basis of meaning in history, and the evolution of consciousness is the only type of progress admitted. What this argument neglects is civilizational activity as an independent source of meaning in history. From this perspective, any attempt to invest it with autonomous significance is ill-conceived. That, of course, is the problematic of modernity, which brought about an enormous flourishing of civilization, but at a price. The underlying premise of this critique of modernity seems to be that the tension between the life of the spirit and civilizational activity causes the latter to become a threat to the former if it is invested with much independent significance.

There is an ironic parallel here between Voegelin and a tendency that he criticizes in early Christian thought about history, represented by Paul and Augustine. Voegelin maintains that their view was defective because they denied adequate meaning to the ordinary affairs of society. They reduced earthly existence to a mere time of waiting for the end, so that politics, culture, economic life, and the other activities that customarily occupy people's lives suffered a drastic loss in significance. This created an intolerable situation, and the eventual result was the triumph of gnosticism. The void left by Christian indifference had to be filled.

Voegelin's work as a philosopher of history is designed to address this dilemma. His interpretation of the eschatological symbols eliminates the time of waiting, and the emphasis on the balance of consciousness counters the tendency toward world alienation that was a part of Pauline and Augustinian thought. At the same time, however, other tendencies are operative in this perspective, and it is not clear that there is actually a sharp break with Pauline and Augustinian assumptions. In point of fact, it was not simply eschatology but also their view of the relation between spirit and civilization that caused early Christians to slight secular concerns, and even if Voegelin's eschatology is different, the view of human life does not appear to be that dissimilar. Here, too, is a bipolar conception of human existence, with "pulls" from "above" and "counterpulls" from "below"; here, too, the way of truth involves dying to the concerns of this world. The more one reflects on the view of life delineated in the later work, in fact, the more Pauline and Augustinian it becomes. In turn, it also becomes more difficult to imagine how the dilemma posed can be solved on its own terms.

It seems appropriate at this point to consider briefly the orientation of *The Ecumenic Age* within the context of the program of *Order and History*. Candid as it may appear, the author's explanation of the break in the original plan of the *History* only complicates an understanding of what has actually taken place. The argument elaborated on at the beginning of this chapter cannot be taken literally. If it is, it cannot be reconciled with the remainder of what Voegelin articulates in *The Ecumenic Age*. If the modes and symbols of order cannot be arranged in any intelligible succession at all, and if the complexity of the history of consciousness precludes distinguishing any topical blocks, then the author would need to repudiate a substantial portion of the earlier argument of the *History*. In point of fact, that does not occur. The principal claims presented in the earlier volumes are repeated, with only minor modification, in *The Ecumenic Age.* Once again, the pivot on which the analysis turns is the distinction between cosmological and existential reality; once again, Voegelin assumes that the latter emerges from the former through a process of development of consciousness; once again, Voegelin assumes that the latter represents a more adequate and advanced level of understanding. Historical consciousness may antedate Israelite prophetism and Greek philosophy by centuries, but these fundamental differences still affect the ways in which different people in different ages experience and symbolize reality. There is an "absolute epoch," moreover, even without an "axis-time"; and despite the volume's emphasis on the pluralism of religious life in this period, it does not treat all of the developments equally. The Israelite, Greek, and Christian instances are given special attention because they represent the differentiation of consciousness in the full sense. They also represent the development of *historical* consciousness in the full sense.

There *is* order in history, therefore, and it becomes apparent precisely through the history of order. The original principle has not been abandoned; the scope of the analysis has simply been expanded to include a broader range of materials. These materials have complicated the analysis by raising new issues and forcing qualifications of the argument. But the thesis of *Order and History* has not changed fundamentally.

Still, there has been a break. *The Ecumenic Age* continues the original program of *Order and History* insofar as it pursues analysis of the history of the symbols and experiences of order, but at the same time other interests intrude. In particular, a theory of the structure of existence comes to the forefront of the analysis, and the emphasis is much more on the permanent or recurring features of human experience than the innovations that evolve through development. Voegelin has apparently decided here that the most adequate protection against the many misunderstandings of history to which people have proved vulnerable is a platonic stress on permanence, so in the later work the order of history tends to be eclipsed by the order of existence. Voegelin has also manifested an increasing interest in ontology, developing a distinctive process theory of being. That, too, constitutes part of the argument of *The Ecumenic Age,* and while in the author's understanding it is complementary to the philosophy of history, the tendency is for the philosophy of history to be absorbed into ontology.

The major critique of modernity found here is that through a complex process, proceeding through various stages, the classical order of existence has been inverted in the language and practice of modern political thought. Instead of the humanity-society-history sequence found in the classical and Judeo-Christian symbolization of existence, we have the inversion history-society-humanity in various ideological constructions. Specifically, the process proceeds from deforming symbols in the attempt to protect them from compromise or corruption. This includes wrenching them from their experiential contexts and reifying them into dogmas or propositions instead of treating the philosophical or scriptural text as a unity, along with the motivating experience that produced it. Such a process led to the revolt that attacked not only the deformed symbols but the experiences that engendered them. Only a recovery of the experiential basis of foundational historical experience, as distinguished from a mere reassertion of past symbols as doctrines, can succeed in reversing this centuries-old trend.

Ethnographic Authority

Having concluded this brief look at *Order and History*, it might be good to say a word about Voegelin's heavy reliance on Western source materials in interpreting Eastern thought and culture, as well as his relative neglect of these cultures in his overall scheme. This is not the place to enter into a complex debate over "Orientalism" à la Bernard Lewis and Edward Said. Rather, a few fundamental remarks will have to suffice.

Every type of knowledge concerned with culture is historical knowledge, and consequently is founded on discernment and interpretation. This is not to imply that facts do not exist, but that facts attain their significance from their construal in interpretation.

Knowledge of other societies is thus particularly susceptible to inaccuracy and the vagaries of interpretation. Yet understanding another society is attainable if the investigator is responsible to and autonomously relates to the society under consideration. The context for most of what the West understood about other civilizations was colonialism. The European intellectual consequently approached a subject from a posture of dominance, and writings were composed with little reference to research other than that of consociate European scholars.

Knowledge of the social world is fundamentally interpretation: It achieves the status of knowledge by diverse means, some of which are intellectual, many others social and even political. Interpretation is contingent on a process of intentionality, molding and forming the objects of its attention with care and reflection. Such an enterprise develops in a particular time and place and is undertaken by a specifically located person with a particular personal history in a particular situation for a specific purpose. Consequently, the interpretation of texts—the primary foundation for knowledge of other societies—neither occurs in an antiseptic environment nor makes claim to impartial findings. It is a social enterprise linked to the situation out of which it initially developed, which then either bestows on it the status of knowledge or rejects it as unacceptable for that status. No interpretation can avoid this situation, and no interpretation is comprehensive without an interpretation of the situation. Thus authoritative accounts of other ways of life are contingent fictions, presently contested in postcolonial contexts: Who possesses the authority to speak for the authenticity and identity of any culture?

At this juncture it is important to clarify our understanding of the *comparative* nature of the study of civilizations. Recently, comparative work in the field of civilizational study has come under fire for a number of reasons. First, the effort to typify entire cultural traditions, like China, the Near East, and the West, then to compare them with each other in general terms, is liable to oversimplification. Such an orientation neglects and obscures the complex and intricate variations and divergences within each tradition and consequently distorts, rather than clarifies, cultural phenomena. Also, the comparative study of civilizations has frequently been undertaken for apologetic reasons, either overt or covert, and this calls into question the objectivity of the results. Finally, attempts have been made on the basis of comparative study to derive theories that claim to explain the origin and development of civilizations. Yet these theories, again because of the multiplicity of phenomena they encompass, are hard to test. Comprehensive theories of civilization, like those of Toynbee, are often perceived as more speculative than rigorously analytical.

Order and History analyzes the way civilizations have symbolized their understanding of the world, the way they have attempted to represent their cultural experience. The first volume is mainly concerned with ancient Israel, but it also touches on a number of other societies of the ancient Near East (Mesopotamia, Persia, and Egypt). The second and third volumes are concerned with Greek culture and thought. The fourth volume is a study of the ecumenic empires, including the Chinese ecumene. It needs to be said in passing that the treatment of Mesopotamia, Egypt, and Israel in places conveys an impression that they serve as more of a background for the consideration of Western thought and culture to follow in later volumes. Specialists would want more analysis of these cultures in their own terms and for their own sakes. It is also inadequate, for an integral interpretation, to scrutinize only a relatively few selected texts from various traditions, as is done with the traditions of the East in *The Ecumenic Age*. Nor is it sufficient to analyze only the official accounts of nonliterate practical beliefs. Apart from the obvious need to test comparative proposals against a wider range of materials, it is necessary to compare the normative practical teaching of groups such as Confucianists, Taoists, Tibetan Buddhists, and Shi'ite Muslims with the lived teaching in those traditions. A rule of thumb in the history of religions is that a discrepancy is likely between the ideal beliefs of a tradition and the daily operational beliefs of practitioners. *Order and History* makes no real contribution to analyzing that discrepancy since it mainly restricts itself to the normative traditions.

Voegelin has thus chosen to focus mainly on the history of the Western and ancient Near Eastern civilizations. This attempt to appropriate the intellectual substance of Western civilization is a wide-ranging one. Yet significant areas and salient questions about its fundamental presuppositions have been passed over. *Order and History* does not give much consideration, for instance, to nonliterate cultures, Chinese religion, Buddhism, Hinduism, or Islam. The system of thought employed does suggest the way these communities fit into the story of world civilization, but anyone wanting to study Africa, China, or India in depth, for example, has to expand such suggestions in correlation with new anthropological and historical information.

Any notion of the way in which history should be broken up into periods is correlative with a definite set of ideas about human nature. Western civilization provides the matrix that Voegelin found most effective in his attempt to understand the causes of differences and similarities among civilizations. His theoretical principles are concerned with the problem of understanding the relationship among the parts of sociocultural systems and the evolution of such relationships, elements, and systems. The universal structure of sociocultural systems posited by *Order and History* rests on biological and psychological constants of human nature. Thus any case for periodization will encounter many questions, including those from critics who believe that any schematization of history interpreted in terms of "development" or western dominance is opprobrious.

After completing the first three volumes of *Order and History,* Voegelin came to the realization that the type of unilinear history he had thought to be engendered turned out to be a cosmological symbolism. Thus, in his interpretation of the history of Western civilization, he slipped into a type of pattern that was prominent from the time of the Sumerians and Egyptians, through the Israelites and Christians, right up to the modern philosophies of history from which he had been trying to distance himself. This pattern of symbolization was inappropriate for the level of differentiation of consciousness on which he was attempting to work and consequently conflicted with his overall thinking. He came to understand that such a conflict was actually a manifestation of a type of cultural imperialism by which one's own cultural group tries to interpret history as centering solely on itself and thus virtually denying significance to other societies. This insight eventually led to the subject matter of *The Ecumenic Age.*

What are some of the implications of the interpretations articulated in *Order and History?* In retrospect, tracing evolution toward more complex levels of consciousness will appear prominent, but these evolutionary developments themselves do not determine the significance of any one particular civilization. Thus, even though the "Western" dimension of the developments may be perceived as an ethnocentric depreciation of the East, in reality it need not be. Because a good deal of this interpretation of history and the human condition originates from an evolutionary theory of the development of consciousness—a theory delineated and refined in the West—it is vulnerable to the criticism of misinterpreting non-Western cultures. It is true that the achievements of the classical Greek philosophers did enter into the fabric of subsequent Western culture, and thus may be termed Western. Yet there are also analogues to the Greek philosophical experience in China and India. *Order and History* does develop some of these cross-cultural parallels, but it makes no pretense of doing justice to the construction of full-scale comparisons.

While Voegelin did make serious attempts to comprehend the East, his writings in this area lack the type of empathy displayed when describing ancient Israel, Greece, or Christianity. Fundamentally, his position is a Eurocentric one. One of the unfortunate implications of

some of the sections of *Order and History* is that Eastern thought is
not of the same calibre as Judaism, Christianity, or Greek philosophy.
The characterization is that the Eastern religions never entered existence in historical form, did not interpret reality as a "flowing process," the structure of which is transparent to reason. Consequently,
according to this portrayal—where past, present, and future are the
same—no *experience* of history can exist.

Yet by way of counterexample, Voegelin did not actually perform a
thorough analysis of a certain type of "Eastern" mental state: that of
the "saint." This mental state is similar to differentiated consciousness
while still ultimately incompatible with it, for this type of consciousness transcends differentiation. If the West has created the symbolism
of universal humanity, the East has fashioned that of "all sentient beings." The symbolism of universal humanity is rooted in Greek philosophy. It implies an ecumenic humanism rooted in historical existence
that is not actually congruent with the diverse strands of Eastern
thought. A nondifferentiating consciousness is an imponderable. It appears to a Westerner as an atemporal rejection of the knowledge of the
very process of reality. This may well be one of the reasons for Voegelin's lack of empathy with the civilizations of the East. Yet overall
Voegelin's analyses are oriented toward universalism. He has, for instance, written of the equivalence—or fundamental similarity and
equality—of all human experience.

Other authors continue attempting to apply the type of methodology
found in *Order and History* and Voegelin's other works to cognate
fields of research. One such work, *Einführung in die antike politische
Theorie* (vol. 1, *Die Frühzeit* and vol. 2, *Von Platon bis Augustinus,*
[1976]), by Peter Weber-Schäfer, was written in order to introduce
German students to the political theory of antiquity. In *Political Philosophy and the Open Society* (1982), Dante Germino dedicates his
study to Voegelin, "who has laid the foundation for any authentic philosophy of the open society." In *Interpreting the Religious Experience*
(1987), John Carmody and Denise Lardner Carmody extensively employ Voegelin's categories to their analysis of the history of religions.
This book makes a concerted effort to deal with materials that Voegelin did not adequately come to terms with in *Order and History,* that
is, materials concerning India, China, and Islam, and sets a good precedent in extending the reach of Voegelin's fundamental insights and
methodology to other areas of ethnographic analysis.

After all this, it may be thought that Voegelin's major accomplishment consists of the immense wealth of new historical materials he made available, together with the "opening" (in an academic sense) of civilizations other than the West. Yet I think that, particularly given some of the limitations in his explorations of other cultures, the primary achievement is rather in the philosophical analysis performed in the course of dealing with the historical materials. And his reappropriation of political theory will succeed as he would have wanted it to, as it continues to be communicated, not in the form of propositional data, but in independent scholarly investigations by individuals who share the same motivation: to think, write, and live against the disorder and inhumanity of our age.

Finally, I would like to offer some notion of the shape of future ethnographic research that might begin where Voegelin's ended. Voegelin's own work, as we have seen, mainly concerned the development of Western civilization. Future work, however, needs to respond to forces that question the hegemony of Western cultural forms. Rather than emphasizing the "order of history," the ideology of order must also be analyzed: order for whom and for what ends? Another theme needing stress is the pervasive condition of decenteredness in a world of distinct systems of meaning, a state of being in society while observing society. This condition responds to the unprecedented tapestry of modern traditions. A contemporary ethnography of conjunctures, perpetually moving between cultures, does not aspire to survey the entire range of human diversity. It is constantly displaced, both regionally focused and broadly comparative.

This type of orientation oscillates between local and global perspectives. It concentrates on strategies of writing and representation, strategies that alter historically in response to the overall shift from the high colonialism of 1900 to postcolonialism and neocolonialism after the 1950s. It would demonstrate that ethnographic texts are orchestrations of multivocal exchanges taking place in politically charged situations. The subjectivities produced in these frequently unequal exchanges—whether of "natives" or of visiting participant-observers— are constructed domains of truth. Once this is recognized, diverse inventive possibilities for postcolonial ethnographic representation emerge.

Intervening in an interconnected world, one is constantly "inauthentic": caught between cultures, implicated in others. Since discourse in global power systems is articulated vis-à-vis, a sense of difference or distinctness can never be located completely in the continuity of a tradition or a culture.

It is a questionable endeavor to return to "original" sources, or the gathering up of an authentic tradition. Such claims to purity of intent are in any case subverted by the need to stage authenticity in opposition to external, often dominating alternatives. Thus the "Third World" plays itself against the "First World," and vice versa. If authenticity is relational, there can be no essence except as a cultural, political invention. Future research might question more incisively some of the local tactics of Western ethnography.

Since 1900, inclusive collections of "mankind" have become institutionalized in academic disciplines such as anthropology and in museums of art or ethnology. A restrictive "art-culture system" has come to control the authenticity, value, and circulation of artifacts and data. Any collection may thus plausibly be said to imply a temporal vision generating worth and rarity, a metahistory. This history determines which groups or artifacts will be ransomed from a disintegrating past and which will be defined as the dynamic, or tragic, agents of a common destiny. Future analyses would bring out the local, political contingency of such histories and the contemporary collections they justify.

The time since the completion of Voegelin's own work has been marked by rapid changes in the terms governing cross-cultural representation. Any text written within a "Western" context that abrogates for itself the authority to represent a unified history of the human race is now questioned. Modern identities no longer presuppose continuous traditions or cultures. Everywhere communities as well as individuals improvise local performances from recollected pasts, drawing on foreign media, symbols, and languages.

The primary goal is to open space for cultural futures, for the recognition of emergence. We need to be skeptical of relegating exotic cultures to the collective past. More than a few "extinct" cultures have returned to haunt the Western historical imagination.

To reject a single metanarrative is not to deny the existence of pervasive global processes unevenly at work. The world is increasingly connected, though not unified, culturally and economically. No historical narrative can lay claim to panopticism. The histories of emergent differences require other forms of discourse. Future work must survey several hybrid forms of cultural representation, forms that foretell an inventive future.

11

The Polarity of Existence

Fundamental to classical political theory is a symbol derived from Plato, that of the "Between" (*metaxy*) of human life. To employ a spatial metaphor, the *metaxy* is a field which lies between the "poles" of the "noetic height" and "apeirontic [boundless] depth." These poles establish the limits of the philosopher's inquiry into the nature of reality, and one "cannot transcend these limits but has to move in the In-Between . . ."¹ It was Plato who developed a symbol for the experience of the person's intermediate status "between" the human and sacred. Consciousness of this status played a significant role in his philosophy.

Within the context of the early Greek philosopher Anaximander's symbolization of reality, one can speak of the *metaxy* in connection with two modes of reality, that is, (1) "reality in existence," comprising the realm of all created things, including human beings in their mortality, and (2) "reality in non-existence," or noncreated reality out of which all existing things emerge, which Anaximander designated by the term *apeiron*—the Infinite or the Boundless or the Limitless or the "timeless *arche* of things." "Reality was experienced by Anaximander . . . as a cosmic process in which things emerge from, and disappear into, the non-existence of the Apeiron." Reality in the mode of existence, therefore, is experienced as "immersed in reality in the mode of non-existence and, inversely, non-existence reaches into existence. The process has the character of an In-Between reality, governed by the tension of life and death."²

Awareness of life takes place within historical movement, as can be perceived by following the trail of symbols from the elemental nature of the old myth to the noetic differentiations of consciousness in

1. Eric Voegelin, "On Hegel: A Study in Sorcery," *Studium Generale* 24 (1971), 335–68, (see note 9) at 350. This has also appeared in *The Study of Time*, ed. J. Fraser et al. (New York: Springer, 1972), 1:418–51 at 434.
2. Ibid., 360.

Greek philosophy and Judeo-Christian revelation, which require a new mythical language about the experiences of coming into and passing out of existence.

Events such as the vision of the *Agathon* by the platonic Socrates, of the burning bush by Moses, and of the resurrected Christ by Paul allow people to become fully aware of the range of their humanity and their intermediate status between mortality and immortality. This leads to an awareness that here and now one continues to exist in the cosmos and cannot achieve immortality within time.

Yet this language contains an apparent ambiguity: the *metaxy* portrayed both as *reality in movement* and the awareness of reality in movement. The ambiguity is not attributable to carelessness of language, however, but is inherent in reality itself. We experience reality only through consciousness; at the same time we are aware of participating in a reality that is greater than consciousness. Consciousness is not the whole, but a process within the whole. Therefore a truth *of* reality as a process in the "between" moving beyond itself can be distinguished from a truth *about* reality conceived of as an object eternal to a (self-contained) consciousness.

The reality of life (or political reality in the full sense) can be experienced only through participation from within; it is not a "something" apart from the consciously participating human being about which we can advance propositions. Adequate symbols in political philosophy portray the participatory character of reality. These are supple and fluid, moving with the flux of reality itself both as to range and depth. Inadequate or deformed language about political reality expresses itself in doctrine and propositions and is based upon the eclipse of part of the experiential field. The "clarity" of deformed political language is purchased at the price of the simplification, reduction, and reification of experience. It is, of course, possible to object that closed existence on the basis of reduced and simplified experience is preferable to open existence in response to historical events. A reply to that kind of objection would in principle be the same as Plato's in *Philebus* (16–17) or the prophet Jeremiah's (Jer. 45). For life is not a given, and the psyche is the locus of conflict between life and death. The basis of the preference for the pull of openness over the pull of closure—is the love of life.

But why, a critic might continue, should one be bound by the language of past events, and above all, by the "parochial" vocabulary of the Greek, Judaic, and Christian philosophers? Why not allow for a certain freedom in fashioning one's own novel vocabulary? One reply is that no abstract language of political evaluation exists, only the actual language fashioned in the articulation of the event. Consciousness itself is not an abstract entity facing an abstract reality but the awareness of a person living in a society and moving within its modes of experience and symbolization. It is fallacious to attempt to abolish the historical process of consciousness; such an attempt can and does lead only to deforming both our symbols and our humanity.

The study of the trail of symbols that is history reveals us to be capable of posing the question, Why should the cosmos exist at all, if we can do no better than live in it as though we were not of it, in order to make our escape from the prison through death? This is the critical question. The human race participates in a cosmos by its existence; we are endowed with cognition of the reality in which we are partners; consciousness differentiates in a process called history; and in the process of history we discover our identity.

Because of the uncertainty and ambiguity permeating our life, and because of the fragility and vulnerability of that condition, we are tempted to construct a closed system in whose prison we might find the substitute security lacking in life. Particularly since the development of consciousness brought on by Greek philosophy and the Judeo-Christian revelation—both of which dissolved the elemental nature of the cosmological myth—the temptation to engage in system-building has been extremely powerful. The spiraling development of consciousness has decisively increased the range of human possibilities for both good and evil, and we are left with the freedom either to form or deform our humanity. Specifically, in thinking inclined to gnosticism there lies the danger that balance may be lost because of pronounced concentration on the pull of the eschatological Beyond to the neglect of our anchorage in the cosmological Beginning. A Gnostic thinker needs to forget that the cosmos does not emerge from consciousness, but that our consciousness emerges from the cosmos. Particularly after the ascendency of Christianity, with its pronounced eschatological emphasis, the risk of deformation is a serious one.[3]

This brings us close to the center of a framework for political evaluation. Nowhere is Voegelin's intention to walk the tightrope over the twin abysses of fanatical certitude and dogmatic skepticism more clear

3. Ibid., 20.

than in his essay "Equivalences of Experience and Symbolization in History."[4] Although reality has a structure, life itself is a condition of flux and tension between truth and the deformation of reality. Therefore, ultimate doctrines, systems, and values are delusions. The constants that we discover to emerge in life are not dogmas or a catalogue of disembodied propositions, but tensional symbols that illumine the character of life as occurring between imperfection and perfection, mortality and immortality, order and disorder, harmony and revolt, sense and senselessness, truth and untruth. If we split these pairs of symbols and hypostatize the poles of the tension as independent entities, we destroy the vitality of life as it has been experienced by the creators of the tensional symbols. We may then fall prey either to apoliticism or obsession with ideology.[5] Dream life then replaces waking life, in the language of Heraclitus and Plato.

The language of politics may be evaluated in terms of its correspondence with "reality," provided that reality be conceived of not as an object external to the consciousness of the investigator but rather as a process within which that person is situated and seeks to render intelligible. The question regarding the beginning of the reality in which we live is answered initially by the myth of the cosmos as sacred—that is, as a creation of the gods and later by the great construction of Genesis I—while the question regarding the beyond is addressed by the "saving tale" of the philosopher's myth of the immortality of the person and the promise of resurrection and redemption proclaimed in the gospels and letters of Paul. The danger always exists that the tension may collapse and a chimera may be substituted for symbols illumining the complexities of life. When symbols are deformed, so are human beings because, though they do not live by symbols alone, they cannot orient themselves to the process of reality without recourse to adequate symbols.

From this perspective, then, there is the perpetual danger that we will yield to the temptation to collapse the tension of life and substitute a "second reality" that reflects our own compulsions and imaginings. This results in an attempt to expand the closed self, or ego, to the point where it opens up false standards or norms for action in the world. Thus the symbols engendered by a Plato, a Jeremiah, or a Paul reflect an authentic tension.

4. "Equivalences of Experience and Symbolization in History." In *Eternità e Storico*, 215–34.
5. Ibid., 220.

Discourse and Counterlogic

From a study of an extensive range of evidence—that is, the comparative study of symbols engendered over the millennia by those who have raised the fundamental questions about the human province—Voegelin concludes that the modern world is in the throes of a crisis of unprecedented proportions. The central symbols of our political discourse have become distorted with "second-reality" connotations. Political science, under the impact of the positivism that has done so much to restrict the range and depth of political inquiry and, in fact, of the concept of the political itself, has largely lost the capacity thoughtfully to raise great questions of political philosophy. Accordingly, it has been a negligible force in combating the fallacy of the two realities that lie at the root of ideological thinking and in exposing the inversion of the proper sequence of humanity-society-history in so much of contemporary political and social analysis.

A common form of the ritualistic rejection of philosophical reflection is "positionism." That is, if one can label a thinker something different from one's own position, then one dispenses with the burden of having to think seriously about what that person has to say. Voegelin maintains that the intention throughout his work is not to advocate a position, but "to follow empirically the patterns of meaning as they reveal themselves in the self-interpretation of persons and societies in history."[6] He is poles apart from the ideological doctrinaire, who imposes an a priori pattern upon events. Thus, after two chapters of relentless criticism of the epistemology and "ontology" of Marx in *From Enlightenment to Revolution,* Voegelin credits Marx with having "laid his finger on the sore spot of modern industrial society," that is, the growth of economic institutions into a power of overwhelming influence on the life of every single person. He argues that Marx treated under the heading of "alienation" the problem that the individual is not the master of his economic existence in an industrialized society. Voegelin also castigates economics as a discipline for its failure to follow Marx's path-breaking analysis of the relationship between humanity and nature to the point where it would have developed a philosophy of labor.[7]

6. *The Ecumenic Age,* 56.
7. *From Enlightenment to Revolution,* 299–300.

In many works, but principally in his major undertaking, *Order and History*, Eric Voegelin has provided an analysis that is relevant to the problem of political evaluation in our time. Although much of his analysis of modern developments accents the negative, his writing is by no means without hope, and he recognizes encouraging signs of intellectual resistance to the symbolic impoverishment that has been a tendency of modern politics, and beyond that the possibility of experiential and linguistic reactivation and renewal. But though he is scarcely without hope, he is modest in his expectations about the impact of his own work on the crisis of our time.

Over two centuries ago, Rousseau's sudden revelation on the road to Vincennes ignited the "Counter-Enlightenment" of Romantic art and egalitarian social ideals that championed the intuitive and affective dimensions of experience and challenged the increasing fragmentation of the individual into competitive roles and statuses. Despite Rousseau's attack, the Enlightenment model of *l'homme machine*—a kind of bipedal calculating instrument later admired by utilitarians and laissez-faire economists alike—was to find penultimate application in the development of advanced industrial society.

What has brought about the contemporary loss of the balance of consciousness? Voegelin's critique of the Enlightenment thinkers, of Hegel and Marx, constitutes an attempt to answer this question.[8] It is a noteworthy addition to the illustrious lineage of social criticism spawned by the vision of Rousseau. To Voegelin, the history of Western civilization, seen from the two crucial vantage points of metaphysics after Plato, and of science and technology after Aristotle and Descartes, is no more and no less than the story of the "loss of the balance." The twentieth century is the culminating but perfectly logical product of this process.

This is the situation aimed at in the critique of modernity: In what precise psychological and material ways does the condition of the modern Western individual represent or act out the loss of the balance of consciousness? What manner of life do we lead in a landscape of reality from which a central awareness of and reflection on the enigma of life has all but disappeared? The attempt to provide a thor-

---

8. *From Enlightenment to Revolution* focuses on Bossuet, Voltaire, Helvetius, Turgot, Comte, Bakunin, and Marx. For a critique of Hegel, see "On Hegel: A Study in Sorcery," *Studium Generale* 24 (1971), 335–68.

ough answer inspired Voegelin's numerous discussions of the sterility of contemporary political theory, of the current crises of alienation and dehumanization, of that pervasive phenomenon that he names gnosticism.

The insistence on questioning, with the concomitant emphasis that any logical analysis, let alone formal definition of the human condition, would be inadequate continues throughout Voegelin's writings. In *Anamnesis,* for example, the accent falls on the nature of the questioning process, on the way in which this interrogation-in-progress fits or does not fit our private and social condition. What Voegelin persistently stresses is the need for more attendance to thought. Thought can, at best, do little more than trace its almost impalpable furrows in language. The source of genuine thought is astonishment, astonishment at and before life. Its unfolding is that careful translation of astonishment into action, which is questioning. There is a fatal continuity between the predicative, definitional, classificatory idiom of Western metaphysics and the will to rational-technological mastery over life.[9] A program of willful sovereignty exists in the Cartesian *ergo.* Furthermore, a vital connection joins the suppression of questions and the construction of a system. Whoever reduces life to a system cannot allow questions that invalidate systems as a form of reasoning. Highly rationalistic techniques of argument and systematization prevent us from putting our thoughts into the register of interrogation.

This conviction underlies a type of "counter-logic," the design to replace the inquisitorial discourse of Aristotelian, Baconian, and positivist investigation with circuitous, but nevertheless dynamic dialectic. In Aristotelian analysis, nature is made to bear witness; Bacon speaks of putting natural phenomena on the rack so as to make them yield objective truths. In the questioning of life itself, an activity so central that it defines the humane status of man, there is no programmatic thrust from inquisition to reply. To question is to enter into concordance with that which is being questioned. Far from being sole master of the encounter, the questioner remains open to that which is being questioned. The answer called forth by authentic questioning is a correspondence. It accords with, it is a response to the core of that *after* which it inquires. The questioner who employs the tactic of counter-logic is the contrary of a Baconian inquisitor.

9. See in particular, *Science, Politics and Gnosticism.*

In all of Voegelin's critiques of the Enlightenment thinkers, particularly in *From Enlightenment to Revolution,* a distinction is made between what is "questionable," and what is "worthy of being questioned." The questionable pertains to the contingent, to the pragmatic spheres of positive investigation. In this sphere, which we might compare with the world of facts, are answers of a kind that leave the question settled and therefore inert. In the contemporary argot, there is really not very much to be gained from asking yet again why the shape of DNA is a double helix. We *know* the answers. That which is worthy of questioning, on the other hand, is inexhaustible. There are no final answers to the question of the meaning of human existence or to the meaning of "justice as fairness," as advanced, for example, by John Rawls in *A Theory of Justice.* The worthiness dignifies the question and the questioner by making the process of interrogation and response an ongoing dialogue.

12

The Archimedean Point

As both a historian and a political theorist, Eric Voegelin was concerned with the nature and sources of order in society and the individual. Like Plato, who was probably the most significant single influence on his thought, Voegelin believed that order and disorder in society and history are rooted in the order or disorder embodied in persons according to their success or failure in pursuing an authentic life. This makes Voegelin's thought philosophical in the classical sense since it is more than simply a speculation about objects, their structure, and their place in a universal system.

The starting point of Voegelin's work is consequently not an analysis of speculative constructions or a history of ideas, but an investigation of historical experience. Experience, conceived in this way, is always concrete and becomes in each person the first step in a process of developing critical self-awareness by reflecting on the symbols through which experience articulates itself in consciousness. Historically, the modes and patterns of symbolization take shape and change over time. For instance, the civilizations of ancient Mesopotamia and Egypt, with which *Order and History* begins, developed cosmological myths to represent their experience of participation in the creation of societal order and their attempt to achieve consonance with a source of order. Some later cultures—such as Israelite, Greek and Christian—developed different symbols to articulate a further understanding of the meaning of order. Or else, as in the case of modern ideologies, a society uses symbols to articulate more restrictive notions developing out of relatively static and inflexible patterns of thought. The difference between open existence and closure, according to this way of thinking, lies in the willingness or unwillingness of an individual to be aware of the important qualities of his or her experience and to accept its basic structure, which involves an awareness of both human limitation and a desire for the type of perfection represented by such symbols as "God," and the "Beyond" (Plato's *epekeina*). Voegelin's term for this basic desire as a significant quality of human experience is "tension" (*Spannung* in his German works), and he maintains that this "tension of existence" is the central dynamism of thought and activity. When interpreted inadequately, its energy can become destructive. Such destruction is frequently manifested in the belief that perfection can be achieved with a transfigured human race in this world. This belief is often accompanied by coercive efforts to force such a development.

If Voegelin's formulation of many of the central questions facing society today appears inadequate to his readers, in *Science, Politics and Gnosticism* he fully acknowledges that the Western positivistically honed intellect will derive this impression since its relations to the world still consist of amnesia and determinism.

But is this an adequate response? Has any content or method of understanding susceptible to either support or refutation been communicated to us? Or are his models of inward-circling questioning and response simply irrelevant to our predicament? Does Voegelin speak in tautologies? It may be that "*Bewusstsein vom Grund*"[1] means nothing or does not translate out of itself. Yet this would still leave open the issue of whether the questions are or are not worth posing, whether they are or are not the most significant questions put to us.

There is another way of viewing the matter, and that is to suggest that these writings are simply a variation on the dominant themes of Western metaphysics—in spite of Voegelin's affirmation that he was attempting to develop an alternative to Husserl's notion of an egologically constituted consciousness.[2] The work could then be seen as a reformulation of well-known principles in the history of Western philosophy, making the distinction between concrete particulars and the essence of their own and all existence a restatement of the fundamental platonic distinction between the phenomenal and the ideal, between the visible realm of contingent singularity and the invisible but real world of ideas. And in Husserl's phenomenological reductionism, with his insistence on the intentional structure of all thought and perceiving, one would discern the core of Voegelin's facticity.[3]

1. Cf. *Anamnesis*, 287–315.
2. *Anamnesis* [Niemeyer, ed.], 10.
3. "Consciousness is always consciousness of something." Ibid., 166.

Seen in this light, the critique of the systematic unfolding of Western thought is at best strategic; the emphasis on "Eternal Being in Time" is, in fact, yet one more phrasing of that dual edifice of understanding and the correlative attempt to proceed from the sensory to the purely intelligible, which historically have been the agenda of Western cognitional theories.

One's judgment as to whether "Consciousness of the Ground," and "Eternal Being in Time" is an esoteric variant on long-established philosophical themes does have intellectual and political consequences. While the implications of such a judgment are beyond the range of this relatively schematic account, a tentative estimate should still be offered.

First, in spite of the uniqueness of its style, the theory of consciousness set forth is actually part of a more extensive, recognizable movement of intellectual history. The identification of the individual loss of the balance of consciousness in the modern world and the anxiety that is both the manifestation and countermeasure of this loss of balance has a dual source. It originates, first, in the tradition of Augustinian Christianity. Also, Voegelin's knowledge of Marxism is wide-ranging even where, or exactly where, it is most contentious. It would be problematic to conceive of some of his most typical writings on the depersonalization of modern life or the often exploitative orientation in science and technology without the precedent of *Das Kapital* and Engels's censures of the social malignancies accompanying industrialization.

The central notion of the decadence from classical realism—an authentic experience of world and truth—to the resignation to mechanistic determinism in naturalism possesses affinities with the distinction between authentic and inauthentic life within the tension of existence. The mandate here is for a technology of responsibility, for a return to the classical scale of the person. The political ends of these impulses are those of reaction. Voegelin's contribution to this tradition is the belief, partly metaphoric, that the instruments of order represented by the ancient gods are fundamental to life and that they can be revivified and brought into dynamic relation with the human psyche.

This plea for a return to the truth of being, of thought, of language, which Voegelin locates at least partially in platonic thought, is one of the most striking personal elements in his philosophy of consciousness. Here are echoes of Heidegger. Even one of his last essays, "Wisdom and the Magic of the Extreme: A Meditation,"[4] eloquently excoriates the vagaries of the utopian imagination.

The questions posed about the nature and meaning of existence have compelling significance. By posing them repeatedly, Voegelin has brought into focus many areas of human behavior, social history, and the history of thought. Even in the areas where we dissent from it, his philosophy of consciousness is seminal and compels us to rethink the very notion of thought. Only a significant thinker can roil so innovatively.

This essay has in part attempted to illustrate both a method and a position concerning the interrelationship among knowledge, politics, and history. The interaction of historical experience and political will is the implicit theme behind a number of issues that run through the book. Neither the historian nor the statesman can afford to minimize "necessary" or "contingent" explanations or understandings. When they bring them together to explain or influence world affairs, they are making a political statement or taking a political decision.

The dreams of Marx and Montesquieu have been shattered, and the unparalleled, though not unlimited, barbarism of the twentieth century has destroyed the received idea of "civilization" (a joint legacy from the previous two centuries). In fact, it is the barbarism of limits (of the limit as a barbarous act) that has foiled the notion of civilization as a process of breaking down limits. Yet again, history has not unfolded as it ought to have done and the collective has failed in its obligation. Still, in history and politics there can be no final determinism.

Voegelin's cultural pessimism is his way of understanding the type of maturity that Kant perceived as the opportunity offered by the Enlightenment. A classical realist such as he cannot fail to point out the tragic dimension of life—past, present, and future. When he focuses on the twentieth century, this tendency is reinforced, especially in his warnings against dogmatism and illusory thinking, which are often associated forms of thought.

Yet it is possible to remain within his context and agree with its fundamental assumptions and be either more reformist or more tradi-

---

4. Originally a lecture given at the Eranos Conference in 1977 in Ascona, published in *Eranos Yearbook* 46:1977, Insel Verlag, Frankfurt. Also given as the thirty-eighth lecture in the Edward Douglass White Lectures on Citizenship, Louisiana State University, April 22–23, 1980. Also published in the *Southern Review*, n.s. 17, 2 (Spring 1981), 235–87.

tionally oriented than he himself was. His comparative, empirical approach to society leads to a pragmatic reformism. How to reconcile this with tendencies toward abstract neo-Kantianism and a belief in certain fundamental truths and the impact, however undetermined, of human reason on history demands a more extensive analysis of his writings than anything attempted here. This is the very problem of liberalism itself, that eclectic and at times ambiguous commitment to both common-sense compromises and absolute principles.

It is frequently difficult to follow Voegelin in his appeals to human nature, the classical tradition, or universal reason. Reappropriation of tradition can be neither absolute nor uncritical, as he himself practiced in his writings, particularly in the collection of essays in *From Enlightenment to Revolution*. A fully interpretive theory of consciousness must consequently be a critical theory. It must acknowledge the nature of its own existence as the product of a particular culture at a specific point in time. And it must be willing to begin the task of striving to examine and critique both its relation to its own subject matter and its own historical situation—the social, political, and economic contexts from which its own interpretive practices have emerged. This applies to our examinations of historical consciousness, the theory of interpretation and the social construction of knowledge.

To the extent that we are able to pursue such directions and link them to our encounter with cultural difference, we might begin to realize an interpretive, comparative study of thinking true to its most fundamental possibility—as a dialogue between self and other in which we ourselves are ultimately placed at issue.

Bibliography

Works by Eric Voegelin*

1928   *Über die Form des amerikanischen Geistes.* Tübingen, J. C. B. Mohr.

1933   *Rasse und Staat.* Tübingen, J. C. B. Mohr.
       Die Rassenidee in der Geistesgeschichte von Ray bis Carus. Berlin, Junker and Dunnhaupt.

1936   *Die Autoritäre Staat.* Vienna, Springer.

1938   *Die politischen Religionen.* Vienna, Bermann-Fischer, with a new foreword. Stockholm, Bermann-Fischer, 1939, published in Schriftenreihe "Ausblicke" des Verlages.

1952   *The New Science of Politics/An Introduction.* Chicago, University of Chicago Press.

1956   *Order and History, Vol. I: Israel and Revelation.* Baton Rouge, Louisiana State University Press.

1957   *Order and History, Vol. II: The World of the Polis.*
       Order and History, Vol. III: Plato and Aristotle.
       Plato. Part 1 of *Plato and Aristotle.* Baton Rouge, Louisiana State University Press.

1959   *Die neue Wissenschaft der Politik.* Munich, Verlag Anton Pustet; trans. Ilse Gattenhof; with a new foreword to the German edition of *The New Science of Politics.* Special edition of Stiferbibliothek im Universitätsverlag, Anton Pustet, Salzburg, 1977.

1966   *Anamnesis. Zur Theorie der Geschichte und Politik.* Munich, R. Piper Verlag.

1968   *Science, Politics and Gnosticism.* Regnery, Gateway Editions; translation of *Wissenschaft, Politik und Gnosis* by William J. Fitzpatrick; with a foreword to the American edition. Appendix: *Ersatzreligion.*
       La Nuova Scienza Politica. Turin, Borla; translation of *The New Science of Politics* by Renato Pavetto; with an introduction by A. Del Noce entitled "Eric Voegelin e la critica dell' idea di modernità.'

---

*Adapted from "Bibliographie der Schriften von Eric Voegelin, *Zeitschrift für Politik*, vol. 2, June 1985, 225–35, with permission of its compiler, Peter J. Opitz. I have updated some of the entries where necessary.

1968   *Zwischen Revolution und Restauration. Politisches Denken im 17 Jahrhun-
       dert.* Munich, List Verlag, published in the series *Geschichte des politi-
       schen Denkens,* vol. 1, ed. Jürgen Gebhardt, Manfred Hennigsen, and
       Peter J. Opitz.
1970   *Il Mito del Mondo Nuovo. Saggi sui movimenti rivoluzionari del nosotro
       tempo.* Milan, Rusconi; Translation of *Ersatzreligion und Wissenschaft,
       Politik und Gnosis* by Arrigo Munari; with an introduction by Mario
       Marcolla.
1972   *Anamnesis: Teoria della Storia e della Politica.* Milan, Giuffré; translation
       of *Anamnesis* by Carlo Amirante.
1974   *Order and History, Vol. IV: The Ecumenic Age.* Baton Rouge, Louisiana
       State University Press.
1975   *From Enlightenment to Revolution.* Ed. John H. Hallowell. Durham,
       North Carolina, Duke University Press.
1978   *Anamnesis.* Trans. and ed. Gerhart Niemeyer, Notre Dame and London,
       University of Notre Dame Press. Partial translation of the German edi-
       tion with a new first chapter.
1980   *Conversations with Eric Voegelin.* Edited and with an introduction by Eric
       O'Connor, S. J. Thomas More Institute Papers 76, Montreal. Transcript
       of four lectures and discussions in Montreal in 1965, 1967, 1970, and
       1976.
1986   *Political Religions.* New York, Edwin Mellen Press; translation of *Politi-
       schen Religionen* by T. J. DiNapoli and E. S. Easterly.
1987   *Order and History, Vol. V: In Search of Order.* Baton Rouge, Louisiana
       State University Press.
1989   *Ordnung, Bewusstsein, Geschichte.* Edited with an introduction by Peter J.
       Opitz. Stuttgart, Klett-Cotta.
       Autobiographical Reflections. Edited with an introduction by Ellis Sandoz.
       Baton Rouge, Louisiana State University Press.

Essays and Articles

1922   "Die gesellschaftliche Bestimmtheit soziologischer Erkenntnis." *Zeitschrift
       für Volkswirtschaft und Sozialpolitik,* Franz Deuticke, n.s. 2, 4–6;
       331–48.
1924   "Reine Rechtslehre und Staatslehre." Zeitschrift für *Öffentliches Recht,*
       Franz Deuticke, IV, 1/2, 80–131.
1925   "Über Max Weber." *Deutsche Vierteljahrsschrift für Literaturwissehschaft
       und Geistesgeschichte,* Halle, Niemeyer, III, 177–93.
       "Die Zeit in der Wirtschaft." *Archiv für Sozialwissenschaft und Sozialpoli-
       tik,* Tübingen, J. C. B. Mohr, LIII, 1, 186–211.
1926   "Die Verfassungsmässigkeit des 18. Amendments zur United States Consti-
       tution." *Zeitschrift für Öffentliches Recht,* Vienna and Berlin, Julius
       Springer, V, 3, 445–64.

"Wirtschafts-und Klassengegensatz in Amerika." *Unterrichts-Briefe des Instituts für angewandte Soziologie* V, 1926/27, 6–11.

1927   "Zur Lehre von der Staatsform." *Zeitschrift für Öffentliches Recht,* Vienna and Berlin, Julius Springer, VI, 4, 572–608.

"Kelsen's Pure Theory of Law." *Political Science Quarterly* 62, no. 2, 268–276.

"La Follette und die Wisconsin-Idee." *Zeitschrift für Politik,* Berlin, Carl Heymann, XVII, 4, 309–21.

1928   "Konjunkturforschung und Stabilisation des Kapitalismus." *Mitteilungen des Verbandes Österreichischer Banken und Bankiers,* Vienna, IX, 9/10, 252–59.

"Der Sinn der Erklärung der Menschen-und Bürgerrechte von 1789." *Zeitschrift für Öffentliches Recht,* Vienna and Berlin, Julius Springer, VIII, 1, 82–120.

"Zwei Grundbegriffe der Humeschen Gesellschaftslehre." *Archiv für angewandte Soziologie,* Berlin, 1, 2, 11–16.

"Die ergänzende Bill zum Federal Reserve Act und die Dollarstabilisation." *Mitteilungen des Verbandes Österreichischer Banken und Bankiers,* Vienna, X, 11/12, 321–28.

"Die ergänzende Bill zum Federal Reserve Act." *National-wirtschaft,* Berlin, II, 225–29.

1929   "Die Souveränitätstheorie Dickinsons und die Reine Rechtslehre." *Zeitschrift für Öffentliches Recht,* Vienna and Berlin, Julius Springer, VIII, 3, 413–34.

"Die Transaktion." *Archiv für angewandte Soziologie,* Berlin, 4/5, 14–21.

1930   "Die amerikanische Theorie vom Eigentum." *Archiv für angewandte Soziologie,* Berlin, II, 4, 165–72.

"Die amerikanische Theorie vom ordentlichen Rechtsverfahren und von der Freiheit." *Archiv für angewandte Soziologie,* Berlin, Junker and Dünnhaupt, III, 1, 40–57.

"Die Österreichische Verfassungsreform von 1929." *Zeitschrift für Politik,* Berlin, Carl Heymann, XIX, 9, 585–615.

"Max Weber." *Kölner Vierteljahrshefte für Soziologie,* Munich, Duncker and Humblot, IX, 1/2, 1–16.

"Die Einheit des Rechts und das soziale Sinngebilde Staat." *Internationale Zeitschrift für theorie des Rechts,* Brünn, Rudolf M. Rohrer, 1930/31, 1/2, 58–89.

1931   "Die Verfassungslehre von Carl Schmitt." Versuch einer konstruktiven Analyse ihrer staatstheoretischen Prinzipien." *Zeitschrift für Öffentliches Recht,* Vienna and Berlin, Julius Springer, IX, 1, 89–109.

"Das Sollen im System Kants." *Gesellschaft, Staat und Recht, Untersuchungen zur Reinen Rechtslehre, Festschrift für Hans Kelsen zum 50. Geburtstag,* ed. Alfred Verdross, Vienna, Julius Springer, 1931, 136–73.

1932   "Nachwort" to *Die Kunst des Dankens,* by Ernst Dimnet. Freiburg, Herder, 1932, 279–96.

1935   Le Régime Administratif. Advantages et Inconvénients." *Mémories de l'Académie Internationale de Droit Comparé,* II, 126–49. Paris, Recueil Sirey.

"Rasse und Staat." *Psychologie des Gemeinschaftslebens*, ed. Otto Klemm, Jena, Gustav Fischer, 91–104.

1936   "Volksbildung, Wissenschaft und Politik." *Monatsschrift für Kultur und Politik*, Vienna, Österreichischer Kulturverlag, I, 7, 594–603.
"Josef Redlich." *Jur. Blätter* 65, 23, 485–86.

1937   "Das Timurbild der Humanisten, Eine Studie zur politischen Mythenbildung." *Zeitschrift für Öffentliches Recht*, Vienna, Julius Springer, XVII, 5, 545–82. Reprinted in *Anamnesis*, 1966, 153–79.
"Changes in the Ideas of Government and Constitution in Austria Since 1918."
Three Reports by Otto Brunner, Eric Voegelin and Gregor Sebba. Austrian Memorandum No. 3 of the International Studies Conference on Peaceful Change, Paris, 1937. League of Nations, Institute for International Intellectual Cooperation.

1940   "Extended Strategy: A New Technique in Dynamic Relations." *The Journal of Politics* 2, 2, 189–200.
"The Growth of the Race Idea." *The Review of Politics* 2, 3, 283–317.

1941   "Some Problems of German Hegemony." *The Journal of Politics* 3, 2, 154–68.
"The Mongol Orders of Submission to European Powers, 1245–1255." *Byzantion* 15, 378–413. German version in *Anamnesis*, 1966, 179–223.

1944   "Nietzsche, The Crisis and the War." *The Journal of Politics* 4, 2, 177–212.
"Siger de Brabant." *Philosophy and Phenomenological Research* 4, 4, 507–26.
"Political Theory and the Pattern of General History." *American Political Science Review* 38, 4, 746–54. Reprinted in *Research in Political Science*, ed. Ernest S. Griffith, Chapel Hill, University of North Carolina Press, 1948, 190–201.

1945   "Bakunin's Confession." *The Journal of Politics* 8, I, 24–43. German version in *Anamnesis*, 1966, 223–39.

1947   "Plato's Egyptian Myth." *The Journal of Politics* 9, 3, 307–24.

1948   "The Origins of Scientism." *Social Research* 15, 4, 462–94. German version in *Wort und Warheit* 6, 5, 341–60.

1949   "The Philosophy of Existence: Plato's *Gorgias*." *The Review of Politics* 11, 4, 477–98.

1950   "The Formation of the Marxian Revolutionary Idea." *The Review of Politics* 12, 3, 275–302. Reprinted in *The Image of Man*, ed. M. A. Fitzsimons, Thomas T. McAvoy, and Frank O'Malley. University of Notre Dame Press, 1959, 265–81. Spanish translation abridged 1950 and with complete text 1951: "La Formación de la Idea Revolucionaria Marxista," *Hechos e Ideas* 22, 1951, 227–50. Italian translation: "La formazione della idea marxiana di rivoluzione, *Caratteri Gnostici della Moderna Politica economica e sociale. 4 saggi di Eric Voegelin*, ed. Giuliano Borghi, with an introductory essay by Gian Franco Lami, published in the Reihe Nuovi Carteggi, Rome, 1980, 81–130.

1951 "Machiavelli's Prince: Background and Formation." *The Review of Politics* 13, 2, 142–68.

"More's Utopia." *Österreichische Zeitschrift für Öffentliches Recht*, Vienna, Julius Springer-Verlag, New Series, 3, 4, 451–68.

"Wissenschaft als Aberglaube. Die Ursprünge des Szientifismus." *Wort und Warheit*, Vienna, Herder, VI, 5, 351–60. German translation of *The Origins of Scientism*, 1948.

1952 "Gnostische Politik." *Merkur* 4, 4, 301–17. Italian translation: Politica Gnostica, *Transcendenza e Gnosticismo in Eric Voegelin*, ed. Giuliano Borghi, with an introductory essay by Gian Franco Lami. Published in the Reihe Nuovi Carteggi, Rome, 1979, 137–75.

"Goethe's Utopia." In *Goethe after Two Centuries*, ed. Carl Hammer, Jr., Louisiana State University Press, Baton Rouge, 55–62. Also printed by Kennikat Press, Port Washington, NY, 57–62.

1953 "The World of Homer." *The Review of Politics* 15, 4, 491–523.

1958 "Der Prophet Elias." *Hochland* 1, 4, 325–39.

1959 "Diskussionsbereitschaft." *Erziehung zur Freiheit*, ed. Albert Hunold. Erlenbach-Zurich and Stuttgart, Rentsch, 1959, 335–72. Reprinted in *Anamnesis*, 1966, 239–53: "John Stuart Mill, Diskussionsfreiheit und Diskussionsbereitschaft." Translated as "On Readiness to Rational Discussion" in *Freedom and Serfdom*, ed. Albert Hunold, Dordrecht-Holland; D. Reidel Publishing, 1961, 269–84.

"Demokratie im neuen Europa." *Gesellschaft-Staat-Erziehung* 4, 7, 293–300. Reprinted in *25 Jahre Akademie für Politische Bildung*, edited by the Akademie für Politische Bildung, Tutzing, 1982, 20–31.

1960 "El concepto de la 'buena sociedad.' " *Cuadernos del Congreso por la Libertad de la Cultura*, Paris, Supplement 40, 25–28.

"Religionsersatz. Die gnostischen Massenbewegungen unserer Zeit." *Wort und Wahrheit* 15, I, 5–18. Translated as "Ersatz Religion: The Gnostic Movements of Our Time," in Eric Voegelin, *Science, Politics, and Gnosticism*, Regnery, 1968, 81–114.

"La Société Industrielle à la Recherche de la Raison." In *Colloques de Rheinfelden*, ed. Raymond Aron, George Kennan, Robert Oppenheimer, et al., Paris: Calmann-Lévy, 1960, 46–64. Translated as "Die industrielle Gesellschaft auf der Suche nach der Vernunft," in *Die industrielle Gesellschaft und die drie Welten, Das Seminar von Rheinfelden*, Zurich, EVZ-Verlag, 1961, 46–64. Also translated as "Industrial Society in Search of Reason," in *World Technology and Human Destiny*, ed. R. Aron, Ann Arbor: University of Michigan Press, 1963, 31–46. "Verantwortung und Freiheit in Wirtschaft und Demokratie." *Die Ausprache* 10, 6, 207–13.

"Der Liberalismus und seine Geschichte." In *Christentum und Liberalismus: Studien und Berichte der Katholischen Akademie in Bayern*, ed. Karl Forster, Munich: Zink, 13–42. Translated as "Liberalism and Its History," *The Review of Politics* 36, 4, 504–20.

"Historiogenesis." *Philosophisches Jahrbuch*, 68, 419–46. Also in *Philosophia Viva*, ed. M. Müller and M. Schmaus, Freiburg and Munich, 1960.

Reprinted in *Anamnesis*, 1966, 76–116. Translated and expanded in *Order and History, Vol. IV; The Ecumenic Age*, 59–113.

1961   "On Readiness to Rational Discussion." In *Freedom and Serfdom*, ed. Albert Hunold, Dordrecht-Holland, D. Reidel Publishing, 1961, 69–284.

"Toynbee's *History* as a Search for Truth." In *The Intent Of Toynbee's History*, ed. Edward T. Gargan, Chicago, Loyola University Press, 1961, 181–98.

"Les perspectives d'avenir de la civilisation occidentale." In *L'Histoire et ses interprétations: Entretiens autour de Arnold Toynbee*, ed. Raymond Aron, La Haye, Mouton, 1961, 133–51.

1962   "World Empire and the Unity of Mankind." Stevenson Memorial Lecture no. 11, 1961, *International Affairs*, London, The Royal Institute of International Affairs, vol. 38, no. 2, April 1962, 170–83.

1963   "Das Rechte von Natur." *Österreichische Zeitschrift für Öffentliches Recht*, Vienna, n.s. 1/2, 38–51. Reprinted in *Anamnesis*, 1966, 117–33. English translation, "What is Right by Nature," in *Anamnesis*, 1978, 55–70.

"History and Gnosis." In *The Old Testament and Christian Faith*, ed. Bernhard W. Anderson, New York, Evanston, London, Harper and Row, 64–89. English translation, *Anamnesis*, 1978, 55–70.

1964   "Ewiges Sein in der Zeit." *Zeit und Geschichte: Dankesgabe an Rudolf Bultmann zum 80. Geburtstag*, ed. Erich Dinkler, Tübingen, J. C. B. Mohr (Paul Siebeck), 591–614. Reprinted in *Die Philosophie und die Frage nach dem Fortschritt*, ed. Helmut Kuhn/Franz Wiedmann, Pustet, Munich, 1964, 267–92. Reprinted in *Anamnesis*, 1966, 254–80. English translation, *Anamnesis*, 1978, 116–40.

"Demokratie und Industriegesellschaft." In *Die unternehmerische Verantwortung in unserer Gesellschaftordnung, Veröffentlichungen der Walter-Raymond Stiftung*, vol. IV of the Walter-Raymond-Stiftung meeting, Cologne and Opladen: Westdeutscher Verlag, n.d., 96–114. Italian translation: "Democrazia e società industriale," in *Caratteri Gnostici della Moderna Politica economica e sociale*, ed. Giuliano Borghi, Rome: 1980, 163–95.

"Der Mensch in Gesellschaft und Geschichte." In *Österreichische Zeitschrift für Öffentliches Recht* 14, 1/2, 1–13.

1965   "Was ist Natur?" in *Historia: Festschrift für Friedrich Engel-Janosi*, Vienna: Herder, 1–18. Reprinted in Eric Voegelin, *Anamnesis*, Munich, Piper, 1966, 134–52. Translated as "What Is Nature?" In *Anamnesis*, ed. and trans. Gerhart Niemeyer, Notre Dame, University of Notre Dame Press, 1978, 71–88.

1966   "Die Deutsche Universität und die Ordnung der deutschen Gesellschaft" In *Die deutsche Universität im Dritten Reich*, ed. Ludwig Kotter, Munich, Piper, 1966. Reprinted as "Universität und Öffentlichkeit: Zur Pneumopathologie der Deutschen Gessellschaft." *Wort and Wahrheit* 26, 8/9 (1966), 497–518.

"Was ist Politische Realität?" *Politische Vierteljahresschrift* 7, I (1966), 2–54. Reprinted in expanded form in *Anamnesis*, 1966, 283–354. English translation, *Anamnesis*, 1978, pt. 3, 143–213.

1967 "On Debate and Existence." *The Intercollegiate Review* 3, 4–5 (March/April), 143–52.

"Immortality: Experience and Symbol," Ingersoll Lecture 1965, Harvard Divinity School. *The Harvard Theological Review* 60, 3, 235–79.

"Apocalisse e rivoluzione." Lecture given on May 18, 1967, to the Camera de Commercio di Milano. *Caratteri Gnostici della Moderna Politica economica e sociale*, ed. Giuliano Borghi, Rome, 1980, 45–79.

1968 "Configurations of History." In *The Concept of Order*, ed. Paul Kuntz, Seattle: University of Washington Press. Discussion by Arnold Toynbee, 43–50. Italian translation, "Configurazioni della storia," *Transcendenza e Gnosticismo in Eric Voegelin*, ed. Giuliano Borghi, Rome, 1979, 95–135.

"Helvétius" with P. Leuschner. In *Aufklrung und Materialismus im Frankreich des 18. Jahrhunderts*, ed. Arno Baruzzi, Munich, 1968, 63–97.

1970 "Equivalences of Experience and Symbolization in History"/"Equivalenze di Esperienza e Simbolizarione nella Storia," 439–54. *Eternità e Storia: I valori permanenti nel divenire storico*, Florence, Vallecchi, 215–34. Italian translation in same volume. A reprint of the English version with some changes by the author, can be found in *Philosophical Studies* 28, The National University of Ireland, 1981, 88–103.

"The Eclipse of Reality." *Phenomenology and Social Reality: Essays in Memory of Alfred Schütz*, ed. Maurice Natanson, The Hague, Martinus Nijhoff, 185–94.

1971 "Henry James's 'The Turn of the Screw.' " With a prefatory note by Robert Heilman, 2. A letter to Robert Heilman, 3. Postscript: "On Paradise and Revolution." *Southern Review*, n.s. 7, 1 (Spring 1971), 3–67.

"The Gospel and Culture." In *Jesus and Man's Hope*, vol II, eds. Donald G. Miller and Dikran Y. Hadidian, Pittsburgh Theological Seminary Press, 59–101.

"On Hegel—A Study in Sorcery." *Studium Generale*, no. 24, 335–68. Reprinted in *The Study of Time*, ed. J. T. Fraser, F. C. Haber, G. H. Müller, Heidelberg and Berlin, Springer Verlag, 1972, 418–51.

1973 "On Classical Studies," *Modern Age* 17, 2–8.

"Philosophy of History: An Interview," *New Orleans Review*, no. 2 (1977): 135–39.

"Reason: The Classic Experience." *Southern Review*, n.s. 10, 2 (Spring 1974), 237–64. Reprinted in *Anamnesis*, ed. and trans. G. Niemeyer, 1978, 89–115. Italian translation: "L'esperienza classica della ragione." In *Transcendenza e Gnosticismo in Eric Voegelin*, ed. Giuliano Borghi, Rome, 1979, 41–93.

1975 "Response to Professor Altizer's 'A New History and a New but Ancient God.' " *Journal of the American Academy of Religion* 18, 4, 765–72.

1977 "Remembrance of Things Past." Chap. 1 of *Anamnesis*, ed. and trans. G. Niemeyer, 1978, 3–15.

1981   "Eric Voegelin to Alfred Schütz." Two letters from Voegelin to Alfred
        Schütz, one dated 1 January 1953 concerning Christianity and another
        dated 10 January 1953 concerning gnosis; also the text: "In memoriam
        Alfred Schütz" (also to be found in *Anamnesis*), English translation by
        G. Sebba. *The Philosophy of Order: Essays on History, Consciousness
        and Politics*, ed. Peter J. Opitz and Gregor Sebba, Stuttgart, Klett-Cotta,
        1981, 449–65.
        "Die Symbolisierung der Ordnung." German translation of the introduc-
        tion to *Order and History*, vol. VI, 1–14. Translated by Peter J. Opitz,
        Politische Studien 32, 255 (January/February 1981), 13–23.
        "Der meditative Ursprung philosophischen Ordnungswissens." (An ap-
        proved translation of the recording of a lecture given at the symposium
        "Philosophie heute," 22–24 September 1980, in Tutzin.)
        Zeitschrift für Politik 28, June 1981, 130–37.
        "Menschheit und Geschichte." German translation of the introduction to
        Order and History, vol II, 1–24. Trans. Peter J. Opitz, *Politische Studien*
        32, 275 (May/June 1981), 231–36.
        "Wisdom and the Magic of the Extreme: A Meditation." Lecture pre-
        sented at the Eranos Conference, 1977, in Ascona. Also presented at the
        Douglass White Lectures on Citizenship, Louisiana State University,
        April 22–23, 1980. *Southern Review* 17, 2, (Spring 1981), 235–87.
        "Equivalences of Experience and Symbolization in History." A version of
        the first publication rewritten by the author in *Eternità e Storia: I valori
        permanenti nel divenire storico*, Florence, Vallecchi, 1970. *Philosophical
        Studies*, 28, The National University of Ireland, 1981, 88–103.
1982   "The American Experience." (Selected portions of an autobiographical in-
        terview conducted with Voegelin, by Ellis Sandoz). *Modern Age*, 26, 3–
        4, (Summer/Fall 1982), 332–33.
        Epilogue, *Eric Voegelin's Thought—A Critical Appraisal*, ed. with an
        introduction by Ellis Sandoz, Duke University Press, Durham, NC,
        199–202.
        Response to Professor Altizer's "A New History and a New but Ancient
        God?" Reprinted in *Eric Voegelin's Thought—A Critical Appraisal*, ed.
        E. Sandoz, 189–97.
1984   "Consciousness and Order: Foreword to 'Anamnesis.' " In *The Beginning
        and the Beyond: Papers from the Gadamer and Voegelin Conferences*,
        ed. Fred Lawrence, Scholars Press, Chico, CA.
1985   "Quod Deus Dicitur." *Journal of the American Academy of Religion* 53,
        569–84.

Reviews

F. Kaufmann, *Logik und Rechtswissenschaft—Grundriss eines Systems der reinen
    Rechtslehre*, Tübingen, 1922. *Zeitschrift für Öffentliches Recht* 3 (1923),
    707–8.

C. Schmitt, *Die Verfassungslehre von Carl Schmitt—Versuch einer konstruktiven Analyse ihrer staatstheoretischen Prinzipien*, Verfassungslehre, Munich, 1928. *Zeitschrift für Öffentliches Recht* 11 (1931), 89–109.

K. Hermann, Die Grundlagen des Öffentlichen Rechts, Berlin, 1931. *Zeitschrift für Öffenliches Rechts* 12 (1932), 630–31.

F. W. Jerusalem, *Gemeinschaft und Staat*, Tübingen, 1930. No. 74 (Recht und Staat in Geschichte und Gegenwart). *Zeitschrift für Öffentliches Recht* 13 (1933), 764.

M. Rumpf, *Politische und soziologische Staatslehre*, Tübingen, 1933. No. 98 (Recht und Staat in Geschichte und Gegenwart). *Zeitschrift für Öffentliches Recht* 14 (1934), 268–69.

D. Schindler, *Die Verfassungsrecht und soziale Struktur*, Zurich, 1932. *Zeitschrift für Öffentliches Recht* 14 (1934), 256–57.

A. E. Zimmern, *Nationality and Government, with other War-Time Essays*, London; A. E. Zimmern, *The Prospects of Democracy and Other Essays*, London, 1929. *Zeitschrift für Öffentliches Recht* 14 (1934), 269.

A. E. Hoche, *Das Rechtsgefühl in Justiz und Politik*, Berlin 1932. *Zeitschrift für Öffentliches Recht* 14 (1934), 270–71.

A. Schütz, *Der sinnhafte Aufbau der sozialen Welt*, Vienna 1932. *Zeitschrift für Öffentliches Recht* 14 (1934), 668–72.

H. Krupka, "Carl Schmitts Theories des 'Politischen,' " Leipzig, 1937. *Zeitschrift für Öffentliches Recht* 17 (1937), 665.

B. Horvath, *Rechtssoziologie*, Berlin-Grunwald, 1934. *Zeitschrift für Öffentliches Recht* 17 (1937), 667–61.

P. Berger, *Faschismus und Nationalsozialismus*, Vienna, Leipzig, 1934. *Zeitschrift für Öffentliches Recht* 17 (1937), 671–72.

G. Mosca, *The Ruling Class*, New York and London, 1939. *Journal of Politics* 1 (1939), 434–36.

" 'Right and Might': J. B. Scott: Law, the State and the International Community." New York, 1939. *Review of Politics* 3 (1941), 122–23.

"Two Recent Contributions to the Science of Law, N. S. Timasheff, *Introduction to the Sociology of Law*, Cambridge, MA, 1939. E. Bodenheimer: *Jurisprudence—The Philosophy and Method of the Law*, New York, 1940. *The Review of Politics* 3 (1941), 399–404.

M. Y. Sweezy, *The Structure of the Nazi Economy*, Cambridge, MA, 1941. E. Frankel, *The Dual State: A Contribution to the Theory of Dictatorship*, New York, 1941. *Journal of Politics* 4 (1942), 269–72.

"The Theory of Legal Science—a Review." H. Cairns, *The Theory of Legal Science*, Chapel Hill, 1941. *Louisiana Law Review* 4 (1942), 554–71.

J. H. Hollowell, *The Decline of Liberalism as an Ideology—With Particular Reference to German Politico-Legal Thought*, Berkeley, 1943. *Journal of Politics* 6 (1944), 107–9.

C. C. Sforza: *Contemporary Italy—Its Intellectual and Moral Origins*, trans. Drake and Denise De Kay, New York, 1944. *Journal of Politics* 7 (1945), 94–97.

F. L. Schuman: *Soviet Politics—at Home and Abroad,* New York, 1946. *Journal of Politics* 8 (1946), 212–20.

G. Eisler, et al., *The Lessons of Germany,* New York, 1945. *American Political Science Review* 40 (1946), 385–86.

Zu Sanders, "Allgemeine Staatslehre," ed. F. Sanders: *Allgemeine Staatslehre— Eine Grundlegung,* Vienna, 1936. *Österreichische Zeitschrift für Öffentliches Recht* 1 (1946), 106–35.

Post-War Governments of Europe, ed. D. Fellmann, Gainesville, FL, 1946. *American Political Science Review* 41 (1947), 595–96.

R. Schlesinger, *Soviet Legal Theory: Its Social Background and Development,* New York, 1945. *Journal of Politics* 9 (1947), 129–31.

E. Cassirer, *The Myth of the State,* New Haven, 1946. *Journal of Politics* 9 (1947), 445–47.

J. Huizinga, *Homo Ludens: Versuch einer Bestimmung des Spielelements in der Kultur.* Basel, 1944. *Journal of Politics* 10 (1948), 179–87.

J. Bowle, *Western Political Thought—A Historical Introduction from the Origins to Rousseau,* London Jonathan Cape, 1947. *The Review of Politics* 11 (1949), 262–63.

L. Strauss, *On Tyranny—An Interpretation of Xenophon's Hiero,* New York, 1948. *The Review of Politics* 11 (1949), 241–44.

G. Vico, *The New Science,* trans. P. G. Bergin and M. A. Fisch. *Catholic Historical Review* 35 (1949/1950), 75–76.

H. Arendt, *The Origins of Totalitarianism,* New York, 1951. *The Review of Politics* 15 (1953), 68–85. Italian translation: *Le Origini del Totalitarismo. Eric Voegelin: Un interprete del Totalitarismo,* ed. Giuliano Borghi, with an introductory essay by Gian Franco Lami and an epilogue by Eric Voegelin, published in the Nuovi Carteggi, Rome, 1980, 53–71.

F. Wagner, *Geschichtswissenschaft,* Freiburg, 1951. *American Political Science Review* 47 (1953), 261–62.

The Oxford Political Philosophers. Review of the following authors: A. D. Lindsay, *The Essentials of Democracy,* Philadelphia, 1929; *The Modern Democratic State (1943),* New York and London, 1947; R. G. Collingwood, *The New Leviathan, or Man, Society, Civilization and Barbarism,* Oxford, 1942; *The Idea of History,* Oxford, 1946; J. D. Mabbott, *The State and the Citizen—An Introduction to Political Conflicts,* London, 1946; E. F. Carritt, *Ethical and Political Thinking,* Oxford, 1947; G. R. G. Mure, "The Organic State," *Philosophy* 24, 90, 1949. See review of Blackwell's Political Texts, ed. C. H. Wilson and R. B. McCallum, in "The Oxford Political Philosophers," *The Philosophical Quarterly* 3 (1953), 97–114. German translation: "Philosophie der Politik in Oxford," *Philosophische Rundschau* 1 (1953/54), 23–48.

J. Wild, *Plato's Modern Enemies and the Theory of Natural Law,* Chicago, 1953. R. B. Levinson, *In Defense of Plato,* Cambridge, MA, 1953. *American Political Science Review* 48 (1954), 859–62.

R. Polin, *Politique et Philosophie chez Thomas Hobbes,* Paris, 1953. *American Political Science Review* 49 (1955), 597–98.

Other Works Consulted

Adorno, Theodor, and Max Horkheimer. *Dialectic of Enlightenment*. Trans. John
    Cumming. New York: Herder and Herder, 1972.
Adorno, Theodor. *Negative Dialectics*. Trans. E. B. Ashton. New York: Seabury
    Press, 1973.
Altizer, Thomas J. "A New History and a New but Ancient God?" *Journal of the
    American Academy of Religion* 43 (1975), 757–64.
Anderson, Bernhard. *Creation versus Chaos*. New York: Association Press, 1962.
———.*The Old Testament and Christian Faith*. New York: Herder and Herder,
    1969.
Aristotle. *Metaphysics*. Trans. H. Tredennick and C. A. Armstrong. Cambridge,
    MA: Harvard University Press, 1969.
———. *The Nicomachean Ethics*. Trans. H. Rockham. Cambridge, MA: Harvard
    University Press, 1969.
———. *The Politics*. Barker edition. Oxford: Clarendon Press, 1946.
———. *Posterior Analytics*. Trans. Hugh Tredennick. Cambridge, MA: Harvard
    University Press, 1960.
Bachofen, Johann Jakob. *Versuch die Gräber Symbolik der Alten*. Werke IV. Basel:
    Schwabe, 1943.
Bergman, Gustav. *Realism: A Critique of Brentano and Meinong*. Madison: Uni-
    versity of Wisconsin Press, 1976.
Bergson, Henri. *Essai sur les données immédiates de la conscience*. Paris: F. Alcan,
    1889.
———. *An Introduction to Metaphysics*. Trans. T. E. Hulme. London: Mac-
    millan, 1912.
Bracher, Karl Dietrich. *Zeit der Ideologien: eine Geschichte politischen Denkens
    im 20. Jahrhundert*. Stuttgart: Deutsche Verlags-Anstalt, 1982.
Bultmann, Rudolf. "Prophecy and Fulfillment." In Claus Westermann, *Essays in
    Old Testament Hermeneutics*. Ed. J. L. Mays. Richmond: John Knox Press,
    1963.
Carmody, John, and Denise Lardner Carmody. *Interpreting the Religious Experi-
    ence*. Englewood Cliffs, NJ: Prentice-Hall, 1987.
Cirlot, J. E. *A Dictionary of Symbols*. Trans. Jack Sage. London: Routledge and
    Kegan Paul, 1967.
Clemens, Titus Flavius Alexandrinus. *Stromateis*. Trans. O. Stahlin. Munich: J.
    Kosel and F. Pustet, 1934–38.
Darwin, Charles. *The Descent of Man*. 2d ed. London: J. Murray, 1984.
Dempf, Alois, and Frederich Engal-Janosi, eds. *Politische Ordnung und mensch-
    liche Existenz: Festgabe für Eric Voegelin*. Munich: C. H. Beck, 1962.
Descartes, René. *Oeuvres philosophiques*. Paris: Garnier, 1963.
———. *Regulae ad directionem ingenii*. The Hague: Martinus Nijhoff, 1966.
Dreyfus, Hubert L., and Harrison Hall. *Husserl, Intentionality, and Cognitive Sci-
    ence*. Cambridge, MA: MIT Press, 1984.
Eliade, Mircea. *Images et Symboles*. Paris: Gallimard, 1952.

Faber, Richard. "Eric Voegelin—Gnosis-Verdacht als polit (olog)isches Strate-gem." In *Gnosis und Politik*. Ed. Jacob Taubes. Munich: Wilhelm Fink, 1984.

Foucault, Michel. *The Order of Things*. A translation of *Les Mots et les choses*. New York: Pantheon Books, 1970.

Freeman, Kathleen. *The Pre-Socratic Philosophers: A Companion to Diels, Fragments der Versokratiker*. Oxford: Basil Blackwell, 1953.

Freud, Sigmund. *Civilization and Its Discontents*. Trans. and ed. James Strachey. New York: Norton, 1961.

———. *Totem and Taboo*. Trans. A. A. Brill. New York: Dodd, Mead, 1918.

Fromm, Eric. *Marx's Concept of Man*. New York: Frederick Ungar, 1961.

Frye, Northrop. "The Shapes of History." In *Northrop Frye on Culture and Literature*. Ed. Robert D. Denham. Chicago: University of Chicago Press, 1978.

Geertz, Clifford. *Local Knowledge*. New York: Basic Books, 1983.

———. *The Interpretation of Cultures*. New York: Basic Books, 1973.

Germino, Dante. *Political Philosophy and the Open Society*. Baton Rouge: Louisiana State University Press, 1982.

Goody, Jack. *The Domestication of the Savage Mind*. Cambridge: Cambridge University Press, 1977.

Guerra, Francisco. *The Pre-Columbian Mind*. London: Seminar Press, 1971.

Havard, William. "The Changing Pattern of Voegelin's Conception of History and Consciousness." *Southern Review* 12 (Winter 1971), 49–67.

Hegel, G. W. F., *Logik. Werke* (July-August) IV. Stuttgart, 1927.

———. *The Phenomenology of Mind*. Trans. J. B. Baillie. 2d ed. London: Allen and Unwin, 1961.

———. *Vorrede zur Phänomenologie des Geistes. Werke.* (July-August) II. Stuttgart, 1927.

Heidegger, Martin. *Einführung in die Metaphysik*. Tübingen: M. Niemeyer, 1953.

———. *Holzwege*. Frankfurt a.m.: V. Klostermann, 1950.

———. *Sein und Zeit*. In *Jahrbuch für philosophie und phänomenologische forschung*. Vol. 8. Freiburg: M. Niemeyer, 1927.

———. *Vorträge und Aufsätze*. Pfullingen: G. Neske, 1954.

Homer. *The Iliad*. Trans. W. H. D. Rouse. New York: Mentor Books, 1950.

Hooker, Richard. *Laws of Ecclesiastical Polity*. Preface, Books I–IV. The Folger Library Edition. Cambridge, MA: Belknap Press of Harvard University Press, 1977.

Hume, David. *Enquiries Concerning the Human Understanding*. Ed. L. A. Selby-Bigge, 2d ed. Oxford: Clarendon Press, 1902.

Husserl, Edmund. *Cartesianische Meditationen. Husserliana* I. The Hague: Martinus Nijhoff, 1950.

———. "Erneürung: Ihr Problem und ihre Methode." *The Kaiso-La rekonstruyo* 3. Tokyo: 1923.

———. "Gemeingeist II. Personale Einheiten höherer Ordnung und ihre Wirkungskorrelate." *Husserliana* 14. The Hague: Martinus Nijhoff, 1973.

———. "Die Idee einer philosophischen Kultur: Ihr erstes Aufkeimen in der geischischen Philosophie." *Husserliana* 7. The Hague: Martinus Nijhoff, 1956–58.

————. *Ideen zu einer reinen Phänomenologie und phänomenologischen Philosopohie. Buch* I. Halle a.d.s.: Niemeyer, 1913.

————. "Die Krisis der Europäischen Wissenschaften und die Transzendentale Phänomenologie." *Husserliana* 6. The Hague: Martinus Nijhoff, 1954.

————. *Logische Untersuchungen. Husserliana* 18. The Hague: Martinus Nijhoff, 1975.

Jaynes, Julian. "The Problem of Animate Motion in the Seventeenth Century." *Journal of the History of Ideas* 31 (1970), 219–34.

Jung, C. G. *Symbole der Wandlung.* 4th ed. Zurich: Rascher Verlag, 1952.

Kelsen, Hans. *Allgemeine Staatslehre.* Berlin: J. Springer, 1925.

Keulman, Kenneth. "The Tension of Consciousness." In *Voegelin and the Theologian: Ten Studies in Interpretation.* Ed. John Kirby and William M. Thompson. New York: Edwin Mellen Press, 1983.

Kierkegaard, Søren. *Der Begriff Angst.* Trans. E. Hirsch. Düsseldorf: Eugene Diederichs Verlag, 1958.

König, Marie E. P. *Am Anfang der Kultur: Die Zeichensprache des frühen Menschen.* Berlin: CE Br. Mann, 1973.

La Barre, Weston. *The Ghost Dance.* New York: Doubleday, 1970.

Leishmann, J. B. *Translating Horace.* Oxford: Cassirer, 1956.

Levenson, Joseph. *Confucian China and Its Modern Fate: A Trilogy* (1st combined ed.). Berkeley: University of California Press, 1968.

————. *Revolution and Cosmopolitanism: The Western Stage and the Chinese Stages.* Berkeley: University of California Press, 1971.

Lévi-Strauss, Claude. *La Pensée sauvage.* Paris: Librairie Plon, 1962.

————. *Mythologiques.* Paris: Gallimard, 1979.

————. *Structural Anthropology.* Trans. Claire Jacobson and Brooke Schoepf. New York: Doubleday, 1967.

Löwith, Karl. *Meaning in History.* Chicago: University of Chicago Press, 1949.

Machiavelli, Niccolo. *The Prince and the Discourses.* New York: The Modern Library, 1940.

Macquarrie, John. *Principles of Christian Theology.* New York: Scribner's, 1966.

Marx, Karl. *Capital.* Trans. S. Moore and E. Aveling. New York: The Modern Library, 1906.

————. *Economic and Philosophic Manuscripts of 1844.* Moscow: Foreign Language Publishing House, 1960.

Marx, Werner. *Heidegger and the Tradition.* Evanston: Northwestern University Press, 1971.

Merleau-Ponty, Maurice. *Phenomenologie de la perception.* Paris: Gallimard, 1943.

Neumann, Erich. *The Origins and History of Consciousness.* Princeton: Princeton University Press, 1954.

Niebuhr, H. Richard. *The Meaning of Revelation.* New York: Macmillan, 1941.

Niemeyer, Gerhart. "Eric Voegelin's Philosophy and the Drama of Mankind," *Modern Age* 22, 1 (Winter 1976), 22–39.

Opitz, Peter J., and Gregor Sebba, eds. *The Philosophy of Order.* Stuttgart: Klett-Cotta, 1981.

Parsons, Talcott. "An Approach to Psychological Theory in Terms of a Theory of Action." In *Psychology: A Study of a Science*. Ed. Sigmund Koch. New York: McGraw-Hill, 1959.

Petit, P. "Wittgenstein, Individualism and the Mental." In *Erkenntnis und Wissenschaftstheorie*. Ed. P. Weingartner and J. Czermak. Vienna: Holden-Pichler-Tempsky, 1983.

Plato. *Philebus*. Ed. with introductory notes and appendices by Robert Gregg Bury. New York: Arno Press, 1973.

———. *The Republic*. Trans. and ed. James Adam. 2d ed. Cambridge: Cambridge University Press, 1963.

Popper, Karl, and John Eccles. *The Self and Its Brain*. New York: Springer International, 1977.

Rawls, John. *A Theory of Justice*. Cambridge, MA: Belknap Press of Harvard University Press, 1971.

Ribot, Théodule. "La Pensée Symbolique." *Revue Philosophique* 49 (1915), 381–92.

Robinson, James M., ed. *The Nag Hammadi Library in English*. San Francisco: Harper and Row, 1977.

Rousseau, Jean-Jacques. *The Social Contract and Discourses*, Everyman edition. London: J. M. Dent and Sons, 1923.

Ryle, Gilbert. *The Concept of Mind*. Chicago: University of Chicago Press, 1949.

Sandoz, Ellis. *The Voegelinian Revolution*. Baton Rouge: Louisiana State University Press, 1981.

Sartre, Jean-Paul. *Critique de la raison dialectique*. Paris: Gallimard, 1943.

———. *L'être et le néant*. Paris: Gallimard, 1943.

Schlesinger, Max. *Geschichte des Symbols*. Berlin: L. Simion, 1912.

Schütz, Alfred. *Alfred Schütz: Collected Papers*. Ed. H. L. van Breda. The Hague: Martinus Nijhoff, 1967.

Schütz, Alfred, and Thomas Luckmann. *The Structure of the Life-World*. Trans. Richard M. Zaner and H. Tristram Englehardt. Evanston: Northwestern University Press, 1973.

Seligman, Edwin A., Editor-in-Chief. *Encyclopedia of the Social Sciences*. New York: Macmillan, 1963. 15 vols.

Steiner, George. *Martin Heidegger*. New York: Viking Press, 1978.

Toynbee, Arnold. *A Study of History*. 2d ed. 12 vols. Oxford: Oxford University Press, 1935–61.

Unger, Roberto Mangabeira. *Knowledge and Politics*. New York: The Free Press, 1975.

Valéry, Paul. *Oeuvres*. 1st ed. Paris: Gallimard, 1957.

Wallace, Alfred Russel. *Contributions to the Theory of Natural Selection*. 2d ed. New York: Macmillan, 1971.

———. *Darwinism: An Exposition of the Theory of Natural Selection*. London: Macmillan, 1889.

Weber, Max. *The Sociology of Religion*. Trans. Ephraim Fischoff. Boston: Beacon Press, 1963.

Weber-Schäfer, Peter. *Einführung in die antike politische Theorie* (Vol. I: *Die Fruhzeit*; Vol. II: *Von Platon bis Augustinus*). Darmstadt: Wissenschaftliche Buchgesellschaft, 1976.

Westermann, Claus. *Essays on Old Testament Hermeneutics*. Ed. J. L. Mays. Richmond: John Knox Press, 1963.

———. *Genesis 1–11*. Darmstadt: *Wissenschaftliche*, Buchgesellschaft, 1972.

Wiser, James L. "Voegelin's Concept of Gnosticism." *The Review of Politics* 42 (1980), 92–104.

Wittgenstein, Ludwig. *Philosophical Investigations*. Trans. G. E. M. Anscombe. 3d ed. New York: Macmillan, 1968.

Wolf, Friedrich August. *Prolegomena ad Homerum*. Halis Saxonum: Orphano-trophel, 1795.

Indexes

Name Index

Subject Index